Roses

and

Thorns

Roses
and
Thorns

The Memoirs of
Isabel Ramos Aguilar

As Told to
Barbara Elliott Carpenter

Isabel Aguilar

authorHOUSE®

AuthorHouse™
1663 Liberty Drive
Bloomington, IN 47403
www.authorhouse.com
Phone: 1 (800) 839-8640

Published by AuthorHouse 12/04/2015

ISBN: 978-1-5049-4824-1 (sc)
ISBN: 978-1-5049-4825-8 (hc)
ISBN: 978-1-5049-5387-0 (e)

Library of Congress Control Number: 2015917259

Dedication

I dedicate this book to my husband, Armando, to whom I have been married for fifty-five years, as of November 5th, 1960; also to my children, Alejandro (Alex), Victor and Christina; to my grandchildren, Alexa, Olivia, Alexander and Lorenzo; and my great-grandchildren, Sarah, Gabriel and Audrey.

IN SPECIAL MEMORY OF

My second son, Armando, (Bebé)

And in memory of Papo and Mami, my parents; and of my maternal grandfather, Domingo Pichardo, who loved me unconditionally.

Acknowledgement

TO BARBARA CARPENTER - You are a wonderful writer, and now you have become my dear friend. I am so blessed. I have learned so much from you. It has been a joy to work together on my book. How many tears! And how much fun we had every Monday afternoon, working together on something that has been my desire for a long time. Thank you, Barbara, from my heart.

Every Monday afternoon we went together to Güines, Havana, Cuba. First we went to the house where I was born, in my father's house, and how many memories! Every memory was renewed inside of me, and now they are in my mind all the time. I had some thorns, but I had more roses. What about a life without roses and thorns? Thank you for my book and for your kind spirit that made it a joy to work together. Thank you, my friend. God bless you! - ISA

Introduction from Writer

Before you begin your trek through the seven decades covered in this book, I would like to share with you how the writing of it came to fruition. The older I grow, the less I believe in coincidence. Many incidents, resulting from this writing, could not have happened by chance.

For example: Renewed contacts between Isabel Aguilar and people she had not seen or heard from for over fifty years….just as she began to tell me stories about her life with them in Cuba: A phone call from the daughter of an old friend who stayed in Cuba, moments into a discussion about this friend, which led to a longed-for reunion last summer. Amazing is over-used, but I have been amazed by many things during this process.

I remember the day in 1968 when I first saw the Aguilars, a striking couple with two dark-haired little boys. They and the Rubio family, who had arrived a few years earlier, caused quite a stir in the small town of Salem. It was not every day or decade that two families from another country settle within its city limits.

For years, I saw Dr. Aguilar and his lovely wife, Isabel, around town, in restaurants, grocery stores and shops; but we did not become acquainted until many years later. In 1989, my family took a seven-year-hiatus from our church and began attending where the Aguilars were members. I found myself in a Sunday school class with Isabel, who intimidated me just a little.

Always cordial, she didn't speak much in class; but there was something about her, a bit like still water in a quiet stream—deep, serene and calm. Just being in the room with her was comforting to me. We were friendly, but not yet friends. One day I complimented her on the lovely purple blouse she wore.

"I will give it to you," she said, smiling. Quickly I shook my head, assuring her that I had no designs on her clothing! But that was Isabel—generous to a fault.

After the seven years, my family returned to our roots; and one day I was amazed and happy to see the Aguilars in the congregation for a time. Again, we were friendly, but not yet friends.

Time passed. In 2007 Dr. S.E. Rubio approached me about writing his memoirs, a genre with which I had no experience. I was still in the process of writing the third book of a trilogy, but I agreed to work with him. In 2008, I finished both my book and his, and they were released within a few weeks of each other.

Among the notes and messages I received about Dr. Rubio's book was a beautifully addressed envelope from Isabel Aguilar. Pleasantly surprised, I opened it and found a letter, expressing how much she had enjoyed the book and that she had read it with tears, reliving moments from her life in Cuba.

Dr. Rubio passed away in November, 2012. As I was leaving the cemetery following the burial service, I heard someone call my name. I turned to see Isabel Aguilar coming toward me. It was a sunny, blustery day.

"I have been wanting to talk to you," she said. I smiled at her delightful Spanish accent, one of the things I have always found most charming about her. "I have been praying, asking God to help me find someone to write my story, write my book. I read Dr. Rubio's book, and I know that you are the one! You are the one who is supposed to write my book!"

I could not have been more dumbfounded, more at a loss for words if she had suddenly sprouted wings! Well, possibly not. I had just finished writing the memoirs of Bryan Davidson, the founder of WJBD; and I had promised myself that I would never, under any circumstances, write another memoir! The process is just too draining!

So I hedged. I don't remember all the excuses I started to list, all of which she listened to, as the wind tossed our hair this way and that.

"But I know that you are the one! I have prayed and prayed and God told me that you are the one!" She was convinced.

So I took a deep breath and told her to call me after the holidays. If she were still interested in telling her story, we could talk. She agreed. I thought that she might change her mind by then, and I would be reprieved. At that time, I did not know Isabel Ramos Aguilar!

Near the end of January, 2013, my phone rang. I looked at the caller ID, and there, bold as brass, was the name of Isabel Aguilar. She had not lost interest in telling her story. My first thought was, "How can I tell God, 'No.'" I was so hooked.

Our weekly sessions began. Most Monday afternoons would find my car parked in her driveway, Isa and me sitting at her dining room table, tape recorder flashing its blue light as she told her story. The more I listened, the more I became involved in her past. It was as if I were seeing, experiencing her memories.

I watched her eyes as she told me of her life, from her earliest memories to our last taped session. Her animated expressions, smiles, laughter, frowns as she spoke drew me in; and it was as if I could see what she saw, feel what she felt, wipe away tears that she cried.

I was the one who took the little girl's cookie. I was the one who cried herself to sleep in that first boarding school, who hated Miss Kelly, who loved Sonia, who hated hair bows, who loved chocolate. I petted the stone lions along Paseo del Prado in Havana, danced, sang and vicariously lived the Cuban experience. I knew first the hope, then the disillusionment, then the terror of losing friends in the madness brought to Cuba by Fidel Castro.

It has been a long journey, lengthened by bouts of illness for both of us, vacations, holidays, two weddings in my family, and other little interruptions that cropped up. Both of us became grandmothers again. In November, 2013, my grandson and his wife became parents of their second son, which gives me two great-grandsons. In January, 2014, Isa's daughter and her husband welcomed a third little boy to their family, another grandson for Isa and Armando. What is more fun than two grandmothers sharing photos and swapping stories about their offspring?

This collaboration has also been a delightful coming together of two minds, two languages, two cultures that have blended and culminated in a story that is compelling, funny, dramatic, romantic, tragic, and finally, a beautiful book, titled Roses and Thorns.

Isabel Ramos Aguilar is a magnificent woman, proud of her Cuban heritage, but prouder still that she is an American citizen. She is the woman described in the last chapter of Proverbs, whose worth is above rubies, whose children all rise and call her blessed. Her faith in God is more than words; it is a combination of attitude and action, of creed and compassion, of wisdom and works.

Isabelita is also a series of contradictions. She moves with the confidence and elegance of a model, which hides a vulnerability seen by very few. Her sense of humor is sometimes surprising, accompanied by sparkling brown eyes that can also demonstrate flashes of temper, which, I'm sure, could probably rival tempestuous Caribbean hurricanes.

I'm glad she chose me to tell her story; but, for me, the best thing to come from this joint effort is that Isabelita and I are no longer just friendly. We have become forever friends, the kind we can depend upon, no matter what. We have prayed for each other during some difficult times, and we have laughed until we both dissolved into hysterical giggles.

After months of hard work, some nights with little sleep and consecutive hours at the computer, I can say, "Thank you, God, for allowing me to tell the story of Isabel Ramos Aguilar."

Welcome to the saga of Isabel Ramos and Armando Aguilar, two people who were destined to be together, who defied a Communist dictator to gain their freedom and whose marriage not only survived, but was strengthened by the loss of a beloved son. Theirs is a remarkable story.

Barbara Elliott Carpenter

PART ONE

Isabel Ramos Pichardo

Preface

The troubled history of Cuba, its various conquerors and rulers before Castro, can be found easily through many sources on the internet. Several movies and documentaries have been produced and are available, so I'm not going to elaborate on those eras.

Like many young people, I had little interest in my country's past. My concerns focused on pretty clothes, movies, friends and handsome boys. When I was a girl, the "boys" part consisted merely of looking, for girls never, and I mean *never*, shared the company of a boy without a chaperone!

My Cuba of long ago now seems like a lovely dream; but I know that the twenty-six years I spent on that beautiful island were real. While my life was good, my pampered childhood sheltered me from the harsh reality that many people on the island faced extreme poverty and want every day. Those who struggled to provide shelter and food for their families, always on the edge of starvation, were ready to embrace any person or creed that promised a different way of life. No one can blame them.

History proves that Batista's government was corrupt. His connection to and traffic with the so-called "American mafia" is well documented. When Batista realized that Fidel Castro's "revolution" and his rag-tag army was on its way to Havana, Batista fled the country like the coward he was, taking millions and millions of dollars with him. His final actions on Cuban soil proved that he had never cared for the people. Like many, if not most, politicians, his concerns were focused on his personal power and wealth.

Fidel Castro, driven by his belief in his own destiny, had within his power to establish a government, a democracy that would have improved living conditions for the poor without destroying Cuba's rich heritage and culture. He could have been recognized for organizing a way of life beneficial for all citizens of Cuba. The people were expectant, and they called him their savior, ready to embrace the man who drove away Batista. My generation believed in him, at first.

Initially an idealist, Castro wanted to "level the playing field and to share the wealth." To him, eventually that meant taking houses, land, possessions, money and companies from those who owned them and giving them to others. Most of the "others" had no idea how to farm, run a grocery store or any other kind of business; so they failed. At that point, Fidel's solution was to insist that people work harder, do without personal gain, tighten their belts and *work harder*!

Like every other tyrant who ever forced communism upon a country, Fidel Castro let loose a brutal storm that, in the end, destroyed the land he claimed to love. He not only betrayed the peoples' trust, within a short period of time he destroyed any hope of freedom for those who were unable to escape.

I will always be grateful for my father's assistance when it became necessary for us to follow him and so many others out of Cuba. I shudder at the thought of how our children would be living now, if, like so many others, we had been denied a way of escape.

There are people in the world who now think that Fidel Castro is some kind of hero. They praise his schools and they approve of what they call "his fair, peaceful country." Most of them are college students or graduates whose socialist-leaning professors either don't know or don't care about what really happened in Cuba. Those of us who actually lived through those years know the truth.

All my life I have received a great deal of pleasure from colorful flowers. I loved the many sweet-smelling tropical flowers and trees that bloomed so freely in Cuba. Diverse scents and beauty can soothe and brighten any day. The rose continues to be my favorite, especially in shades of yellow and the delicate, salmon-edged pastel. These long-stemmed beauties have come to represent the many joys that have filled my life.

Perhaps one thing that makes them so intriguing is that they are surrounded by thorns, capable of inflicting painful, bloody injury to the unwary. While roses convey joy, thorns cause pricks and cuts that can leave scars, some larger than others.

I carry many thorn-pricks and scars, but two of them caused the most pain. Fidel Castro proved to be the most painful thorn of my early life, and he left the biggest scar. However, I was able to escape from him and his oppressive government.

One of the sweetest roses that graced our lives was our second son, Armando, whom we called "Bebé." After a long, courageous struggle with brain cancer, Bebé passed away at the age of nineteen. Death, the cruelest thorn of all, tore our hearts when it took our son.

Without the love and grace of our Lord Jesus Christ, my family and I could not have survived the pain caused by that thorn of agony. Without a doubt, Jesus is the brightest rose, the Rose of Sharon, whose sweet scent fills every day of my life.

I am not the only person who has experienced the pain and loss of home and freedom, or suffered the loss of a beloved child; but mine is the only story I can tell. Mine is the only heartbreak I know how to relate; and mine is the only victory I can share. My desire is that my story will help or bring comfort to other broken hearts.

Please don't think that I am bitter or that grief destroyed my joy in living. The roses far outweigh the thorns in my life. I loved to laugh when I was young, and I still do. Although I had bouts of extreme shyness, I also acted on spur-of-the-moment whims that either landed me in trouble or resulted in outrageous laughter from my classmates.

All these years later, my old friends and I reminisce about the good times and laughter we shared when we were young. Working on this book has triggered even more memories and has resulted in renewed friendships, as well as very expensive telephone calls to Cuba! It would be my pleasure to know that this story brings a tear to your eye, a smile to your lips or causes you to remember something happy from your past, as I have.

A Little Family History

Güines, Cuba, was a beautiful city of around 37,000 people in 1937, the year I was born. My roots in Cuba are deep, deeper than I have been able to ascertain; but I do know a bit about my father's father, Juan Ramos Rivera.

Family genealogy statistics can be boring, so I have only a few to share. During the Hispanic-American War, my paternal grandfather took medicines to the wounded on the battlefield. I don't know if he was pressed into doing this or if, as a pharmacist, he felt it was his duty. As a result, he placed himself in great danger, so I like to think of him as a hero.

He married Isabel Montero, for whom I have very little history. I am her namesake. They had ten children. I know that my grandfather must have been well-thought of. In a town near Güines is a lodge named for him: The Juan Ramos Rivera Masonic Lodge. When we left Cuba in 1963, the lodge was still standing.

I know a little more about my maternal ancestors. My great-grandfather, Rafael Pichardo, was born in Santa Ana, Matanzas Province, Cuba; but I don't know the year. All I know about his wife is her name, Victoria.

Their son, my grandfather, Domingo Pichardo, was also born in Santa Ana. I will share much more about him later. He married Juana (nicknamed Juanita) Albrecht Muguruza, who was born in Limonar, Matanzas Province, Cuba. Juana's parents were Justo Albrecht and Valentina Muguruza, who was of French and German descent.

I mention this bit of genealogy to show how strongly I was tied to Cuba. Only names now, my grandparents and great-grandparents go far back into the 1800s, almost to the late 1700s. What a tremendous amount of recorded Cuban history they watched unfold. I wish they had been able to record at least something about their lives.

Warm, balmy Caribbean breezes continually waft across the land and fill the air with fragrant, unbelievably sweet, floral scents. Waters off the shores of Cuba shine like turquoise, a sweeping vista of azure and every shade of blue and green imaginable. Hard as one might try, it is impossible to describe with words. Even the best photography cannot do it justice.

Many, many decades before I was born, a system of irrigation, leading from the Mayabeque river was developed, patterned after those used in Europe. It was responsible for the lush vegetation and productive farms and gardens in and around the city of Güines. Hundreds of canals led from the river into and through the town, along streets that led even into the countryside.

I have heard that the channels through which the water flowed have been neglected, some ruined, and that the river is not as beautiful as it was fifty-five years ago. If that is true, it certainly cannot be blamed on a booming economical civilization. A stifling, dictatorial Communist government can take the credit.

CHAPTER ONE

The Child

The oldest of three children, I was born January 30th, 1937. My mother was twenty-two, and my father, nearly twenty years older. He was one of ten children, apparently the most responsible one. It became his duty to see that his brothers and sisters were educated and cared for, which is why he married later in life than was common.

The long wait to have a family of his own could account for the fact that my two younger brothers and I were the center of our father's universe. Juan was two years younger than I, and José Julián arrived when I was twelve. It seemed that our lives in Cuba, my island Eden, would always be happy, safe and secure.

When I was a child, I thought my life would never change. My home, parents, grandparents, friends and extended family would remain the same, placed there to care for me and meet all my needs. I suspect that many of my "needs" were only "wants." Most of them were supplied, the result being a pampered, spoiled little girl.

My father's horizons were broader than those of my mother. He travelled a good deal when he was younger, which included a trip to the United States before he met my mother. He had a serious problem with his eyes, so he saw an ophthalmologist in Stanford, New York, where he stayed for a long time. While there, he acquired a good understanding of the English language, which would prove valuable to his family in the coming years.

His interests were many; and although not wealthy, he became a man of substance. His primary occupation was president of the Nuñez Bank (*Banco Nuñez*), but that was not his only job. As an agent for various insurance companies, he would eventually spend most of his evenings at the dining room table in his home, going over his insurance accounts.

My father brought his bride to the house where he grew up, the home where his parents reared their children. I think that Papo and Mami, my parents, loved each other very much, although they did not express affection in public nor in front of their children. I have no way of knowing whether or not all Cuban marriages of that era were as private. I wish I had just one memory of them embracing or sharing a tender kiss.

One of my treasured photographs, taken before they were married, shows them gazing into each other's eyes. On the back is a romantic note written by my father in English. Like most Cubans, Spanish was and is our native language, so I was surprised that he wrote such lovely words in English all those years ago. I know there must have been an attraction between them at some time, for I and my brothers were born!

At times I have been surprised by the vivid memories from early childhood that still linger in my mind. One triggers another and another. It would be wonderful if a printer could instantly print out those mercurial memories, all in chronological order. In the meantime, we click away on computers, grateful that we have progressed from paper and pencil.

During my childhood, we often spent summer months on the upper eastern beaches of Cuba. My father rented various houses for us, sometimes big enough for two families; and we stayed at each location for three months at a time. They took furniture, bedding and everything else we needed. Miguel, a young man my father hired to work around our house, helped us make our summer moves both to and from the beaches.

One summer my parents rented an especially large house on the beach at Santa Cruz. We shared it with my Aunt Sara, her husband, Panchito, and their son, Panchitín, who was my age. We were no more than three, four at the most, but we already loved to dance. One day Panchitín came into the house and called to me.

"Isabelita, come dance with me!" He began to sing the words of a happy little chorus that everyone knew. *"Pan con queso, guayaba, no!"* Loosely translated: "Bread with cheese, guava, no!" Guava is a fruit, made into a hard paste that we sliced and put on bread. The chorus has a catchy tune and a distinct beat. Ta-ta-ta-ta--ta-ta-ta-TA! The two of us danced and laughed, and the memory of my little cousin is still very sweet.

One of the places most memorable for its beauty is called "*La Loma de Candela*," the Hill of Fire. Again, I was no more than three or four, but I remember how much we enjoyed this place in the country, close to my home town.

Every morning my mother took me for a walk in the scenic hills that surrounded *La Loma de Candela*. The scent that greeted me on those outings was so appealing—fresh, sweet, unusual. The early morning light seemed golden and new each day.

(I make a practice of going into our yard to smell the fresh air and look at the flowers every summer morning, and one day something in the air triggered my memory of the Hill of Fire. I don't know from what local flower the aroma comes, but it is the same sweet scent that filled the air on that Cuban hillside so long ago. Perhaps it is a combination of summer breezes and flowers.)

For us, Santa Cruz and Santa Fe were the best beaches on the northeastern side of the island. The sea and sky were incredible—clean sands, not pure white like some of the other beaches in Cuba, but very nice. I wish I could describe it adequately; but words cannot convey how the sun sparkles on the water, or how sea breezes feel on the skin.

A vivid image in my mind from early years at Santa Cruz is of my mother. She was slim, and she swam with skill and grace. I was only three years old, but I can close my eyes and see her, strikingly beautiful in her brown swimsuit, sunlight bouncing off her wet arms and legs as she laughed with the pure joy of being young and vibrant. I can understand why my father had been enchanted with her.

My father's youngest sister, Omaira Ramos, lived with us until she married. She is in my earliest memories, and I loved her like an older sister. I was very territorial with her, thinking that she belonged only to me. She played with me, babied me and spoiled me; so how could I not believe that she was mine alone?

So pretty and full of life, she loved to dance as much as my mother did. During our summer days on the beach, the radio played music all day long. Our many cousins often wandered in and out of the beach houses, and dancing could break out at any time.

In thinking of Omaira, my mind skips to many sudden, bright images of times I spent with her. One of them took place on the beach at Santa Fe, where we sat in chairs to watch the regatta. Long, slim crafts filled with determined young men rowing in unison raced through the azure water. Sun-tipped ripples sparkled in the wake of so many vessels, and the breeze off the water felt good on my face.

However, the most memorable thing to me then, and today in memory, is a handsome, brown-skinned young man who sat in front of us. I stared at him, because he was all I could see. He was right in front of me and I could not see around him. One is never too old to appreciate beauty, whatever its form.

During one of those summers in Santa Fe, Annette, the granddaughter of people who owned the house beside us, became my friend. Her home was in the United States, where she lived with her parents. I think that Annette's parents had grown up in Cuba, and they brought their daughter to see her grandparents, perhaps to become acquainted with the country of their childhood, as well.

Not only did Annette and I play together, she introduced me to new breakfast foods. In Cuba, we did not eat much for breakfast, not like the huge meals served in the United States. This girl ate a big breakfast! I was amazed at the amount of food her grandmother served for the morning meal.

She had poached eggs and toast, and the moment I saw them, I wanted them, too. I insisted that my mother poach eggs for me, like Annette had; and Mami did it! I laugh at myself, even now, for desiring whatever new or luscious food caught my eye; or was it my appetite! I have never been afraid to sample new foods.

From my perspective, we lived happily for several years in the house that had belonged to my Papo's father. The windows were tall throughout the house; but the wall in the dining room that opened onto the big courtyard was practically all windows, none of which had screens; and they were always open. Gleaming, hunter green shutters opened and closed, like an accordion, along the windows. The open expanse seemed to extend the dining room into the courtyard.

The woodwork, including doors, shutters and frames, painted the same beautiful, dark hunter green, created a striking contrast against the stark white stucco outer walls. Each room had a door and windows that opened onto the back courtyard, surrounded by the house. Like many houses in

Cuba, red tiles covered the roof. My grandfather's house looked like the happy home it was.

While very small, probably no more than three, I discovered an open place, a slot like one in a piggy bank, along one of the boards in the kitchen. Somehow, I came to believe that I must insert every coin I could find into that slot. No coin was safe from my obsession before my mother discovered why and how money disappeared from the house. If the building is still standing, the money is still there, just waiting for Fidel to put his soft, blood-stained hands on it.

Coins were only one of my passions. Before I was very old, chocolate became a close second. I smile, remembering a visit from my cousin, Ondina, who was closer to my mother's age than mine. I was perhaps five or six, old enough to have developed a loving relationship with Ondina, whom I called "Ondi." She and my mother were close, and Ondi often came to visit. She was so skinny I could wrap my arms completely around her.

My father worked in his home office that evening, while my mother and Ondi sat in comfortable chairs on the big sidewalk in front of the house. I wanted to sit with them, but my mother had put my brother and me to bed. She told me that I needed to sleep, for tomorrow I would have to get up early and get ready for school. I think she probably wanted to spend a relaxing evening with her niece.

Well, I didn't buy it! I wasn't sleepy, and I knew there was a place where I could hide and hear the conversation that would take place between Mami and Ondi. So! If I wasn't sleepy, I must be hungry. I was always hungry! Well-fed, but always wanting something delicious to eat!

I also knew where my mother kept the bars of chocolate she shaved to make her wonderful hot chocolate. I got out of bed and slipped into the kitchen, where I found a bar of that delicious brown stuff of which dreams are made! I ate it. All of it! My mother, happily unaware of my kitchen adventure, continued her visit with Ondi. I decided to get as close as possible to them, for I wanted to hear their conversation.

I passed my father's closed office doors, which had opaque panes of glass that let light pass through while providing privacy. Absorbed in his work, he didn't see me. I crept across the immense living room, drawing closer and closer to the porch before disaster struck. Ondi looked up, saw me and began to laugh.

"Lila, look at Isa's mouth," Ondi chuckled. My mother could do nothing but laugh at the spectacle I must have presented, my mouth and chin completely circled with delicious chocolate. Delighted with the laughter of the two women I adored, I laughed, too. I could have been in trouble, but, surprisingly, my mother chose to ignore my disobedience. She helped me wash off the chocolate, and she put me back to bed. By then, my sleepy eyes drooped and my tummy was quite full!

CHAPTER TWO

Changes

The dining room held a table long enough to accommodate many guests. That's where I spread out my crayons and colored pictures while my father worked on insurance accounts. It's where I later did my homework and where I pretended to play a piano. I can close my eyes and see Papo, absorbed in his work, patiently listening to my chatter. He was a good father.

Many photographs from that time survived my family's flight from Cuba, thanks to the foresight of my father. Until I was in my teens, my mother must have kept her favorite photographer in business. I have many albums filled with professional photos of me and Juan, taken from the time we were very young. Both of us had dark hair and eyes, and the way we were posed in those pictures makes us look like little dressed-up dolls.

Life was about to change in our house, an event for which I was not prepared. It seems that the young man who came to call on my beloved *Tia* Omaira, who had lived with us as long as I could remember, had an ulterior motive. Unknown to me, he intended to marry her! It was bad enough that I had to share my aunt's attention when he came to call. I did not like him, and I didn't pretend that I did!

Each time he came to our house, I placed my little rocking chair right in front of him and my aunt; and I watched them. In Cuba, every unmarried girl and woman had to have a chaperone when they were in the company of a man. My constant presence made another chaperone unnecessary for my aunt, as long as I sat there in my rocker. I was jealous of anyone who took her attention away from me!

I had no idea that a wedding was being planned. On the wedding day, my mother told me that I was very tired and that I must go to sleep. The whole family knew how devoted I was to my aunt. I'm sure they wanted to avoid a scene when it came time for the young married couple to leave. Mami put me in the bed, and I slept; but the sound of many people in the house eventually woke me.

When I sat up, everything was dark. I could hear people talking and laughing. I climbed down from my bed and followed the sound of merriment, never dreaming what I would find. My aunt and her new husband were already getting into their car, ready to begin their honeymoon. Well, that was the end of a peaceful wedding celebration! I must have thrown a royal fit!

"No, no, don't leave!" I cried, but my tears had no power to stop my aunt. My parents told me how I cried and cried when my aunt and her new husband drove away. For many years I hated the man who became my uncle. After their daughter, Elba, was born, I think I forgave him; but I was five years old by then. Elba became my best friend, even though she was so much younger.

Divorce was not common in Cuba back then, but my father's sister, Noemia, was divorced from her husband. I didn't meet him until I was older. I liked him, and he was well-thought of by my family. They had two daughters, Norma and Nivia, who were quite a few years older than I; but like so many of my older cousins, they were very kind and sweet to me, especially Norma.

The girls and their mother lived in a small suite located in a boarding house in Havana. The building itself was beautiful. When I was four, my little brother became very ill with a communicable disease. I don't remember which one, but it was important that I not catch it.

So my Aunt Noemia took me into her home to live with her and her daughters until Juan was well. I was so very sad and lonely. I missed my parents and my home. On the second floor, the apartment was at the top of a long flight of cold, white marble stairs. I remember sitting on the top stair, looking down, wishing I could go home.

Inside the common living room was a piano. Their suite held more furniture than you might expect to be in such a small place, but it was very cozy. Every day my aunt insisted that Norma play the violin, while Nivia practiced the piano. So it seems that I come from a very musical family. They made my time with them as enjoyable as possible, but I was happy when I was able to return to my home.

On most afternoons in Cuban cities, around four o'clock, many people dressed up in nice clothes and sat on their front porches or patios. Neighbors and strangers who walked along the streets stopped to chat with those who sat in their finery, waiting for such an opportunity.

"How sweet you look in your pretty dress." Time after time, passers-by greeted me in this way, until I thought it was what everyone should say. My mother told me that one day I ran into the house, crying, broken-hearted.

"Mami!" I cried. "A lady walked by the house and she did not tell me how pretty I look in my dress! Why did she not tell me?" I think this set the precedent for me, the practice of dressing up, of wanting to appear always at my best as much as possible. It was drilled into me from an early age, possibly instilling in me a sense of entitlement at that age.

When I was in kindergarten, at the age of four, that sense of entitlement proved to be my undoing. If I saw something I wanted, I assumed that I should have it. It never occurred to me that acting on a "want" might be construed as stealing. So I took it!

I loved the snacks provided to the kindergarten, especially the cookies. Their sweet, luscious filling just seemed to provide more temptation than I could resist. In fact, one afternoon after I had eaten mine, I took one from another little girl, who cried and cried. The teacher stood me in the corner for a while, to punish me; and then I was the one who cried! I was angry, too, I think; for I escaped from that awful place where they dared to punish me!

I ran the three blocks to my home. I can only imagine how Mami must have felt when her little four-year-old daughter walked into the house. Furious, she marched to the school, demanding to know how and why I had left my class. When she discovered that no one, not one person, had noticed my absence, she was livid! She took me out of the school that day.

I don't know why she didn't enroll me at another school in our city. Instead, she sent me to a school in the town of Cidra, where her parents lived. Cidra is located in the province of Matanzas, a good distance from Güines. Perhaps Mami thought that it would be good for me to spend time with her parents, which it turned out to be.

My grandparents were wonderfully loving, caring people. They were materially poor, but life with them was good. Some of my cousins lived nearby, and I was allowed to visit and play with them for hours. I loved it! I missed my mother and my home, but I had no problems in school; and I loved my grandparents' house.

How vivid are my memories of my nights there. My grandmother made up my bed with clean, crisp white sheets that she starched and ironed. My bedroom opened onto the living room, so I could see them sitting there at night. Without fail, my grandfather and grandmother had devotions. He read from his Bible and they prayed together, something I had not seen before.

(Although my mother was not active in a church when I was a child, she had memorized a great deal of scripture in her youth. I recall her quoting Psalm 23, as well as many others. She never drew away from the teachings of her father. Further into my story, I will share more about her, about the unusual path it took for her to find what was always with her.)

In spite of the lack of money, my grandfather never left the house in summer without being dressed in a white linen suit. In winter he wore a dark one, always with a bow tie. One of my cousins still describes him as "a real Dandy." My grandmother washed their clothes by hand and ironed every piece. My poor grandmother had to work so hard. How amazed she would be to see how easy it is to do laundry today.

A short sidewalk from their front door led to concrete steps, which had a handrail that allowed my grandmother to walk down them safely. Every Saturday, she moved carefully down the steps and walked a short distance along the public sidewalk to the nearby bus stop, where she boarded a bus to Matanzas, the large city that is the capital of Matanzas Province.

She managed to save enough money to keep her standing appointment at a beauty shop where she had her hair done. Like most woman of her day, she kept her newly-styled hair covered with an ugly hairnet! To me, that is similar to people who cover new furniture with throws or blankets, protecting it from soil and wear. Unfortunately, they never really see their beautiful furniture.

For as long as my grandmother was able, she kept those appointments. She set the standard for looking as well-groomed as possible. My mother continued that practice, and I have tried my best to follow their examples.

This routine, like brushing our teeth, was instilled in us at an early age, to look our best, no matter how we feel or what our financial circumstances are.

My grandfather founded the Presbyterian church in Cidra. They no longer attended services, but I went to church with my cousins every Sunday. I remember how safe I felt, sitting with them on the hard benches. Someone played a piano, and we sang hymns. There were classes, one for men and one for women. I don't know how many, but I'm sure that much of the congregation consisted of members of my extended family.

Among his many interests, my grandfather had been a writer for a newspaper called The Mogote Eco (*El Eco del Mogote*). What I didn't know at the time was that he had once owned and operated a theater in the building next to his house, when my mother was a girl. It's difficult for me to imagine my grandparents in that light, for I knew them only as devout people of faith.

The shows featured singers, dancers, performers of all kinds from Matanzas, including a clown, created by my Uncle Mayito, who also sang. Another uncle, Enrique, sang quite well; and Aunt Sara performed beautiful operatic solos. She had a wonderful voice.

After I went back to my parents' home, my grandfather sent a large picture of my kindergarten class to me. On the back he wrote a sweet dedication, still special to me; and I am including a photo of it in these pages. His handwriting was beautiful, an art that, to my knowledge, is no longer taught in classrooms.

In thinking of my grandfather, I feel again that sense of being special. He called me "*Belica*" and "*Chabela*," endearments that expressed his devotion. I missed him and my grandmother after I went back home. They could not travel easily from Cidra to Güines, but we went to see them often.

During those few years before they came to visit, I had taken piano lessons, unknown to my grandparents. They heard me play for the first time when I was nine, and my grandfather cried. I played a Strauss waltz, "The Blue Danube," for him; and I can still see the tears of pleasure and pride on his face.

It pleases me to know that his house still stands in Cidra, where so much of what once was beautiful has deteriorated or been destroyed. My cousins have restored it, and they keep the house in good condition. They have managed to keep our grandfather's desk, and it remains where it stood when I lived with them. It was from there that he wrote articles for the newspaper.

My cousins have sent a current photo to me, which I am including in the book. Two of them now live in the house, hopefully a sign that one day all of Cuba will be restored and free again. That is the hope which lives in the hearts of every Cuban who remembers what Cuba once was, even when reality whispers that our hope is dim.

There is one thing I know: My love for the cookies that caused the exodus from my home to the house of my grandparents still exists! They remain one of my favorites; and I order them often from a supplier of Cuban foods and delicacies in Florida. At times, as I enjoy one of those cookies, I smile, remembering the one I took from that other little girl so many years ago; and I wonder if she ever forgave me.

CHAPTER THREE

The Girl

Some of my earliest memories are of Consuelo, the woman who became our cook when I was three years old. Not only did she prepare good food, she made us feel loved. I loved her, too; and I thought she was just another member of our family, which she was as long as she was with us.

Like many children, I was a picky eater. In spite of mothers who fear that their little ones are not getting enough to eat, toddlers will not starve themselves to death. When they get hungry, they will eat. I think my mother did not believe that statement to be true, for she contrived a number of inventive ways to insure that I ate what she thought I needed.

She once sent Consuelo to rent a big bicycle and bring it to our house. The cost for the bike was five cents for one-half hour, ten cents for one hour. The rental stand wasn't far from our house, and my mother was willing to try anything to make me eat.

They placed me on the bicycle seat, and Consuelo fed me *almuerzo*, our noonday meal, a spoonful at a time. She was so patient and loving, and she would prove to be important to me when I grew up, just as she did when I was a child. As for eating, I don't remember ever being encouraged to feed myself, maybe not until I went to kindergarten.

My mother also employed a housekeeper, which was common for Cuban households. Many of them also had gardeners and chauffeurs, but we did not. Our laundry was sent out to be washed and ironed, also common. This practice was a benefit to both the user and provider of the service.

I went to the Kate Plumer Bryan Memorial School, which was known as The American School, through first and second grades. My cousin,

Panchitín, was in my class, which was wonderful for me. We had been part of each other's lives since we were babies.

By the age of six, I was able to write legibly. We were taught the Palmer method, and I loved making circles, long loops above and below the lines. My skill with pencil and paper paid off quite well for me, not long after I learned to connect all those beautiful letters into sentences.

One of my father's insurance clients was Raymundo Rosa, who owned a shoe store only a few blocks from our house. Every evening, my mother took me with her to visit her sister, a short distance past the shoe store; so we walked by it, going and coming. In the window display I spied a pair of beautiful red sandals, the prettiest shoes I ever saw! I wanted them so badly I knew they must have been made just for me. Unfortunately, I had to wear what I considered ugly orthopedic shoes!

The night Raymundo Rosa came by to see my father was, I knew, heaven-sent! Carefully, I crawled into my father's office where he met with his evening clients; and I crept beneath the desk, beside Papo's chair. On a scrap of paper I wrote this note: "Papo, I want the pair of red sandals in Señor Rosa's store window." I raised the paper and slipped it atop the table, where my father could see it.

He laughed, read the note and said, "Then get them." Señor Rosa joined in the laughter. Why would he not? He knew that he had just made a shoe sale! Young as I was, perhaps I thought that he might have had the shoes with him! Who knows?

I never would have attempted such a thing with my mother. I was very young, but I had already learned who was more likely to give me what I wanted and who was not! I loved those red sandals, and I wore them as often as Mami allowed.

The shoes were only one of many indulgences given to me by Papo. On another evening, sitting with him as usual at the dining room table, I voiced another of my wants.

"Papo, I want a piano. I know that I can play it."

"Do you think so?" Papo's voice was gentle, like his spirit. I had a small piano, a toy, like many small children owned; but I wanted a big one.

"Yes, Papo." I flexed my fingers along the table, showing him how capable of playing the piano I would be. With my whole heart I desired one. It was not long before my father brought home a piano; and I started to take lessons.

My father's brother, Narey, and his family lived in Encrucijada, Las Villas, a province on the other side of Matanzas Province. *Tío* Narey's daughter, Nayce, played the piano very well. The first time they came to visit, following the acquisition of my piano, she performed for us. I watched her fingers fly nimbly over the keys, especially her left hand, as she played a pretty, lively waltz called "Isabelita." I was entranced.

I had an ear for music; and after they left, I sat down and picked out the melody, listening to and remembering the sounds of each key. I played that waltz, not as perfectly and skillfully as my cousin; but I played it! After all, I thought that the piece was named for me, since all my family called me "Isabelita" most of the time. *How could I help but think that the world revolved around me?*

I know that my mother's intentions were to provide only the best for me, and she thought that a boarding school would offer a good education and discipline. So when I was seven, entering the third grade, she enrolled me in a boarding school in Matanzas City in the province of Matanzas, the same province where my grandparents lived.

It was then, at seven years old, that I became truly aware of what went on around me. I suddenly awoke to a world that no longer held my parents, my little brother, my cousin, Panchitín, and my other little friends. Going to a strange place in a strange town certainly did not seem the best to me. It wasn't unusual for children to be sent away to school, and I'm sure it was not unusual for them to go through a period of adjustment. I never did adjust.

The Irene Toland School, a Methodist school run by Americans, was a beautiful place in 1944. A big auditorium had just been built. The buildings and grounds were well kept, filled with flower beds and climbing roses. I was too young to be so far from home, and I was miserable, suffering from homesickness to the point of constant tears. I missed my house with its white stucco walls and Hunter green trim.

My mother came to see me every weekend, and sometimes she came during the week. She missed me, too. She sometimes took me to see two of my aunts who lived in Matanzas. They took me out to eat, for one of my greatest dislikes at the school was the food. I hated it.

In retrospect, it might have been better if Mami had not come to visit. When she left, our heartbreak was a repetition of the first time—both of us crying and clinging to each other. I wonder if this separation anxiety might have been responsible for my mother's reluctance to allow me out of her sight, even as I grew older. She would be overly protective until the day I got married. On the other hand, Cuban mothers were known for holding tight reins on daughters, but not so much on their sons, part of the Cuban culture.

On Wednesday nights, the girls from the dorm attended chapel, which was mandatory. During every service, I became very sleepy as I listened to the devotions. One particular Wednesday night was different. At the end of the service, the congregation began to sing *At the Cross,* which was familiar to me; but I had never paid attention to the words.

That night, for some reason, every word touched my heart. In my mind, I saw Jesus, dying for me. Although I was so young, I was ready to respond to my inner vision and the words of that song. If an invitation had been given, I know that I would have answered it; but there was none. I experienced a joy in my heart for some time; but there was no one to explain to me the plan of salvation. It would be many years and many tears later before I found that for which I sought.

I was happy only during my piano lessons. The campus had a Music Building with several small rooms, all of which held a piano. Each room had a large window, covered with wrought iron grills, which allowed a sunny view of the grounds; and outside the windows grew the most beautiful red roses. They climbed upward, winding through and around the iron grills; and their scent filled the air. One of those roses would prove to be my undoing.

I was not totally alone in the school. An older second cousin of mine also attended, and my mother gave her money to keep for me. Any time I asked for something, the money was available to me. The food served in the dining room was so awful, I didn't eat much. I still won't eat something I dislike!

Every afternoon at the same hour, we were allowed a certain time on the playground. I'm sure it was no coincidence that a man came every day at just that moment to sell ice cream. I always wanted some, and my cousin gave me money to buy it. Oh, it tasted so good! Of course, I went back for seconds; and my cousin gave me more money. Ice cream and my piano lessons were the brightest spots in my days at the Irene Toland School.

One day after I finished practicing my piano lesson, I spotted a perfect red rose climbing up the iron grill on the window. Its beauty enticed and tempted me beyond endurance, but the rose eluded me, just out of reach. Determined to have it, I found a small stool, pushed it as closely to the wall as possible and climbed onto it. I reached through the ironwork and grasped it, ignoring the thorns that scratched my skin. I didn't see Miss Kelly, the director, on the grounds; but she saw me.

"What are you doing?! How dare you pick my rose!"

Not only was Miss Kelly the director, she took care of the flowers and roses that grew so beautifully on the grounds; and she was furious with me. I knew I was in trouble, but I didn't understand her fury. I had to appear before her in her office, where she scolded me without mercy. I cried and cried, so miserable and unhappy that I could have drowned in my tears.

In spite of my unhappiness, I participated in a Halloween play in the magnificent auditorium. It was the first I had heard of such a holiday. I was so very shy; but I managed to say my one line, "*Calabaza!*" (Pumpkin), and hit the swinging piñata.

Somehow I survived until Christmas, when students were allowed to go home. I loved Christmas vacation; but as the day neared that I must return to school, I cried so long and so pitifully that my mother did not take me back to the boarding school. She reenrolled me in the American School in Güines, where I was reunited with my friends and my cousin. I don't know who was happier, I or my mother. Since she made the decision during Christmas vacation, there was time to have uniforms made for me.

After I finished third grade, my mother transferred me to a small academy close to our house. Gloria Troncoso, the teacher, was very stern. She maintained order in the classroom much as a military sergeant might. Her strict rules allowed no room for leniency should they be broken. I didn't like her, but she seemed to like me well enough. I made good grades, and I memorized poems easily.

Every Friday, the students gathered on the outside patio where we saluted the flag. Many times, following the salute, Gloria asked me to recite a poem, something I did without being afraid or self-conscious. I memorized a lot of poems, some of them quite long and dramatic. I remember tears falling down my face as I recited sadder ones. Perhaps that is why my teacher asked me to recite so often.

Still, my mind sometimes wandered when she was teaching, explaining something or telling us facts we were expected to remember. One such day, I began to draw little figures on a piece of paper. I drew a boy, so pretty, and a girl, so pretty, and beneath them I wrote Tony and Virginia, and I drew a connecting line, indicating that they were sweethearts.

Aware that the teacher was walking toward my desk, as quickly as I could I scratched out the drawing. At least I covered the names! Too late! With a stick made especially for the task, she struck my hands. I was mortified. From that moment I hated her, even into adulthood. It didn't help that Gloria was a family friend. By family, I mean my parents. My father was a Mason, and my mother and Gloria belonged to the "Daughters of Acacia," a part of the Masons I still know little about.

When I got home from school that day, I said to my mother. "Look, Mami, what she did to me!"

"What did you do that made her punish you?" Mami knew me well. I don't remember what I told her, but I'm sure it wasn't the whole story. I endured school in Gloria's academy until I entered fifth grade.

(Skipping ahead in my story. Not long before I was to be married, while sitting in the house where I would live with my husband, my mother called my name from the front door.

"Isa, come here. Gloria has come with a wedding gift for you." I ignored her, not wanting to see the woman who had dared to strike me when I was a child!

"Isa, I am calling you! Gloria is here. Come here!" Mami would not give up. So I stood and went to the door, where my nemesis handed to me her gift. It was a good deal of money, more than I expected from her.

"Thank you very much," I said to her, probably not as graciously as I should have. She was not invited to the wedding, for she was not a relative, close friend or business acquaintance of my father's. It was during the course of writing this book that I learned why the woman had a kind of fondness for me. While visiting over the phone with my cousin, she told me that Gloria had been my father's girlfriend before he met my mother.

If you don't know this about Cubans, let me tell you that we are a nation of very territorial women when it comes to married relationships, whether our parents, our siblings or our spouses. Just the thought of my father once having any kind of feelings for a woman other than my mother was enough to make me livid! If I had known of this when Gloria came to give me a wedding gift, I might have ordered her out of my house! I am probably joking, but I'm glad I didn't know then that Gloria and my father once had any kind of relationship!)

Around the time my mother rescued me from boarding school, I became friends with Sonia Romero, a girl my age who lived in our neighborhood. We didn't go to the same school, but we became the best of friends. Sonia came often to my house to play. Whatever I had, she wanted one like it, from shoes to clothing. We were practically twins! More than anything else, she loved to watch me practice my piano lessons.

"Oh, I wish I could play the piano," she said to me. "I love it so much."

"Well, you could take piano lessons, too." My suggestion was well-meant.

I had no concept of life style or economic differences. I didn't know that Sonia's family could not afford a piano and lessons. Children don't care about "poor" or "rich" or anything in between. Nor do they care about race. To me, Sonia was simply my dearest friend, not the little black girl who lived down the street. All I saw was my good friend, with whom I laughed and played. We had no prejudices.

If I had realized why Sonia had no piano, I probably would have insisted that my parents give Sonia piano lessons, too; and we could have practiced our lessons together in my house. Had I suggested such a thing, my father probably would have agreed to it. He was a kind, generous man. Sonia proved to be not only bright, but very determined and talented beyond my comprehension.

When I was nine, we moved from my father's childhood home to a huge house above the bank, where he worked. I lost touch with Sonia. It would be a few years before we saw each again, as teenagers. What she accomplished in that short time still boggles the mind.

Beyond that, the following decades would prove how resourceful and talented, even brilliant she was. Sonia will appear and reappear throughout my story.

CHAPTER FOUR

Happy Times

By the age of nine, I was very tall for my age; and I'm not much taller now than I was then! My mother insisted that I wear big, fluffy bows and ribbons in my hair, which did not help my self-esteem. She bought them to match every dress I owned. One of my cousins once told me that the huge bows with trailing ribbons looked like a kite, maybe even a helicopter on my head!

That same summer, my mother let me go for a visit with my Aunt Blanca in Havana. Very few people owned cars, so the majority of Cubans rode buses. A bus would fill up with passengers at the first stop of the day, as a rule; so there was usually a crowd of people waiting for the next bus, and the next, and so on.

My mother packed my suitcase, choosing what she wanted me to wear while I was away. She included a yellow dress, which I liked; but with it she placed a huge, matching hair bow. She told my aunt to be sure to put the bow in my hair when I wore that dress. However, when we arrived at my aunt's house, and it was time to dress for an excursion to an amusement park, I begged my aunt.

"Please, Blanca, don't make me wear that bow! I hate it!" She had mercy on me, and I didn't have to wear that big floppy thing. It would have made me taller than my aunt, for she was as short as I was tall!

We had a wonderful day. I thought she was old, but Blanca rode every ride with me and enjoyed our time together as much as I did. Riding the roller coaster seemed a little daunting to me, but my aunt insisted that we ride it.

"Don't be scared," she told me. "Have fun! Let's ride everything!" And that's what we did. The roller coaster turned out to be one of my favorite rides! She made each new experience for me something to remember.

During my visit, she took me shopping, and she bought a two-piece swimsuit for me. I loved it! Somehow, during the checkout process, the package containing the swimsuit disappeared. Someone must have taken it from the counter. I cried and cried. My aunt and my cousin felt so sorry for me that they bought fabric; and my cousin, who was a good seamstress, made a cute little two-piece swimsuit for me.

They knew and I knew that I could never wear it around my father. He didn't like to see midriffs exposed or shorts on his wife and daughter. Although he was loving and generous, there were a few things he would not tolerate.

"Don't worry," Tia Blanca told me. "We'll go to the beach here, and you can wear your new swim suit. We'll have a good time." We did! Those few days still stand out in my memory as some of the happiest days in my childhood.

Somewhere among my boxes and boxes of photographs is one of me in my lovely new swimsuit, but it didn't come from those of my parents! My father never knew about my two-piece swim suit. I didn't care that Papo wouldn't like it. During the time I spent with my aunt and my cousin, I swam and splashed in the water, knowing that I looked as modern and cute as all the other little girls.

Tia Blanca took me on many excursions around the city of Havana that summer. A wide staircase graces the front of the Capitol building, magnificent in style and construction, steps that I ran up and down as my aunt watched me play. Across the wide street from the steps were outside restaurants.

Bands performed on the broad sidewalks, and my favorites were comprised of women musicians. My aunt took me to see them several times during my visit. There were no armed guards to bar the way, no green, fatigued-clad thugs carrying machine guns; and no one asked for our identification papers. Little did I know or care that the seeds of revolution already grew in the heart of a man who would become "The Supreme Ruler" of Cuba.

Along the beautiful *Paseo del Prado,* a boulevard that stretches for blocks and blocks through the center of Havana, are shops and colorful buildings with arches and columns. The street is more like a park, paved with stone and tile in geometric designs, impossible to describe adequately.

In one area, I played and danced around magnificent statues of lions, huge and glorious, frozen in time and motion. They had stood there for many years, and they would stand for many more. A few years after my playful interchange with them, their blank stares would look upon unbelievable atrocities, beatings and executions. I had enjoyed my brief time of freedom from hair bows and my mother's sharp eyes; but at that time I had no concept of what freedom truly is.

My aunt and I walked along those lovely streets of Havana and looked into shop windows, at the mannequins dressed in beautiful clothing and jewelry, the very latest in haute couture. I fantasized about being all grown up, my imagination filled with visions of myself clad in such finery.

Outlandish? Not with a mother like mine! I think that she lived to dress me in the prettiest clothes she could find or have made for me. Perhaps that is why it is so easy for me to remember my dresses from long ago. I don't know if an occasion was made special to me by the dress I wore, or if the dress made an event special. Possibly both.

Living in our new house above the bank was an adventure in itself. The most wonderful thing was the balcony, which stretched all along the front of the house. It provided a wide view of the streets below and around us, a source of entertainment for me. I enjoyed watching men and women, dressed in fine clothes, go in and out of the stores.

A lovely park with magnificent grounds covered two or three blocks right across the street from the bank. Large trees and beautiful flowers accented the green lawns, and benches were placed conveniently where people could sit and enjoy such peaceful surroundings.

In the center of the park, a Catholic Church's classic lines and steeple called the faithful to worship every Sunday. At the back of the church, visible to us, was a fountain. In front of the church was a beautiful gazebo that provided an area for people to gather nightly to promenade and visit with friends and neighbors.

At the end of our block, an Emergency Care Clinic, *La Casa de Socorro*, provided walk-in patient care, as well as ambulance service. Businesses of various kinds lined the other two sides of the park.

Owners of some of the shops had living quarters behind their establishments, but no other single-family dwellings were available on the three blocks. A taxi stand, with a line of several taxis, was among the businesses. The Balerdi Building (*Edificio Balerdi*), was built on the left side of the church, across the street. The bank was on the opposite corner.

Living so high above the streets, from our balcony we watched all the parades, the carnivals (*carnavales*), the bands, singers and dancing groups. It was the perfect place to live.

Not long before the next big change that would take place in my life, I acquired something that would be uniquely mine forever. One evening while my mother attended a meeting for women at the Masonic Lodge, my brother, Juan, and I entertained ourselves on the porch of the building, which was really beautiful. We decided to play baseball.

We had a ball, but no bat; we determined where the bases would be, and we began our game. As I ran from one base to another, I tripped on a bootjack, a metal devise conveniently placed for people to clean the bottoms of their shoes before entering the building. I fell hard, landed first on my knees; and my mouth hit the metal.

The pain was horrendous! I cried and cried. Blood poured from my mouth, and my knees were cut and bloody. The janitor, Ventura, came to help me. He had a first aid kit, complete with everything he needed to stop the bleeding. I was more concerned with the pain from my skinned knees than a chipped tooth. Moments later, my mother came downstairs. She looked at me and began to cry.

"Oh, no, Isabelita! Your beautiful teeth! What have you done to your beautiful teeth?" A piece from one of my front teeth had broken away. She took me to a dentist the next day. He examined me and told Mami that he could repair my tooth. She decided to leave it alone, and soon everyone began to like it, even my mother. Still, she kept the chip, a toothy souvenir, for a long time.

All the dentists I have seen since have told me they could repair the chip. Actually, I rather like it. The chipped tooth is a constant reminder of my childhood, of who I was, how and where I lived. It has become just another part of me, of who I am. It turns out that I was sometimes more hazardous to my own wellbeing than a Caribbean hurricane would be.

Tropical storms hit Cuba quite often, but most of them did little damage. We were used to them. Not even the occasional hurricane scared us. There was warning enough for people to put up plywood over doors and windows. What could have been scary for us children became fun-filled parties.

My Aunt Estela lived in a big, solid house, which became our storm shelter. The adults made party foods for us, and we played games, laughing and having the best time. We didn't notice or care that havoc might be occurring outside.

Tornadoes are capricious, unlike hurricanes we experienced in Cuba. Tornadoes can turn on a whim of the wind, while hurricanes are too big to turn quickly. I would much prefer to deal with them than a tornado. In fact, years later, we partied through Hurricane Andrew, while we were visiting family in the southern end of Florida.

(*Fast Forward, Re: Hurricane Andrew. My daughter, Christina, and I attended the wedding of my niece, Aidy, the daughter of my brother, José. Christina was a member of the wedding party. The ceremony took place in Miami, and the dinner-dance reception was held in a beautiful banquet hall. A group of violinists strolled among the tables, softly playing Cuban music while guests enjoyed their dinner.*

The dance that followed was everything a bride and groom could hope for. Laughter, music, family and friends of the couple toasted to their good health and happiness, after which the young couple left the party and went to their suite in the hotel.

During the night, Hurricane Andrew came ashore and did horrendous damage to the town of Homestead, where my brother's house was located. That morning, the groom was told about the destruction of his new father-in-law's house, but he did not tell Aidy, his bride, not wanting to worry her needlessly. They left on their honeymoon cruise, as planned.)

CHAPTER FIVE

Tragedy

During my time in the American School with my cousin, Panchitín, we grew even closer. Not only were we cousins, we were good friends. Always precocious, his curiosity and intellect seemed to have no boundaries. When the teachers asked questions, he raised his hand immediately, indicating that he knew the answer! And he always had the correct one.

Like a flag in a stormy gale, his hand flew up and waved frantically, even in third grade! I just sat there, not sure of anything, amazed that he knew all the answers, in awe of his knowledge. How was it possible that we had read the same books?

Panchitín's father, Panchito, was a brilliant man, an orator, who often spoke at various occasions. He conducted a small academy where he tutored students to prepare them for high school. Perhaps Panchitín's talent and thirst for knowledge was inherited from his father, by either genetics or example, possibly both.

Panchitín could talk about anything, and he was never without words on any subject. He was a bit chubby, a sweet, cute little boy, who captured the hearts of all who knew him. One of the best words to describe him is endearing, for that is what he was. Endearing.

After two years of shared classes with him, I transferred to an Academy, so he and I were no longer in the same school. It was during those two years that Panchitín not only passed me, he completed grade school when he was only eleven and would be entering high school at the age of twelve.

Although he outpaced me in school, Panchitín and I shared some of the same likes and dislikes. He came to our house every Saturday, and together we listened to our favorite radio show, an ongoing Western serial,

Los Tres Villalobos, which we would not miss. We sat there together, eyes glued to the radio, as though we could see the action if we just stared hard enough. How exciting it was for us!

Not only had Panchitín graduated early, he was the valedictorian of his class. Multitalented, he excelled in reading comprehension; and he read fluently, as well as expressing his thoughts well. The boy stood confidently before his classmates and an audience of parents and guests; and he spoke as if it was the easiest thing in the world for him.

The graduation took place in El Liceo, an ornate, spacious building where elegant ballroom dances and other special occasions were held. Huge potted palms for decoration had been hauled by truck from the school grounds to El Liceo, and they had to be returned the next day.

The truck driver enlisted some of the boys to help him load the truck and go with him to unload. Panchitín volunteered, although he was smaller than the other boys who had graduated. Several trips would be required, for the pots were big, and the palms were tall and heavy.

After the pots were loaded on the back of the truck, the boys climbed aboard. Panchitín, for who knows what reason, rode in a seat that was higher than the driver's in the open cab. He was king of the world, able to see everything from his high perch. I don't know how many trips the truck had to make, but on the last one, the driver drove past the home of Panchitín's unmarried aunt, whom he and his sister, La Nena, called Tita.

"Bye, Tita! Bye, Tita!" Recognizing her nephew's voice, she ran outside; and there he was, waving to her from the top of a moving truck.

"*¡ Panchitín, why are you on top of the truck!*" She went back inside, and the next moment she heard a crash. The truck driver, who turned out to be drunk, had hit an electric pole. The crash sent Panchitín flying high into the air, over the electric lines, landing on the street.

About three blocks away, I glanced through the open door to the balcony and called to my mother. "Mami," I cried. "Look at the electric lines! They are swinging!" She came running, and we looked over the balcony, where we could see a line of cars, many of them beginning to honk their horns.

The electric lines were still moving. A few minutes later, we saw a flatbed truck pull up to emergency care at La Casa de Socorro, near the bank. We could see an injured person on the truck bed, but we didn't recognize him. In a very short time, an ambulance emerged with the victim and headed to a hospital in Havana.

Meanwhile, my uncle, Panchito, was sitting in the bus he took every day from Güines to Havana, where he worked in the main branch of the Nuñez Bank, which owned the bank where my father worked, right below our house. Caught in the long line of traffic, bus passengers speculated as to the cause, while a crowd of spectators had gathered along the streets.

"What happened?" From an open bus window, a passenger called to them.

"Panchito Hernandez's son has been badly hurt in an accident."

Even as I relate this story, I am struck anew by the horror and disbelief my uncle must have felt at that moment. To hear that your only son has been hurt, perhaps dying, only a short distance away, well, it is every parent's worst nightmare.

A competent, well-known neurosurgeon in the Havana hospital operated on Panchitín. Unfortunately, his head injuries were massive; and he died on the operating table. His body was returned to Güines. A few days later, the funeral for the son of Panchito and Sara was held at the same school from which the boy had just graduated.

That day I saw my Aunt Sara, sitting in a rocking chair in the second grade room of the school, quietly sobbing. In the corridors, her husband paced endlessly, his grief audible and horrible as he cried, "*Dios mio*! My God! My son, my son!" Pacing and pacing, inconsolable, he was wild in his grief.

Panchitín's little sister, Maria Magdalena, whom we called La Nena, sat holding a doll beside her mother. Something on the doll broke, either an arm or a leg; and the little girl began to cry.

"Oh, Mami, look what happened to my doll!" La Nena sobbed. I believe that the broken doll simply gave this child the opportunity to cry. She was so very young, I'm not sure she understood what had happened to her brother, or that he was gone from their lives forever. Seeing her parents cry and witnessing their grief must have been traumatic for her.

As I stood in the middle of all that pain, I grieved for my young cousin. More, young as I was, my heart ached for my Aunt Sara; and I thought how awful it must be to lose a son. Decades later, I would remember that moment and those grieving parents; and only then would I be able to comprehend the magnitude of their loss. The difference was that my son would not die suddenly.

I truly do not know how my poor aunt and her family coped with the loss of Panchitín; but I know that they did. Somehow, life does go on. We keep breathing and getting through the days, until one day we notice that the sky is blue and the sun is shining. And God is still in His heaven.

As family tragedies played out and the citizens of Cuba, wealthy and poor, continued about their daily lives, Fidel Castro entered law school in the University of Havana. He became involved with Communist groups, laying a foundation for what was to come. For a while he practiced law with a group of other attorneys.

An attractive young woman served as secretary for this firm. She was not impressed with Fidel, neither as a man nor as an attorney. Her name was Norma, and she was one of my first cousins, in whose home I had stayed often. At the time, Fidel was one of the attorneys she worked for. She could not know how he would impact her life, changing its course forever.

How different our lives could be if it were possible to discern, even a tiny bit, what goes on in the minds and hearts of those around us. It is only in hind sight that we say, "If only I had known!" But that is how our stories are told

CHAPTER SIX

Buenavista

In the autumn after Panchitín died, my parents enrolled me at Buenavista in Havana. It accepted students of elementary school age, preparing them for Secondary (*Bachillerato*) school. (high school) By then, I no longer suffered from homesickness; and I enjoyed going to school in such a beautiful place. I loved it from the beginning.

Construction on the current buildings began in 1913, but the original college was founded in 1899 by Southern Methodist Episcopal church missionaries. Buenavista, a women's college located across the street from Candler, was founded by The Women's Board of Missions of the Methodist Church in 1920. The school was open to students of all protestant denominations, including Jewish and Catholic; and students came from other countries, as well.

The majority of Methodist teachers and staff were Cuban. However, American missionaries and teachers were also part of the faculty. English was one of the many courses in the curriculum. An American high school that offered the same classes as those in the United States was also available. The whole campus was lovely. How could we not enjoy being resident students in such a place?

Buenavista's buildings and grounds were well-kept. Flowers, a spectacular Framboyans tree that spread like an enormous, flowering umbrella, and numerous other trees created beautiful surroundings on the campus that served both schools. The girls' dorm, where female students of both schools lived, was located in what had been a privately owned mansion, complete with marble floors and inside columns.

Years later, I heard a story that the original owner of the mansion had been buried outside a sealed window of the building. If I had heard that story while I was living there, I probably would never have slept!

At the beginning of my years at Buenavista, my parents received a list of clothing that all students had to wear. Girls wore identical uniforms, white skirts and blouses, with black scarves, worn sailor fashion. The tips of the scarves had to be in the most precise position at all times. They were measured! Even our shoes and socks had to be identical.

They told us how many and what kind of uniforms we must have. There were some for daily wear, Physical Education classes, and one called "gala," that was for church—only one, because it was sent to the cleaners during the week and returned before the following Sunday.

We also had a special navy sweater, the final garment of the ensemble, all of which was supposed to be purchased from *El Encanto*, an elegant department store in Havana, comparable to Saks Fifth Avenue in the United States.

My parents bought one of each uniform for me, and they had others made by a professional seamstress. This was allowed only if the correct fabric and design were exactly like the purchased uniforms and perfect in every detail. With every student in school uniforms, there was no competition or jealousy. Everyone looked the same. The interesting thing about those uniforms is that they were identical to those worn at The Irene Toland School, for the two schools were affiliated with the same religious organization.

A story about the origin of the uniforms is still told at school reunions. Whether or not it is true, I don't know. It seems that the principal fell in love and was engaged to a young sailor in the US Navy during World War II. He did not return from the war. The story goes that she was so in love with him that she never dated anyone else and she never married.

In fact, she became a missionary for several years, working out of the United States. Later she was sent to Cuba; and that's how she became the principal of Buenavista. I don't know what the uniforms were like before I enrolled. At any rate, the story goes that she designed the girls' uniforms in honor of her lost love. The same style of uniforms was used by the older girls in Candler, as well.

Every Friday afternoon we had to make a list of the soiled clothing in our laundry bags for the *lavanderas* to gather for washing. We took the clean outfits, every piece of which must have our names on it. There were several ladies who took care of our clothing.

At Buenavista we learned social graces, as well as discipline, etiquette, culture, a well-rounded curriculum that included English, as well as Spanish classes, preparing students for college upon graduation.

The chapel at Candler was an important hub of the college. It was a beautiful place, used not only for worship and religious training, but as a theater for music programs and school theater productions. Until the nationalization of all schools in Cuba, graduation ceremonies were also held there. Both campuses had access to this chapel.

Every spring, a music recital by Buenavista students took place in the chapel. I became a member of the rhythm band, comprised of the younger students; but eventually the director appointed me to accompany them on the piano. Another girl and I played together, called a "four hands" presentation. I located a photo depicting one of those events, and I smile every time I see it.

As before, piano was my favorite course. I had an excellent teacher, Senorita Querol, who came from Spain. As I had from the age of seven, I loved to play the piano more than anything else in my life. I worked hard to learn all this dedicated woman could teach me.

I also took clarinet lessons and became a member of the school band. The director, whose name I cannot recall, although he was well-known, also directed the Municipal Band. Buenavista's music department was exceptional. I loved being a member of it.

After band practice, we were required to store our instruments in the music room closet. As usual, I was late, the last one to enter the closet; but everyone stayed in the room, visiting and talking. While I was in the closet, an American boy in the band closed and locked the door on me. I suppose he did it as a joke, hoping the others would laugh. To me, it was not funny.

I knew he did it, for I looked through one of several ventilation holes in the door, and I saw him. When he finally opened the door, I screamed at him and I think I tried to kill him! I hit him with everything I could find: books, a chair; and I even kicked him!

Within moments I knew that my reaction had been too fierce. I felt bad for attacking him, and he did apologize for scaring me. "I'm sorry, too," I told him. Something about being locked inside that closet really did scare me. The thought came to me that everyone might leave, that no one would hear me after the outer door closed and that no one else would know where I was.

My apology to him was heartfelt. At least no one outside the room heard the commotion. Practice was held after school, and only the janitors would have been in and around the building. The boy was nice enough, even a bit timid; so I tried to be friendly to him every time I saw him after that incident.

When I started attending Buenavista, my friendships with children I knew in Güines dwindled. We lost touch with each other, and our interests were no longer the same. All my friends were at Buenavista, although their homes, like mine, were in various other cities and provinces, even other countries.

At my final music recital in elementary school, I was the last to perform. I had practiced a very difficult piece, "Farruca," by Manuel de Falla, until I knew it was perfect. I played that piano as if my life depended upon it; and I knew that I had done my very best. As the last chord faded, the audience gave me a standing ovation. This beautiful memory still remains a wonderful ending for a special day.

Lots of activities took place on the girl's campus. For the second time in my life, I experienced a real Halloween celebration. A dance was held for the older boys and girls; and during one of the faster paced ones, the dancers held an apple between their foreheads, not touching otherwise, as they moved to the music. The last couple not to drop the apple won, but I don't recall the prize. There was the usual bobbing for apples in a tub of water as well as the "House of Horrors."

Several rooms had been darkened and decorated in Halloween fashion, and they were actually pretty scary. I didn't like it. Pillows flew at our heads, and we had to touch creepy things we could not see, while disembodied voices told us that the things in our hands were eyes or other body parts. What I hated most was when someone grabbed my legs! I'm certain that such physical contact was not approved by the school!

Most weekends my mother picked me up and took me home. Then my father brought me back to school on Sunday evening. A few weekends, I stayed at the dorm, during which I had a great time! We went to baseball games, to the beach, movies, to the zoo, took long bicycle rides.

One time we rode through the *El Bosque de la Habana,* a hilly, treacherous road full of curves. One of the girls had a bad accident, and an ambulance was called to take her to a hospital. Of course, we always had a chaperone, Mrs. Ferry, who oversaw every trip I took.

Mrs. Ferry, a sweet-natured lady, didn't live in the dorm; but she had a little stand in the patio, where she sold food items: candy bars, crackers with cheese or ham, fruits, sodas and such. I was one of her best customers, for I didn't care for the food that was served in the dining room. Nothing unusual about that!

Other chaperones accompanied small groups of girls to many regular activities off campus, similar to the weekend programs, all of which were great fun. We had excursions to the beach, and we went to the movie theaters, one of the most important sources of entertainment in the 1950s. I loved the social events!

Buenavista students had to study hard, and every night we girls gathered in a basement classroom, in total silence. Our dorm mother patrolled, and no one was allowed to talk, to doze or to read any book outside of classroom materials. If additional study was required, the student must go to the library on the first floor.

Another room in the basement held school books and all school supplies. I enjoyed spending time in the supply room. I didn't especially like to study, but I loved to get new notebooks and pencils and pens. It gave me pleasure to line them up neatly and admire how pretty they looked.

A heavier, burnt orange paper, used as a book cover, was sold by the yard. I learned how to make perfect covers for my books. If one of them got a scratch or mark, I went down to the supply room and bought more orange paper. I might not have been the best student, but I certainly carried the most attractive books.

Etiquette took precedence over food in the dining room. The girls had to wait outside the dining room, while two girls held open the two big entrance doors, until the principal passed through them. We then entered after her, in order. We went to our assigned tables and stood at our designated places until she pulled out her chair and was seated. Only then were we allowed to sit.

She seldom, if ever, smiled; and she wore severe-type clothing that did nothing to flatter her. Nor did her hair style. She wore it pulled back from her face and forehead, drawn into a bun so tight I think it must have tightened her skin. She walked as if a steel rod was attached between her shoulders, even when she sat. Meals did not begin until she was seated.

The principal, directors and teachers sat at the head of the tables, and students took turns sitting at the other end. To my chagrin, I sat beside the principal on my very first day at Buenavista. We were required to remove the napkin from the napkin ring, fold it in half, and place it in our laps. Our left hands remained in our laps at all times, unless we needed to gently pat our mouths with the napkin. Wiping the mouth would have been considered grossly bad manners.

Two serving dishes were placed near the head and the foot of each table, and those who sat in those places were required to fill each student's plate as they were passed around. Serving ourselves was not an option, although we were allowed to say if we wanted only a little of a particular food as we were served from the four dishes.

Servers in uniforms brought drinks to us, usually milk or chocolate milk. After everyone finished eating, the head of the table rang a small bell. She then called for the servers to remove the dishes and bring in dessert. In spite of my complaints about the food, it was decent most of the time.

We had to eat every bit of the food on our plates. Those who had a problem doing so must remain at the table while the rest of the students were excused. Those left at tables had to at least try to eat the food on their plates, which became great incentive to take small portions.

Even so, there were times when even the smallest bit of a particular food was impossible to swallow. It wasn't uncommon for an occasional student to invent ways to avoid swallowing these foods. Morsels might become entrapped within folds of a napkin, or "accidentally" dropped to the floor. Not that I ever attempted anything like that!

These sly tricks did not fool whichever teacher or supervisor served as head of the table. The scolding these girls received reminded me of the one given to me by Miss Kelly, the day I plucked a rose at the Irene Toland School.

Buenavista's principal did not like me. I've speculated as to why over the years, whenever I've thought of her; but I could not think of a reason. I wonder if she might have sensed a hint of rebellion in me, although I was never disrespectful; and I didn't break rules—not when she was looking, anyway.

She remained a thorn in my life during the whole time I attended Buenavista/Candler College; but I didn't let her keep me from having a wonderful time while I was there. Of course, I was older, not so easily scared; and I even became a bit daring. Perhaps that's what the woman resented.

One of my friends, Carmita Rubio, and I sometimes studied together. She and two or three other girls convinced me to join them for a raid on the pantry one night. Carmita tells the story how they waited until everyone else was asleep, and then took a pillowcase and tiptoed down to the big pantry in the kitchen, hoping to find something good to eat. If they were successful, getting back to our rooms undetected presented the greatest challenge.

That night they found a lot of apples on a big round table, which was covered with a cloth much too big for it. The sides dropped all the way to the floor. They wanted something rich and sweet so they tiptoed to another source of food. Unfortunately, someone tripped or caught her fingers in the tablecloth; and the apples fell to the floor like stones.

They knew that someone would surely wake up, so they went running as fast and quietly as they could back upstairs. They had to pass the principal's quarters on the first floor. An American pupil, Monica, didn't move fast enough to get out of the pantry.

Monica heard someone coming down the basement stairs, so she crawled under the table and arranged the tablecloth in folds, hoping it would hide her, hoping that the principal would not pull it aside. The woman inspected the room, trying to find the source of the commotion, while Monica trembled in her hiding place, certain that she would be discovered at any moment.

After an unsuccessful search, the principal left the basement. Monica remained under the table for a long time. She wanted to be certain that everyone had gone back to sleep before she crept from her hiding place. I don't remember if she took food or not. She got back to the rooms without being caught. It was my first attempt at stealing anything from the pantry.

After we ate breakfast the next morning, the woman confronted us, outraged indignation showing from her pulled-back bun to the tips of her shoes. She was furious that any of her Buenavista students might dare to do such a thing as trespass into the pantry, even more, to take food! Luckily, none of the girls were identified.

It's surprising that any of us had actually done so, for we were terrified of that woman's anger. I was just happy that I had not been called to her office. Her anger did not stop the girls from continuing the late-night forays down to the kitchen pantry. It was too dangerous for me, but Carmita and some of the other girls continued to bring goodies from the kitchen, and we all enjoyed them.

Some of the girls were expert at bringing back food on the late-night excursions. One was always hungry, so maybe that was her incentive. She and the other girls took pillowcases to hold the contraband food, which were perfect for the task. They brought back bread, jars of marmalade, apples, oranges—whatever they could find and carry.

I think they did it more for the fun and the challenge than the food. I don't remember what we did with the scraps, but I know that there was no way we ate everything. Safely back in our rooms, we laughed ourselves breathless. We loved the excitement of getting away with breaking just one rule. Looking back, I am amazed at some of the things I did.

My mother never would have believed it! I cannot imagine what my punishment might have been if she had learned of my involvement in midnight raids for food in a college dorm kitchen! I never did tell her of my escapades at Buenavista, not even after we came to the United States. She probably would have felt even more justified at having kept her teenaged daughter on such a tight leash. She might even have sent me to my room!

CHAPTER SEVEN

Candler College

When I entered Secondary School (Bachillerato) in Candler, girls attended classes with the boys, our only coed contact. We had separate sports activities, field trips and socials. We girls always had "boyfriends," but there was no actual social contact with them. Smiles, long looks, maybe a small note passed along by someone else was the extent of it. The faculty was very strict about that.

Freddy Morris was my boyfriend. I smile, remembering; for having a boyfriend back then was such a sweet, innocent part of a girl's life. It could also have been a kind of status symbol, an indication to classmates that a handsome boy thought we were special. Cuban girls were protected and shielded from anything questionable or potentially harmful. The nearest thing we saw to actual romance occurred in the American movies, made during the 1940s and 1950s, all of which were shown in movie theaters all over Cuba.

Freddy's father was an heir of the Philip Morris Tobacco Company, a large American cigarette manufacturing company with production in Cuba. Freddy's mother was Cuban, which automatically made him a citizen of Cuba. Born of an American father, Freddy had American citizenship, as well.

Twice a week, Candler and Buenavista students attended Chapel. As always, the boys would already be seated when the girls entered, but the groups were segregated. While no physical contact was allowed, the boys had ample opportunity to observe the girls, which I'm sure they did, boys being boys!

How can I describe the essence of the young Frederick Morris? Tall, slender, but broad shouldered, he had dark brown hair and dark, smiling eyes. In thinking about him now, I can still recall the impression he made on this young, teenaged girl. In short, he was really cute!

I remember the night I first met him, even what I was wearing. My mother had bought the dress at El Encanto, the department store where our uniforms were purchased. The skirt was made of light aqua corduroy. Soft wool knit, in matching aqua, formed the bodice. The collar and cuffs of the short sleeves were made of corduroy; and a belt with a silver buckle completed the outfit. I felt like a princess in the dress.

That night a large group of students from Candler and Buenavista, boys and girls, walked to a nearby Methodist Church to attend a social with the young people in their congregation. Some of Candler's students with us that night did not live in the dorms. Freddy Morris, who lived not far from campus, was one of them.

I walked with a group of girls, talking, laughing and having a good time. Barely into our journey, fifteen-year-old Freddy Morris fell into step beside me, as naturally as if we had been friends all our lives. Confident and at ease, he began to talk to me; and I talked to him, which was not like me at all. I tended to become tongue-tied and self-conscious; but with Freddy, I felt free to be myself.

Somewhere along the way, I was suddenly aware that Freddy had taken my hand! On this beautiful evening, walking to a Methodist Church, holding hands! Unheard of, especially since any kind of physical contact was not condoned, regardless of how innocent it might be.

We arrived at the church, and for most of the evening we played games and visited with young people we had just met. Opportunities such as this, meeting and getting acquainted with people from different towns, provinces and countries were part of the Candler experience, one more event that made my life here so wonderful.

On our way back to the dorm, Freddy walked beside me, all the way to Candler, which was out of his way, since he didn't board at the college. That might have been one of the reasons why the principal of Buenavista did not like him.

Boys and girls who did not board on campus were called "externos and externas," since they only attended classes. Whatever her reasons, if she had seen us walking together, there would have been consequences! I couldn't understand why the chaperone, Mrs. Ferry, didn't seem to notice.

On his way to and from Candler College, Freddy often walked along the sidewalks outside the girls' dorm. Around that time, I developed a problem with my feet, and an orthopedic doctor prescribed a course of exercise. He recommended that I try to skate every day. The only place available was on the sidewalk, outside the dorm.

My mother asked the principal if it were possible for me to do that, and permission was granted. I didn't want Freddy to see me skating outside, alone; and I certainly didn't want to explain to him why. What kind of story could I have told him that didn't make me sound like an invalid in my early teens? Thankfully, he didn't come that way while I was skating; but I was always on the lookout, afraid that he might.

My old school friends still tease me about the way I used to run from window to window to watch Freddy as he passed the dorm every day. Well, it was my only opportunity to see him at all!

Freddy's actions got me sent to her office twice! I think that Freddy must have known my schedule; for one day he tossed a small necklace to me, through a hedge that grew along the sidewalk. Unfortunately for me, a supervisor saw the exchange.

"Isabel Ramos, you will go immediately to the principal's office!" I don't know why the lady was so angry with me. I had done nothing wrong. She didn't scold Freddy! It seems that all the responsibility for decorous behavior fell upon the girls. Apparently, we were responsible if a boy even looked at us. I went to the dreaded office and took the scolding. I believe that she could have made even the most righteous feel guilty about something!

Another day, a friend approached me on the way to class. As we talked and walked along the sidewalk, she passed a small box to me. Yes, it was another gift from Freddy! Impossible as it might seem, I looked up to see yet another of the missionary supervisors staring right at me, anger and disapproval on her face. I tossed the box aside, terrified to be seen with it. But it didn't matter. Yes, that meant another visit to the principal's office. She must have thought that I was a true Jezebel!

I continued to be surprised how circumstances worked out for Freddy and me to be together. One night, Mrs. Ferry chaperoned my group of girls to a movie. When we entered the theater, Freddy miraculously appeared and told everyone to let me go first. Then he sat down beside me. Looking back, I see a small conspiracy here. Freddy lived with his aunt and uncle, who just happened to be neighbors of Mrs. Ferry. They knew each other well.

On another occasion, when Mrs. Ferry chaperoned us to the beach one Saturday morning, Freddy was waiting for us. I think that Mrs. Ferry and Freddy's relatives might have set things up as he wanted them. I thought nothing of the "coincidences" at the time, for I was happy to see Freddy.

In spite of my shyness, I sometimes did crazy things, for no reason. While playing volley ball one afternoon on the grounds, I decided to climb a big tree near the court. Climbing up was relatively easy, but I could not climb back down! I simply couldn't get out of that tree.

Someone called the grounds gardener, Guillermo, who brought a ladder and held it against the tree for me to climb down. Poor Guillermo. I once asked him to put wooden heels on my shoes. I wanted them to make clicking sounds like taps when I walked, which would have required some kind of metal. He was probably not surprised when I needed to be rescued from a tree. Now why would a usually shy teenager do something like that? It seems that I had my moments—several of them.

Our dorm mother, Angela, was nice enough; and we liked her. After the nightly bell rang one evening and lights were out, something devilish swept over me! I changed my voice and began to call her name.

"Angela," I called. Pause. "An...gel...i...ta." My high-pitched tone of my voice must have sounded like a disembodied spirit. She came into our room and turned on the lights. Everything was fine until one of the girls, Aida, began to laugh, which caused the other girls to join in; and laughter reigned. Thank goodness our dorm mother saw the humor, too.

I mentioned that classes at Candler were coed, but boys were already seated when girls entered the classrooms. This way there was a minimum of contact between them. That didn't prevent eye contact, of course. I'm fairly certain that dark brown eyes flashed and secret little smiles might have been exchanged.

Just as the girls were entering the classroom of Dr. Moreno one day, I told Carmita Rubio to push me when we got inside the doorway. Carmita was a strong, big girl; and her push sent me sliding across nearly the whole length of that slippery floor! My slide was perfect…until it wasn't. At the end of my grand entrance, I tumbled onto the floor and became a mass of arms, legs and school uniform, like all the girls wore.

Not surprisingly, the classroom erupted with laughter. The boys, the girls, even Dr. Moreno, laughed for several minutes before he regained order. There was a difference in the classroom, a kind of loosening of the rigid rules, if only for the span of one session. The teacher did not scold me and there were no repercussions. It was a good day.

Dr. Moreno, usually very stern, looked like the classic American movie actor, Montgomery Clift. In Cuba, we saw the same movies and dressed the same way American girls dressed. We also had the same crushes on handsome teachers and boys. We were just not allowed the freedom most American girls experienced.

At any rate, one of the girls in Dr. Moreno's class was hopelessly in love with the man. Vicky's desk was right in front of his, and she spent most of her time gazing adoringly at the poor man, totally crazy! He seemed oblivious to Vicky and her charms. He was probably used to teenage crushes.

My days at Candler College were numbered, but I had no idea how or why they would end. In the meantime, after a really good year in school, my life included a delightful summer in a sweet little house overlooking the ocean that encompassed all the Caribbean Islands.

CHAPTER EIGHT

Rosario Beach

My father bought a house on Rosario Beach one summer when I was in my early teens. It made more sense to buy a house than to rent every summer, since we all loved the beach so much. He was not wealthy, but we lived comfortably.

Rosario Beach was closer to Güines, about ten miles or so; and many people from our home town had houses there. The beach extended from a marsh, La Ciénaga de Zapata, where alligators and other marsh creatures lived, a place we avoided.

An area covered with sharp, rough rocks and sand crabs had to be crossed to get to the house and the cleaner sand of the beach. Miguel, the young man who worked at our home in Güines, helped us move every summer before Papo bought the house on Rosario. Miguel had carried my brother and me across the hard places when we were small. With the purchase of the house, we no longer had to bring furniture from home every summer. The bigger, necessary furnishings came with it.

Rosario Beach might not have been as beautiful as the others, but we loved "Mi Casita," our little house. A very wide porch covered two sides of it. We often played games there, like Dominoes, Bingo and Ping Pong; and we had birthday parties for my little brother, José Julián, who was born in July.

We invited friends to join us, and we played and swam in the ocean every day. My brother, Juan, was twelve; and the two of us loved the beach more than anything else. Many young people lived there during the summer; and every night we danced in an open club, always with a group chaperone.

We had the use of a rowboat, and that year we had a great time. I wish every child could experience the pure joy my brother and I shared with our family that summer. Our younger brother, José, was only two years old. That might account for the bit more freedom Juan and I enjoyed. The usual means of transportation on the beach was by foot or bicycle, but there were a few cars.

Animals roamed freely on Rosario Beach. Chickens were certainly "free range;" and no one seemed to own them. One afternoon several of my girlfriends and I were sitting on the porch floor, playing Bingo, when we saw several chickens in the fenced back yard next to us. Some of the girls went to the back of the yard to go around, but one of the girls and I jumped over the fence, barefooted! We caught two chickens! Our friend, Nidia, had a great idea.

"Hey, I'll go tell my mother about the chickens, and she'll probably make *arroz con pollo* for us."

Nidia's mother, Hilda Quiñones, was famous for her *arroz con pollo*, as well as everything else she made. Her fame as an expert cook spread throughout Rosario Beach. Nidia's father, Quintín, was a pharmacist. None of us could know how our paths would cross over twenty years later, in another country.

Anyway, Nidia's mother agreed to prepare the chickens and make the dish for us. We were thrilled and excited. We had actually captured our dinner, and we were going to enjoy the work of our own hands! What could be better!

Unknown to me, my mother had watched us chase and catch the chickens. We didn't try to hide it, for we saw nothing wrong with catching chickens no one owned. It was an adventure, a challenge that we had met victoriously!

"Mami, Nidia's mother is going to make arroz con pollo for our supper tonight." I must have radiated with excitement.

"Really?" The tone of her voice should have warned me.

"Yes. She told us that if we caught two chickens she would make it for us."

"You cannot go." My mother's words stunned me.

"Mami! Why?" I could not believe it.

"Because you stole the chickens. You took chickens you do not own, and you are not going to be rewarded with a stolen supper."

My mother was adamant, but so was I. I cried, I screamed, I yelled, I was livid! All to no avail, for my mother would not change her mind. My friends enjoyed the fruits of their labor, in this case, chicken; but I did not. I thought about the times my dorm mates and I raided the basement kitchen at Buenavista. If my mother was this upset over a couple of free-range chickens, what would her reaction have been if she had learned of my involvement in that? It is too scary to contemplate!

For a long time, I resented my mother's interference with my plans; but I eventually realized that she was trying to teach me something. Even though the chickens appeared to belong to no one, they did not belong to me. It might have caused me to rethink participating in the food forays when I returned to Buenavista.

It would not be the only time my mother and I were at odds. It seemed to me in those days that the main goal of her life was to stop me from having a good time. I have since learned that most young people feel the same way during their teen years.

Juan and I took the rowboat out often. With sun-warmed water beneath us, soft breezes and spray on our faces, what more could we ask? We knew no fear, for we were well acquainted with beaches and the water. We spent a good part of each day in that boat. Both of us could swim, but there was little danger of drowning. The water was very shallow for several feet offshore, and we didn't go into the deep water.

Danger of another kind often lurked in the deeper waters. At certain times, sharks appeared and came closer to the shore than was safe for unwary swimmers. One day my friend and I decided to swim out to a floating boat dock, a good distance from the beach. Not even thinking about sharks, we glided through the water.

We sprawled atop the dock, where we dangled our feet and fingers in the warm water. For those sun-kissed moments, we had not a care in the world. After a while, we noticed that people had gathered on shore, among them my relatives and friends and neighbors. They waved, so we waved back.

We simply didn't notice the sharks that swam around and around the dock. Eventually, we swam back to shore to find some frantic, worried people. We were happy to feel the sand between our toes, especially after we realized what danger we had escaped.

No modern conveniences were available to most houses on Rosario Beach. A few people had electric plants/generators at their house, but we didn't. No electricity, no TV, no theater, no swimming pools at the houses, no telephones, no radio, no light to read by at night. That might account for the extreme interest and curiosity over our potential danger from sharks. For that matter, anything out of the ordinary could bring out a crowd.

The Bar Ferino, one of the restaurants, offered food delivery, and most people used this service. My family did not order from there often. Eating restaurant food all the time could get boring, since there were only so many items offered on the menu.

Thankfully, there was another place where young people could gather to listen to music and dance. It had no name, so we called it "The Club," and it had an electric plant, which allowed us to play the jukebox. We danced every night and played Dominoes or Bingo. There were not always enough boys to go around, but we girls didn't care. We danced anyway! It was the hot spot of Rosario Beach! Life was simple then, but it was also very good.

Nidia's father, Señor Quiñones, owned a yacht, one of few in the area. Unexpectedly, he invited our whole group of young people to take a short cruise on his magnificent vessel one day. Who could resist? Certainly not any of us.

No one even thought about asking permission from our parents. After all, we knew everyone, so what was the harm? Juan and I had our own personal chaperon/baby sitter, a cousin of my father's. Thelma had no children, and it was a pleasure for her to be included in the unexpected excursion. She became the group chaperone, escorting us everywhere we went.

What fun for us! Juan and I were used to our rowboat, but the yacht offered us an entirely different view of the ocean and the shoreline of Cuba. I don't remember how long our impromptu cruise lasted, but it was an event I never forgot.

Unfortunately, one must wake from all good dreams; and the awakening for my brother and me stood on the beach, arms folded, waiting. The beach houses all faced the ocean, for the back yards were soft and not of much use; so as the yacht neared the beach, it and everyone on it was visible from the front yards.

People knew how protective and strict my mother was, especially with me, her only daughter. I had committed the cardinal sin of not asking permission before boarding that yacht. Knowing that, the whole community gathered on the beach to watch what they considered to be the upcoming show.

Those who witnessed her anger told us later that my mother had been waiting for us outside Mi Casita, watching the yacht, pacing back and forth, arms folded across her chest, anger building. Knowing how angry my Mami could get, I expressed my concern to Thelma.

"Look at my mother!" I told Thelma.

"What is going to happen to you?" one of my friends asked.

"Thelma, what are we going to do? Mami is going to be so mad, and we'll be in so much trouble!"

"Don't worry, Isabelita," she said. "I'll talk to her, and everything will be all right. She will understand that I gave my permission. You and Juan are not to blame."

I still smile at the sight we must have presented: Thelma leading the way, my friends and I lined up behind her, like ducklings, as we came across the beach, dreading what lay ahead. I should have taken her at her word.

Thelma did a magnificent job! She disarmed my mother with her explanation, and neither my brother nor I were punished. I can't help but wonder if the crowd that had gathered was disappointed when my family did not provide some eagerly-awaited entertainment. Such was life at Rosario Beach.

My first hospital visit as a patient occurred that same year. I was fourteen. I don't remember being deathly ill or even feeling very sick, but the doctor decided that I should have my appendix removed. I said hospital, but the operation was performed in a clinic in Havana. Freddy Morris and several family members visited.

Among them was my cousin, Norma. She treated me as a person, not just a younger cousin. At that time, Norma and her mother, my Aunt Noemia, lived in the spacious home of Dr. Carmona and his wife, Nivia, Norma's sister. My family visited them often.

Norma took me many places in Havana when I was younger. One weekend she took Elba and me to see Liberace at the "Blanquita Theater." Elba and I were crazy about him and the way he played the piano. We were determined to touch him when he passed close to us. We were terrible! We pushed and fought our way through the adoring fans, squeezing between other determined people.

Although Elba and I were so much younger, Norma accompanied us on our mission, all three of us holding hands as we pushed and elbowed our way through and across the battlefield until we reached the prize! We touched Liberace! Norma understood how important our silly whim was, and it was sweet of her to help us.

So when she came to see me in the clinic after my surgery, I was happy to see her. A tall, broad-shouldered, handsome man came with her; and she introduced us to him as her boyfriend. He would soon become her fiancé. I was overwhelmed at the sheer size of him. He was incredibly handsome. With his beautiful blond hair, he looked like an angel!

He was so big that when he sat down in one of the standard clinic chairs, it fell apart! Everyone laughed, and he laughed with them; but laughter for me was horribly painful! I lay there, all bandaged and sore, holding my wounded tummy, laughing in spite of the pain.

I recovered from my surgery and went back to school at Candler College in the fall, without giving another thought to Norma's boyfriend. Or if I did think of him during the next couple of years, it would have been only because he was really big and really handsome, as any teenaged girl might recall.

I had no way of knowing then that a friend of his would occasionally accompany him to the home of Norma's sister. I could understand Norma's boyfriend's presence there. Later I would learn that the friend often intruded into the kitchen of the house that belonged to Dr. Carmona and Nivia.

Aunt Noemia, who was an excellent cook, prepared meals for the household. This friend of Norma's handsome young man had no qualms about taking food, helping himself to whatever he fancied from another man's kitchen, even as my aunt was cooking. She did not like the man at all!

In those early days, when plans for the revolution that would sweep across Cuba were being formed, my cousin, Norma, fell in love with Abel Santamaria, who came with her to see me after my surgery. This man was the best friend of and Number One Man next to Fidel Castro and his revolutionary army. I met Abel that one time, the day he broke a chair beside my bed in the clinic; but what happened to him two years later would haunt me for the rest of my life.

The incident that Fidel Castro would later call the beginning of the revolution to free Cuba from Batista occurred on July 26, 1953. Except for its tragic results for many men, their attack on the Moncada Barracks could be described as a comedy of errors. Many of the would-be revolutionaries were killed, and several more were captured, among them, Abel Santamaria.

In the early, planning days of Castro's dreams, he met with his companions in the home of Abel and his sister, Haydee, both of whom believed in the possibility of deposing the dictator and establishing another government. According to history's account, the men who took part in the attack on the barracks included only a handful of university students, one of them, Santamaria.

Both Abel and his sister were among those captured and taken to prison in Santiago de Cuba. Abel Santamaria believed in Communism with all his heart, but my cousin, Norma, did not. Regardless of his beliefs, Norma loved this handsome, dedicated man, as did his comrades.

Some say that Fidel had already become jealous of Abel's rapport with the members of their fledgling army and that he resented Abel's popularity. It could only help Fidel's popularity when this young man became the first martyr for their cause.

To persuade Haydee to betray members of their revolution, Batista's goons removed the eyes of Abel, her brother, and brought them to her before they murdered him. While some accounts disagree as to the extent of the torture endured by the young man, it is true that he was murdered shortly after his imprisonment. Haydee refused to give them one single name.

I met Abel Santamaria when I was fourteen years old. He was murdered when I was sixteen. The years of murders and retributions against the rebels, led by Fidel Castro, made it easier for many of us to welcome him as a "liberator." It was impossible for us to know that Cuba's people would merely trade one dictator for another.

CHAPTER NINE

Growing Up

Classes at Candler College and Buenavista began in the fall, like in The United States. Now an experienced boarding school resident, I plunged into school activities as if I had never known anything else. The girls continued their night time assaults on food in the basement kitchen. We wholeheartedly enjoyed the extra-curricular field trips, dances, games and movies.

The most anticipated event in a Cuban girl's life occurred on her fifteenth birthday, called her "Quince Años." Similar to a debutante or "coming out" ball in America, no expense was spared, according to each family's finances. This custom is still observed in Cuban communities in Miami and other Latino cities all around the world.

I doubt that it is observed in Cuba, for a number of reasons. Only those involved with the government make enough money to afford the formal clothes and party expenses. During his reign, Castro has declared many Cuban customs and beliefs as "bad for the Revolution."

For decades, he forbade any observation of Christmas, saying that the exchange of gifts was a capitalistic practice and would no longer be permitted in Cuba. The appointed block captains took note and reported on everything that happened in every neighborhood, and they probably still do. That's why I doubt that Quince Años parties are held now. It would not surprise me to learn that he had abolished this centuries old tradition.

From the moment of my birth, my mother had dressed me like a fashion doll, complete with bows in my hair and perfect little white socks and cute shoes on my feet. She loved to shop for clothes and pretty things more than anything else in her life.

I assumed that the approach of my Quince Años meant numerous shopping trips to Havana. I knew that Mami would choose the place for my party. She would plan menus, flowers and decorations, musicians and choose a dressmaker. The dress must be designed just so, and the absolutely perfect fabric chosen. I just knew that my party would be perfect.

Disaster struck.

My father told me that there would be no Quince Años party for me. There must have been a great number of reasons, or perhaps there were no reasons. He would not even discuss the possibility of a party. Distraught does not describe my disappointment. For weeks I tried to change his mind, to no avail.

At last I had to accept that the party wanted by every girl in Cuba would not be mine. Many girls held the parties at home. They invited friends and relatives and had music so that everybody could dance. At the very least, I wanted something like this; but my father was adamant. There would be no party. January 30th would come, and I would be fifteen years old—without a party.

The weekend before my birthday, my mother picked me up at Buenavista, as she usually did. When we entered the living room of our house, I stopped, awestruck. Standing before me was the most beautiful baby grand piano I had ever seen! I could not imagine that it was truly mine. The room was large, a big, elegant room; and the piano looked as if it had been designed especially for that space.

Looking back, remembering that gorgeous piano standing there in such glory and beauty, it represents to me one of the most special roses in my life, not just because of the instrument. I realize anew how much my parents truly loved me and wanted me to be happy, something I might doubt in days to come.

But at that moment, my heart felt as if it might break from sheer happiness. It took away the sharp thorn of disappointment at not having the longed-for birthday party. I could forgive my father just about anything right then.

Oh, but that was not the only surprise! Imagine my delight to discover that my cousin, Meli, an excellent seamstress, was working on a beautiful dress—for *me*! A strapless bodice of the palest, softest pink you can imagine topped the cocktail length skirt, which consisted of yards and yards of the finest tulle in different pastel colors.

Meli had already reached the point that demanded fittings, and that was the moment I knew that my party would actually take place. The finished garment fit perfectly. My cousin could not have created a more beautiful dress for me.

That same evening they told me that the band, "La Orquesta Sori," would provide music for my guests and me to dance. You cannot imagine my happiness, my joy at my parents' generosity and love for me. But there was more.

When I went into my bedroom, I discovered that a new bedroom set had been delivered and installed in the room. Overwhelmed is not adequate to describe how I felt.

The next week was Saturday, February 2nd, 1952; and I was probably the happiest girl in Güines when I woke up in my new bed. I was delirious with joy! I viewed that day through rose-colored glasses, but a couple of thorns would intrude before the night would end.

The day began with a trip to the beauty parlor to have my hair done just right. No birthday girl wanted frizzies or even one hair out of place on such a special occasion. For the rest of the day I played my beautiful piano, stroking the keys like a mother caresses her baby, content with everything in my life. What girl would not be?

I played and played, content in the moment, happy to make music for everyone around me, sharing my love and appreciation for such a magnificent gift. I wish there were another way to convey what that day meant to me, for mere words seem inadequate.

Huge as our house above the bank was, it had only one bathroom inside. A half-bath, accessed from the balcony, was used by servants. I don't remember who had bath privileges first; but quite likely, I did. The party was to start at seven, and it takes a lot of time for a girl to get ready for such an event.

Freddy Morris was still my boyfriend, and he would be my date for the evening. He arrived before I had placed the final touches on my makeup and done all those little last minute preparations. He had quite a wait before I could "receive him" as my formal escort.

Freddy waited for me on the balcony that overlooked the streets while I double-checked makeup, jewelry, dabbed on my new Christian Dior perfume, which was a gift from some friends, stepped into my high-heeled silver sandals and made sure that a tube of lipstick, and whatever else I thought I might need, was tucked safely into the little evening envelope purse I would carry.

My ten-year-old cousin, Elba, the daughter of my beloved Tia Omaira, ran from my bedroom to the balcony and back, reporting on Freddy's movements as he waited for me to make my appearance. She told me that he had something small in his hands.

"I think it's a ring, Isa. I think he has brought a ring for your birthday!" Her words made me nervous, for I certainly didn't want a ring. I told her to go back and check again, to find out what he had in his hands. So Elba made another trip to the balcony to spy on Freddy. When she came back to my bedroom she had my answer.

"It's candy!" Just remembering makes me laugh at the nervous teenager I was and my little cousin who acted as my secret agent, spying on my unsuspecting boyfriend.

By then I was really anxious, suddenly hesitant to appear before Freddy, dressed as he had never seen me. I didn't want to go to the balcony where he sat, waiting for me. I had no choice. I had to go. So I ventured out to the open balcony, where Freddy sat, by now eating his candy, a sucker, of all things!

"Hi," I murmured. Freddy stood up.

"Hi. You look very pretty, Isa."

I hope I thanked him, but I really don't remember if I did or not. By then it was time for us to make our way to the Brage Yacht Club, which overlooks the Mayabeque River. The river, which supplies many cities with water, flows from far inland, covering many miles before it reaches the Caribbean.

Freddy rode with my mother and my brother, Juan, in a taxi. My father and I waited for a bit, for we had to be the last members of the party to arrive at the Club. One of the sudden rainstorms had hit the city, and rain came down in sheets. My father called another cab, and we had to use umbrellas to avoid ruining our party clothing. By the time we arrived at the Club, the rain had stopped, not unusual in Güines.

My nerves felt like tightly strung piano wire, jittery and electrified. While I enjoyed having fun, I didn't like to be the center of attention. I dreaded the drama of driving with no lights up to the darkened Brage Yacht Club. Completely open, guests inside were able to see us arrive, unless the driver turned off his lights. I think they could see us anyway, for nothing blocked their view!

My father and I were the last to arrive. As we stepped from the car, the lights inside the Club came on, and the band began to play "Happy Birthday." With all that beautiful Cuban music and different, intricate beats, they still played the traditional birthday song. It seems almost silly now.

My father escorted me to the center of the dance floor, and the band began to play a waltz. Papo, an experienced dancer, whirled me around the floor. The many layers of tulle in my skirt flared and swirled around my legs, and I felt like a princess in a fairy tale.

Halfway through the waltz, my cousin, Orlando, who was a twin, cut in; and I finished the waltz with him. Without taking a collective breath, the band began to play some American Swing. Orlando danced like a professional, and we performed as if we had spent days rehearsing, which we did not. It was a perfect special moment, and I loved every second!

The band continued to play: Salsa; Cha, Cha, Cha; Rumba, Pasodoble, Boleros, Mambo; and everyone got up to dance. I forgot my shyness, for I loved to dance almost as much as I loved to play the piano. One of the things I have missed during my years away from Cuba is the music and dancing, the abandon with which Cubans used to dance.

It was as if Orlando and I had no bones, only flesh and muscle, all limber and rhythmic, able to become one with the music. We *felt* the music, the beat, the drums, as if we spoke to it with our bodies, in a conversation without words. I still miss that feeling, that sense of freedom to be who I really was on my Quince Años.

While guests danced, the staff of waiters brought out food and set up every table with plates and drinks. I don't remember the dishes. I was too excited to pay close attention, but I know that all of it was prepared in the Cuban way, and very delicious.

I received another surprise when a carful of students from Candler arrived at the party. A missionary chaperone from the school accompanied them, which turned out to be a disaster in more ways than one. The woman, dressed in drab, dark clothing and black and white "spectator pumps" with socks, could have been albino, she was so white—her skin, eyebrows and lashes, her hair, what could be seen of it beneath the scarf she wore.

The girls, some of my friends from Candler, had come to party! They danced and had a wonderful time. They even began to cheer for me, like they did for ballgames, making so much noise that the band stopped playing until the girls finished. I doubt that such a thing had ever occurred at a Quince Años before, and probably not since!

Because of my father's position as president of the bank, he had provided an open bar for his guests, many of whom were his business associates. He felt that providing it was a necessity, especially since we lived above the very bank where he worked. None of the young people were allowed alcohol, and none of us drank.

That poor missionary lady chaperone trotted all over the dance floor, trying to keep her charges in sight and under control at all times. She looked so out of place among the bright, glittering lights and beautiful evening clothes. Her head needed a swivel, for she tried her best to see all the girls at the same time, an impossible task. The girls laughed and were not still for a moment. The woman finally gave up. She ordered all of them into the car, and they went back to the dorm at Buenavista before the party was over.

My father was uncomfortable with something other than alcohol. He did not want me to dance with all the boys, but I was looking forward to it. A boy had called me that morning and asked me to dance with him at the party, but he would not tell me his name. All evening, I kept waiting for this anonymous boy to ask me to dance, but it didn't happen. It would be many years and many miles later before I would discover to whom the mysterious voice belonged.

Papo relented and told me to dance with any boy who asked me, but he didn't have to worry about that! They all knew that Freddy was my boyfriend, so not one of them asked me to dance! It was the biggest party of my life, and the boys were afraid to ask me to dance!

Like most of us Cubans, Freddy danced beautifully. At one point, guests cleared the floor to watch us dance, which was one of the highlights of the evening. The party lasted until midnight, and it was fun, fun, fun! A beautiful, perfect evening.

After we left the Club, a group of us went to our house for another party, where we played the piano, sang and danced for a long time. There were a lot of gifts, one of which was a gold bracelet, given to me by the staff and employees of the bank. The bracelet is a circlet of embossed roses, and it is a miracle that I still have it, thanks to the foresight of my father a few years later.

Such happiness filled the rooms of that big house that night. I don't remember what time it was when I finally slipped out of my lovely dress and climbed into the new bed. It had been a perfect day, and I would never forget it.

Not knowing what the future holds is a good thing. While my wonderful party had been the high point of my young life, it would prove to be the catalyst that caused my departure from the school I loved—Candler College

CHAPTER TEN

La Progresiva

Still basking in the afterglow of my party, I looked forward to going back to school the next evening. My mother drove me to Candler, and I couldn't wait to tell the other girls all about the exciting events of my birthday. I was not prepared for the message that I was to go to the principal's office.

I had no idea what I had done, of even *if* I had done something to merit a trip to see her. I had always known that she didn't like me. I didn't like her much, either; but my opinion didn't count in that prestigious house of learning.

With a bit of fear and trembling, offset with curiosity, I knocked on the door of her office.

"Come in."

There she sat, hands clasped atop her desk. Dressed in her usual dignified suit, hair pulled into its habitual bun atop her head, she watched me approach.

"Isabel, I am very disappointed." She paused. I said nothing. "I received a report that your parents hosted a party at the Brage Yacht Club this past Saturday evening. Is this correct?"

"Yes, my Quince Años party." She looked down at her hands.

"Some of your schoolmates, escorted by one of our staff, attended this party, did they not?

"Yes."

"I am not only disappointed, I am appalled." The woman fixed her eyes on me, accusatory and stern. "What kind of people *are* your parents? How could they host such a party for their daughter, where there was such outrageous behavior? ***Drinking alcohol? Wild dancing? Smoking?*** Is this true? Did your family and you take part in such things?"

"No...well, yes, but..."

"Our code of conduct does not permit these things, Isabel. We have high standards of behavior, and this is just not acceptable."

"But every girl in Cuba has a Quince Años party. Yes, there was an open bar at my party for the adults, but none of my friends drank. Neither did I! None of us smoke! My father allowed the bar for his business guests. It is the acceptable thing."

Her steely eyes stared at me. I had no idea what she was thinking, but I knew that it was probably uncomplimentary.

"I'll have to think about this, Isabel. It's hard for me to understand how any mother and father could subject their daughter to such behavior." She looked down at her hands, then back up at me, her lips in a thin line. "You may go to class now."

Just like that, I was dismissed from her royal presence. I didn't go to class. I stopped at the receptionist's desk outside the office and asked to use the phone. I called my mother and told her everything the principal had said to me. Mami told me to wait for her, which I did.

My mother called a taxi, and as soon as it was humanly possible, she arrived at Buenavista. I don't know what all was said inside that office when Mami went in and closed the door behind her. It might have resembled a small atomic explosion, but no blood was shed!

My pretty mother, as strict and unreasonable as I thought she was, turned into a mother tiger when her cubs were threatened! I wish I could turn back the clock and somehow hear what she said to the rigid mistress of Buenavista! Sad as the outcome was for me, I cannot help but grin at the thought of my mother verbally attacking the reigning monarch of the school.

I know this: my mother, in her anger, was a sight to behold! Unlike the girls who resided in the dorms, she was not intimidated by the principal, nor anyone else, for that matter. I don't know how long the confrontation between them lasted, but it seemed like a long time to me. The result was that my mother took me out of Buenavista that day, and I never went back. Not having a choice in leaving a school I loved remains one of the most painful thorns in my life, and it left a scar.

Not one to sit and cry "Woe is me!" it wasn't long before my mother hired a tutor for me; and my schooling continued. She employed one of my father's second cousins, and this man laid out a course of study for me.

I'm sure that I cried a lot, moped a lot, felt sorry for myself a lot. What just-turned-fifteen-year-old girl would not, under those circumstances? There were some pluses, too. I took ballet classes, and I continued with my piano. There might have been a small sense of freedom, but my mother would not allow me to skimp on my class and study time with Papo's cousin.

Freddy came to see me several times. Young as we were, with only chaperoned time and no school in common, those occasions dwindled down to fewer and fewer, until they stopped. Another thorn. I lost touch with my Buenavista/Candler friends.

Keep in mind that there were no cell phones, no emails, not even telephone calls allowed, for they were expensive. Our only means of communicating with distant friends and relatives was by mail. Letters are nice, wonderful, in fact; but long distance relationships have a tendency to diminish over time.

Shortly after I left Candler College, an old friend came to see me; and I was so glad to see her I could have cried. Sonia, my childhood friend who had loved my piano, whom I had not seen for several years, dropped in to visit. We had a good time, just catching up with each other's lives.

"I heard that you have a new grand piano," she said. "Would you play something for me?"

Proud of my skill, I sat down at the piano and began to play. All those years of lessons came bouncing off the keys, and playing lifted my spirits. I don't remember what I played; but feeling very proud of my performance, I looked up at Sonia.

"May I play it?" she asked.

"Of course!" I slid from the bench, and Sonia sat down. Placing her hands above the keys, she hesitated for a few seconds. I could not imagine that she played at all, for I remembered that there had been no piano in her house. I think I might have felt a bit smug.

Sonia's fingers struck a resounding chord, and then she filled the house with the most spectacular piano solo I had ever heard! Stunned, I stood there as she played, from memory, a concerto. I sensed another presence, and I looked up to find my mother, standing quietly, just inside the living room. Her face reflected the same emotions as mine…awe and wonder. We stood, spellbound, until Sonia's hands dropped into her lap.

"Well," my mother said. "I came in to see who was playing, for I knew that it could not be *you*!" I couldn't take offense at Mami's words, for she was right. That day I didn't learn all the details of how Sonia learned to play so well so quickly.

It would be years before I discovered her ingenuity, not only concerning the piano, but also ballet and her many other accomplishments. Our lives took different directions, and it would be a while before we reconnected. After that, it would be decades before we would be reunited. Sonia was, and continues to be, a remarkable person. She will reappear in my story.

So life continued; and I was fine, eventually. Not only did I keep up with my studies, via my tutor, I progressed on the piano and other interests; and my education continued. In time, I applied to the School of Commerce at La Progresiva School of higher learning in Cárdenas. I passed the admissions exam, and there I was--back in a boarding school, making new friends, many of whom are still my friends! At that point, to quote an old song, life was "coming up roses!"

Ah, La Progresiva School of Cárdenas! Founded in November, 1900, the goal of the school was to provide a quality education to students of all economic circumstances. Instituted by The Presbyterian Church of the United States and founded by Doctor Robert L. Wharton, the courses of study began each day with reading from the Bible. In retrospect, this practice was the most valuable one; but in all honesty, the students probably didn't give it the respect it deserved.

La Progresiva was the first Christian college to provide co-ed classes. Until then, none of the higher learning schools in Cuba allowed boys and girls to sit in a classroom together. Students from families who could afford tuition were admitted, but so were those who could not. Parents of these students were allowed to work at the school, providing valuable services while their children received a well-rounded education that included Bible study.

Swimming, basketball, tennis, track, baseball, even gymnastics were offered to the young men; but women's sports were limited to volleyball, basketball and tennis, and only on the grounds surrounding the dorm. La

Progresiva had a music program, but I thought the band and chorus at Candler College were better. I played drums in La Progresiva's band, but I didn't enjoy it enough to merit the time involved. I dropped out after one year.

I was a girl when I left Candler College, but I entered La Progresiva as a young woman of sixteen. Even so, boarding schools have rules; and this one was no different. It was run by the same organization as the Irene Toland School, where I had been miserable as a child. The uniforms were even the same color and style, just worn on a more feminine frame!

The rules of conduct were pretty much the same as at Candler: no contact between male and female students outside of classes, girls would be chaperoned if they went on "dates." I've never been able to understand why the boys/men were never chaperoned! Back then, questioning any rule was unheard of and would not have been tolerated.

The men who lived in the dorms were called "pupilos" and the women were called "pupilas." Students who attended classes but did not live in dorms were called "externos and externas," which means day pupils. Where all students in English and American schools would be called simply "pupils," many Spanish terms have masculine and feminine endings.

During the first week at La Progresiva, the new pupils were required to perform in a show, entertainment for those who lived in the dorms. A group of older students chose who would be in the show, and they picked me to perform the *cha-cha-cha*. The song that accompanied the dance was called "The Deceptive."

In essence, the song tells the story of a beautiful girl. Every day she strutted and pranced along Prado and Neptuno, two busy streets in Havana. The men watched her as she paraded in front of them, displaying her beautiful figure.

The end of the song relates that in this life, we will discover everything that is false, all that is unreal. And that is how I came to be wearing false "supplements" beneath the costume! The voluptuous figure beneath the costume was not really mine!

Since I knew no one at the school, I was able to wear such outlandish fakes and pretend to strut and prance along the make-believe boulevards of Prado and Neptuno. No one knew me, either; so I didn't have to worry about what friends might say. This particular role was not something I enjoyed, although I always loved music. It was just a requirement I met.

Many of the girls who lived in my dorm became my friends, and I am in touch with them to this day. It is still amazing to me how many of us were able to get out of Cuba before Castro dropped his own version of an iron curtain around the island.

On Saturday nights, boys and girls who did not go home for the weekend ate an informal, buffet-type meal in the dining room of the men's dorm. The food was always good, and my friends and I looked forward to delicious dinners.

Just outside the dining room doors, in front of the dorm, was a swimming pool, surrounded by spacious grounds, dotted with beautiful trees. Although the pool was closed, the area was a favorite Saturday night meeting place where couples could stroll or sit together, where groups of friends could visit.

It had been over a year-and-a-half since I'd seen Freddy Morris, but I was not looking for a "boyfriend." I was surprised when someone approached me and my friend, where we sat beside the swimming pool, one Saturday evening. I looked up and noticed that several had gathered in front of the dorm.

"Isabel, a boy over there just asked me if I knew you," she said. "He wants to meet you." She waved her hand toward the group of pupilas and pupilos. Among them was a boy who stood out from the rest. He was tall, slender and very handsome.

My friend and I followed the girl, who introduced me to the young man. We shook hands, and that's how we met. For a while, we chatted with the group; and then we walked around the grounds, talking.

We returned to the pool and sat down together, in the same place I had been sitting earlier. One of my teachers stood near the dorm, a frown on his face as he watched us. I wondered if the professor thought that this boy and I were doing something wrong. We were not; but I knew that rules against physical contact were so strict that even just sitting together might appear to be questionable to an observer.

We talked for a while longer, and then he walked me to my dorm. I don't remember doing it, but later he told me that I had held onto his hand longer than he had expected when we were being introduced. It would be the extent of our physical contact! Chaperones! I can just imagine how my American-born friends and readers are shaking their heads over such restrictions.

I remember a couple who fell in love while they were students at La Progresiva. They were together as much as possible, but only in public, sitting together on the broad steps that led into most of the buildings. They spent all their free time together just talking, gazing into each other's eyes, and everyone could see that they were crazy in love. They held hands all the time, and they were totally unaware that others watched them. Theirs was a true love story. They married, and they are still together, all these years later.

I fell into the La Progresiva routine quickly; and just as quickly, I discovered that my dorm mates were even more adventurous than those at Candler. There were no limits to their imaginations. As at Candler, evenings were scheduled for study time. Haydee, one of my most daring friends, and I decided to dress up and visit the rooms, just to make the girls laugh.

We intended to dress like clowns, and my costume turned out pretty well. Haydee dressed in her room; and when I saw her, I nearly died laughing. To complete her costume, she put a bucket on her head! We had to be very quiet on our journey from the first floor to the second.

Unfortunately, in the middle of the stairs, the bucket fell off Haydee's head; and we had to run really fast to hide before the dorm lady, Señora Caridad, came looking for the guilty parties. I entered a nearby room and slid under the bed. Haydee ran into another room and hid in an armoire.

We could hear the Señora looking for us on the first floor, asking everyone who had dared to disrupt the study time. Repeatedly, the girls assured her that they did not know, but they couldn't stop laughing. She came upstairs, stopped at every room and demanded to know who and where were the girls responsible for the commotion.

Meanwhile, from under the bed, I kept wondering what we were going to do. Finally, Haydee and I emerged from our hiding places and confessed.

"We didn't mean to make any noise," I told her.

"We just wanted to dress up and make the girls laugh, and we're sorry," Haydee said.

"But the bucket fell off her head and bounced down the stairs, and we ran. Please forgive us." It was all we could do not to laugh, even in the face of possible punishment.

La Señora Caridad was furious at first, but little by little (*poco a poco*) she calmed down. I don't recall that we suffered any repercussions. At least, we weren't expelled! This was probably the least of our adventures.

Ah, Haydee. Without getting too far ahead in my story, I can say that I am still in contact with her and other friends from La Progresiva. What I don't remember, Haydee does; and when we visit, we remind each other of the funny, silly things we did during our years in the dorms at La Progresiva.

Quite a sports rivalry existed between Candler College and La Progresiva. Following a ball game at Candler between the two schools, a parade victory was held by Candler. Haydee and Marita, her roommate, joined the parade, posing as Candler students, marching and cheering.

"Ganamos uno, dos, Progresiva, que pasó?" English translation: "We gained one, two, Progresiva, what happened?" They were marching and yelling and cheering with the Candler College victors!

Haydee also reminded me of another parade held in Cárdenas. La Progresiva's band marched in it; and Haydee was a majorette, quite good with her baton—except perhaps that day. While marching, she tossed her baton high into the air, misjudged the distance and lost it. However, quick-thinking Haydee simply grabbed another girl's baton as it came down, and she didn't miss a step.

The girl whose baton she confiscated was not so fortunate. While the parade continued, the poor girl was left behind, desperately trying to find the baton that had belonged to Haydee, who marched cheerfully along with her fellow majorettes.

During those years, many girls wanted the new hair style made popular by Gina Lollabrigida, sometimes called "the pixie or boy cut." I loved it, and I had my hair cut in that style, successfully. Another friend, Rebeca, asked me to cut her hair just like mine, so I agreed to try.

Rebeca had a lot of hair, thick like mine, but light brown, while mine was dark. It was a shame to cut it, for it was long and shiny, like honey; but the girl insisted. The haircut turned out beautifully. I was as thrilled as Rebeca. So I began to give haircuts to all the girls who asked for them.

In turn, they gave me twenty cents or so. (Don't laugh! In those days, one could do a lot with twenty cents!)

Then came Haydee. I am glad that we are still friends. Today, after all these decades, she can laugh; but at the time, it was not funny. Poor Haydee's haircut was, to say the least, not successful. When she looked into the mirror, she cried and cried! I wanted to cry, too! She ran from the room to find La Señora.

"I have to go to the beauty shop *right now*! I'm not going to school on Monday, looking like *this*! Isa, you made me look like a boy!" Haydee was adamant.

I think that La Señora agreed with her, for she found a shop that would take her that very afternoon, although it was already late. Another student, Sarita Monzón, took Haydee to the beauty shop, where the stylist was able to repair the damage.

I was sorry, and I felt terrible; but I had cut her hair the same way I cut the other girls'. That was the day Haydee and I learned that not every cut and hair style is suitable for every girl. I also learned that some things are better left to professionals!

CHAPTER ELEVEN

Transitions

While the first year at La Progresiva held days, weeks and months of good times for me, it was also filled with courses of study that would prove challenging, some even difficult, but all geared to provide me with the ability to get and hold a job. Even so, my new friends and I found, or created, ways to entertain ourselves and those around us.

My parents surprised me one weekend. Perhaps shocked is a better word; for when I went home, they were no longer living in the big house above the bank. I had loved that house so much, and I could not imagine they had actually left it. Even worse, its replacement was tiny! *Miniscule! Microscopic!*

You might think I exaggerate a bit, but the grand piano stood in the middle of the house; and there was barely room to move around it! Our family of five scooted around each other, almost bouncing off each other, laughingly apologetic. Well, perhaps I do exaggerate *un poco,* a little. When I returned to the dorm, I had much more personal space than I did in the tiny house, and that is the truth!

I repeat that having a boyfriend in Cuba in those days was nothing like dating for teenagers in the United States. It is important to keep that in mind. Aside from going to a movie with other friends, or walking to church, or eating together in the boys' dorm on Saturday nights, there was no contact.

If I walked very slowly, and my boyfriend ran to catch up with me, occasionally we could walk a short distance together after classes, on our way to lunch; but we ate in our separate dorms. I didn't see him after school in the afternoon, probably because of his basketball practice. He had a starting position on La Progresiva's team, so he couldn't miss a practice, especially for a mere girl. As a senior, he had commitments and courses that took up lots of his time—which allowed me to be with my friends.

I was no more prepared for what happened the next time my parents picked me up than I had been the last time. Instead of taking me to the little house, they pulled up in front of a truly beautiful dwelling. When the city of Güines was built, no zoning laws had been in place; so this house stood between two or three other nice houses and a corner hardware store.

The neighborhood businesses, including a small food market across the street from the hardware store, were well-kept, taking nothing away from the appearance of my father's latest endeavor to locate a house he wanted as a permanent home.

My mother and father lived a simple life. In comparison with other lifestyles in Cuba, we lived well. My father had worked hard all his life. He was entering middle age when he married, and he wanted the best he could afford for his family; but he was not pretentious.

In comparison to the other houses where we had lived, this one was outstanding, although there were many more elaborate houses in Güines. I learned that the man who owned the house, Señor Sarmiento, had a son who was an architect; and we believe that the son designed this wonderful house.

The entire structure was made of concrete and stucco, roofed with red tiles, like a great many Cuban houses. Tall columns supported the corners of the porch roof. Shiny Italian tiles covered the porch floor that ran the whole width of the house. Two of the three front entrances were French doors, made of dark wood that encased glass panes, protected with wrought iron grills. Both doors opened into the living room, which was huge.

The third entrance was an extra-wide door made of heavy wood. It opened onto a spacious area called the *zaguán*, built to accommodate a car in older, elegant houses. But this house was new, so the *zaguán* was actually a foyer. Since the colorful room, covered with the same beautiful, shiny Italian tile as the porch, was so huge, my father chose it for his office.

Another room beyond the office became his den, where he installed a television and comfortable furniture. It became his favorite place, where he could relax and listen to music, maybe even take a nap. This room was filled with light, for the outer wall was nothing but wide windows and a door that opened onto the central courtyard.

While speaking with a visiting nurse one day in my father's den, I glanced up in time to see a man dressed in a white lab coat, talking to my father in his office. From my position, I could see that the man was very tall, with dark hair; but he was turned away from me; so I could not see his face.

"Who is that?" I asked her. The nurse glanced up.

"Oh, that's Dr. Aguilar." The name was unfamiliar to me, so we went back to our discussion. I didn't give another thought to the stranger who had insurance business with my father. Clients came and went, mostly in the late afternoons and evenings; so I was accustomed to seeing strangers in Papo's office.

Inside the living room, which held my piano, of course, an additional set of French doors opened into the largest bedroom. My mother had chosen it for me, both for its size and the chance to feature my pretty bedroom furniture when the door was open. The elegance of the doors and the size of all the rooms were a bit overwhelming to me. It was even more impressive than the house above the bank.

The main bathroom was between my room and my parent's bedroom, accessible from both rooms, as well as from the hall that ran the length of the house, convenient for all of us. Another bedroom, for my brothers, adjoined Mami and Papo's room; and the large kitchen was the last room on that side of the house.

It opened into a dining room that extended along most of the back courtyard wall, completing the square shape of the entire dwelling. A small, full bathroom, tucked into a corner of the courtyard, was an added convenience. A stone privacy wall extended to the front of the house, the finishing touch to this beautiful piece of property.

I call this outdoor area a courtyard, because it was enclosed on all sides; but it could as easily be called a large patio. Terracotta tiles covered the ground, except for an opening in the center, where a tall tree grew, with branches that spread tall and wide, like an opened umbrella. Beneath its shade and along the *canteros* (stone works) was seating to accommodate anyone who wished to read or relax in comfort.

Song birds in decorative cages provided a musical background. Most houses that faced the streets had sheltered courtyards in the back, but this one was more like a lush, private oasis.

I wish I had a photograph of this place, my favorite of all the houses we lived in during our years in Cuba. I'm afraid we just didn't live there long enough to take pictures. In fact, my nights in the house were not many. My father considered buying it, but it carried a very high price. It was close to downtown, convenient to stores, theaters and anything we could possibly need. My long-distance boyfriend came to see me four or five times when we lived in this beautiful house. It provided a lovely place for us to sit and talk, which was the extent of our dating.

While Papo was keeping the streets of Güines busy with transferring our furniture from one house to another, I was occupied with classes and occasionally seeing the tall basketball player, which was not often.

During my first year at La Progresiva, our courtship, if you could call it one, consisted of going to baseball games held at the school. We ate Saturday dinners together in the dining room at the boy's dorm before we went outside to talk for a while.

The biggest event we attended at the school was the graduation banquet for my boyfriend's senior class in the spring of 1954. The junior class was responsible for all decorations and festivities. The graduation ceremony was held in Teatro Cárdenas, a very elegant, even opulent theater in the city. I loved being able to wear a new dress, taking extra care with my makeup and hair, wanting to look especially good for such an occasion.

On graduation day, I met his parents and sister for the first time. His father was a veterinarian, a career his son meant to follow. I liked his mother immediately, and his sister was also very gracious. They were a warm, wonderful family. I would have enjoyed getting to know them better, but that was not to be.

After the graduation, he sometimes borrowed his uncle's car and came to see me in Güines that summer, before he started school in Havana that fall. On one occasion, he brought his sister with him; and another time my mother accompanied us to the movies. She also served as chaperone when we went to the one and only dance we attended.

The only physical contact we ever had was when we held hands as we were dancing, always a discreet distance apart, closely observed by my mother. I'm not sure, but perhaps there was a brief touching of hands as he would have helped me into the car on our way to and from the dance or a movie. There was a distinct double standard as to what was acceptable behavior for single men and single women. I knew that boys and men did not have chaperones! I might have resented it just a bit.

It was during those summer days that my father came to a decision as to whether or not to buy the house where we lived. As it turned out, the first residential real estate my father bought in Güines was not the beautiful house. Instead, he bought two. We called them the "twin houses," for they were joined. I have photos of them. It would be the last of our homes in Cuba.

While not as pretty as the other house, it was large and laid out well. Across the street from it was a scenic park, where children played and people strolled in the evenings. All things considered, my father made a wise choice.

One of the houses had an occupant, who remained there for quite some time. My parents moved into the adjoining house, and in no time at all, it felt like home to me. After all, it held my family and my piano. What else did it need?

My favorite source of entertainment was movies. During the summers between classes I went to the movies often, sometimes with my friends, sometimes alone. The theater was not far from my home. I loved the movies! For a small admission price, I could pretend that I was the glamorous actress on the screen: Elizabeth Taylor, or Kim Novak, or Audrey Hepburn or Jane Russell.

At five o'clock one warm summer evening, (All summer evenings in Cuba are warm!) I stood in line, alone, outside the theater. I noticed a tall man dressed in a white lab coat, a doctor's coat, standing outside an office beside the theater. He seemed relaxed as he watched people on the street. He was very handsome, literally tall and dark, with striking good looks.

Wearing one of my favorite dresses, I thought I looked pretty when I left our house that late afternoon. Sleeveless, the form-fitting brown dress had a square neckline. Wide, short straps, attached to the back of the bodice, connected to the front with big wood buttons. A sharp pleat fell from the front waistline, giving the impression that the skirt was straight, but allowing freedom of movement. It's possible I liked knowing it fit well.

At seventeen, I felt good about my life, happy to be home for the summer, while looking forward to rejoining my friends at La Progresiva in the fall. The presence of this tall man in his white lab coat was just an added attraction to my evening at the movies. He was as handsome as a movie star, with his unsmiling face, strong jawline and piercing eyes.

Shy as I normally was, I never would have spoken to him; but as far as I knew, there were no restrictions to looking! Besides, I already had a boyfriend; and I wasn't looking for another one. My own code of conduct and ethics included loyalty. My focus on this stranger's appearance was nothing but a pleasant passing of time.

That moment, details of my dress, the muffled conversations of people who stood in line to buy theater tickets—everything became imprinted on my mind. For, suddenly, I realized that the man was staring at me! It was as if a lightning bolt had struck me. I had never experienced such a sensation, and I didn't know what to do, where to look, what to think! (A more fitting description, a loose Spanish translation is: *I didn't know where to put my face!*)

No boy or man had ever looked at me like that, not to my knowledge, anyway! This man seemed to see into my mind when our eyes met, even to read my thoughts. Mesmerized, I stared back at him while his gaze swept from the top of my head to my feet and back again. My mouth was dry, and my heart beat faster. What was wrong with me!

I had never been hypnotized, but I wondered if the feeling might be similar. I think I was afraid to move, so nervous I was trembling. His stare didn't waver. I looked away for a moment, but it was almost as if my eyes were compelled to seek his again. I turned my head, just enough to catch his gaze and found that he had not moved. He was still staring at me, unsmiling, intent.

I turned my back, willing myself not to look at him again, nervously impatient for the crowd in front of me to move! I bought my ticket and hurried into the theater. I sat down in the second seat in one of the back rows, anxious, maybe a little bit scared.

I would not have been surprised if the man had suddenly appeared beside me. What would I do, if he did? What would I say? What would he do? Somehow I sat through the movie, not focusing on the screen; and to this day I cannot remember what I watched! I'm glad my mother didn't ask the name of the movie when I returned home. Normally, I would have been able to tell her the title, the actors and the storyline.

It was a few days before the vision of the man faded. I would probably never see him again. I had a boyfriend. We hadn't been together enough for me to know exactly how I felt about him, but I liked him; and there was that loyalty issue.

My good friend, Zinnia, lived across the street from what I would always call "the beautiful house," the one my father did not buy. However, her house, especially the interior and the spacious courtyard, was truly opulent. I loved to attend parties hosted by her parents. They kept a full-time chauffeur, who was often allowed to drive Zinnia wherever she wanted to go.

One evening she invited me to go along, and together we enjoyed riding around the town. I understand that in the United States during that time, young people who had access to cars spent their evenings the same way, driving along the streets of their cities and towns, looking for friends who were doing the same thing.

I spotted a beautiful Bel Aire Chevrolet coming toward us. Oh my goodness! It was the most gorgeous car I had ever seen on the streets of Güines. The body of the car was a soft mauve. Shiny chrome, a white top and trim were perfect offsets for the opalescent color. I recognized the driver at just about the same time he saw me. It was the man who had stared so intently at me as I had waited in line at the theater! And Zinnia knew him.

It was Dr. Aguilar, the stranger I had seen in my father's office, the man I had ignored weeks earlier. The mystery of his identity had been solved. One thing was certain: The man was as handsome as I remembered! I saw him a few times after that, on the nightly promenades. Then one evening he pulled up in front of Zinnia's house, where she and I sat on the porch together. I don't remember what we talked about, maybe even the weather! He stayed for only a few minutes before he left.

"Isa, what is it with these doctors? You know how much I want to go out with Aurelio Alverez, but he doesn't seem interested at all! I know! Why don't you see if you can get Aurelio interested in you, and I'll go after Agui!" Meaning Dr. Aguilar! Zinnia was serious.

"I would never do that, Zinnia," I told her. "I have a boyfriend. Besides, Dr. Aguilar probably has dozens of girlfriends, so I doubt that he would be interested in either of us." So that was the end of the conversation about the two doctors. I'm not sure that my friend ever forgave me. In the fall I went back to school at La Progressiva. If I thought about Dr. Aguilar again, it was fleetingly. School kept me busy.

The University of Havana, where my boyfriend was enrolled after graduation, is a long distance from La Progresiva, which is in the province of Matanzas. With him so far away, I was free to spend time with my friends; and they proved to be just as fun-loving and daring as ever, even more so. It didn't occur to me to wonder why I enjoyed school so much more when he was not there.

Our lives in La Progresiva were so sheltered we had to find or make our own kind of fun. The patio outside our dorm had very high walls, too high to see over without help. As it turned out, the gardener left his tall ladder against a tree on our side of those walls one day. A group of girls moved the ladder to the tallest tree, and they climbed up and into the branches of the tree. From there they could see the boys on the other side of the wall.

"Señora Felicia is coming!" This woman didn't like any of us, and she would have used any opportunity to report what she considered bad behavior. I don't remember who sounded the warning, but the girls had some scrambling to do. They came down as fast as possible, and my friend, Haydee, was the last one. She jumped from a higher distance than was safe, landing on her left knee. She still carries in that knee the repercussions of her desire to spy on the boys of La Progresiva.

I was not as daring as some of the girls. The few times I agreed to rebel even a little I was too scared to enjoy them! I once agreed to accompany a friend to the small building where sports equipment was kept on campus. Her goal was to smoke cigarettes, which I had not tried. With fumbling fingers, she struck matches to the cigarette, finally lighting it; but we had to keep constant watch out the window. Puff, peek! Puff, peek!

I think I probably attempted to inhale, but all I remember clearly is hoping that no teacher or dorm mother would see smoke coming from a window. Our smoke break didn't last long, and I was more than happy to give up nicotine! If my father had even suspected that I would try smoking, he would have jerked me out of school, which would have ended my scholastic endeavors.

A happier, safer venture for us also took place in the little equipment building. Rebeca and I were part of a girls' band. There were several of us who played instruments, but not the kind we played in the band. We created instruments from whatever we could find. I made a drum from my makeup case, and the other girls formed some pretty funny-looking noise makers. We actually played pretty well, but it just gave us something fun to do when we had free time.

I was never tempted to try to leave campus, but some of the girls actually did. Two of them slipped away one night and went to a nearby bar. They both drank, but one of the girls drank so much she kept falling down on the way back to the dorm. None of the staff caught them, but some of the students noticed and went to help them.

They put the falling-down-drunk girl under a cold shower, hoping to sober her up, but she began screaming and trying to get out of the shower. Her friends tried to help; but when that sick girl began to throw-up, they had more than they could handle. They could not calm her down.

About that time Señora Caridad, the dorm mother, heard the commotion and came to see who was making so much noise. The woman was furious! In the first place, vomiting in the shower was strictly forbidden, no matter how ill a girl became! From there, it all went downhill for the unfortunate girl.

The director was called, and the next day the girl had to appear before him, hangover and all. The end result was that the girl was expelled. I don't recall that any of the girls ever tried such a dangerous excursion again.

Time passed. Sheltered at La Progresiva in Cárdenas, we didn't hear or care about much that was going on throughout Cuba, especially in Havana. President Batista maintained his corrupt government, while college students at the University of Havana protested with demonstrations. These were met with brutality from law enforcement and resulted in beatings and attacks with high pressure water hoses, arrests, imprisonments and torture.

If and when we caught a rumor or saw a newscast, none of us could believe that anyone would be able to rid the country of Batista. He was too powerful, too corrupt and too brutal to be overthrown. So I attended my secretarial classes at La Progresiva, certain that all would return to normal.

In January of that year, close to my eighteenth birthday, my boyfriend invited me to go to an annual dance, held in a beautiful ballroom in Güines. I knew that my mother would not allow me to go, even if my brother and his date would be chaperones. I was too embarrassed to tell him, so I only told him that I didn't know if I could go. I didn't hear back from him, so I thought it was settled that I could not go.

I liked him. I had thought there might be potential for something between us after I finished school; but I could not see past what I thought were oppressive, strict rules of boy/girl contact at La Progresiva. That was not the only reason. I was never away from my mother's watchful eye during every moment when he came to see me. In all fairness, my mother was not alone in her attitude. It was the same with most Cuban mothers.

My parents brought me home the weekend of the dance, but I had not even mentioned to my mother that I had been invited to go. I knew her, and I knew that she would not let me go. The evening arrived, and I didn't get dressed for the dance. I was surprised when I heard my mother greet my boyfriend on the porch. I had not expected him.

Nervous, I sat on the sofa, near the tall marble columns, waiting for him. My mother remained on the porch, within sight and hearing of the living room.

Dressed in a nice suit, he looked very handsome, even eager, as he came through the door. When he saw me, he stopped, a puzzled expression on his face.

"Why aren't you dressed for the dance?"

"I cannot go." At my reply, he stared at me, disbelief on his face.

"But, why?" He pressed. I shook my head, for I could give no reason that would make sense to him. I felt very bad, even heart sick, at what I felt I must tell him.

"I'm sorry, but I have to break up with you tonight."

"Why? I don't understand!" he said.

"I cannot tell you exactly why. It's just the way it has to be." He would not understand anything I told him, when I didn't entirely, myself. I only knew that something was not right and never would be.

"Will you at least open this gift I brought to you?" He took a small, square box from his pocket and offered it to me. "Please. Please, open it."

"No, I cannot do that. I'm not your girlfriend anymore. It wouldn't be right." He knelt on the floor in front of me, tears in his eyes. "Please, Isa, please." I didn't know what to do. I leaned back, putting as much distance as possible between myself and the gift box.

"I can't," I told him. I felt terrible, knowing that I was hurting him, for I liked him. I could see my mother on the porch, listening to every word. "I'm sorry, but I have to break this off. I can't see you anymore." When he saw that I was serious, he stood up.

"Let me talk to your mother," he told me. He went back to the front porch. From there, I could hear him talking to my mother, asking her what was wrong with me, why was I doing this thing. She had no answer for him either.

In all honesty, I have to say that the strict code of separation was not the entire reason. Even though he and I rarely saw each other, going to separate schools so far apart, his attitude had become possessive, even jealous of the most innocent things.

As much as I liked him, it was just a friendship that had no chance of being anything else.. As strict as my mother was, and as far away as he lived from me, there would be no opportunity for us to spend any real time together.

So he left, and I spent the night with my parents, at home, probably playing recordings of Dean Martin or Nat King Cole singing love songs. I have a photo that was taken at the dance that night. It shows my brother and his date, along with my now-former-boyfriend and another girl that my brother had found for him, sitting at a table together. Was I sad? Yes, for a while.

Worse than that was the sense of guilt I carried for a long time, guilt over the way I had ended our friendship. I was not a cruel person. It bothered me that I hurt him, and I knew I had.

Time passed, and a few months later, I saw him for the last time. My neighbor, who lived in the adjoining house, asked me to go with her to visit a friend in the hospital. We had walked about two blocks from my house when I heard footsteps behind us. We kept walking, and they got louder.

"Nenuca, I think someone is following us," I whispered. Somehow, I knew it was my ex-boyfriend.

"Isa." He said my name at the same moment I turned.

"Isa, I want you to return to me everything I gave you." He was very direct. All trace of his ever having cared about me had disappeared, but I really could not blame him. I didn't expect anything else. Oh, but he looked really handsome!

"I'm going with my friend to the clinic," I told him. I looked at Nenuca.

"We can go back to your house, Isa," she told me, "and to the hospital later." So that's what we did. He went back a short distance to a parked car, evidently owned by one his friends; and they drove to my house while Nenuca and I walked. By the time I arrived, he was in the house, talking to my mother! He didn't hesitate to tell me why he had come.

"Isa, I want the letters back, and my bracelet. I need the pictures, too." Prepared for just such an event, I had carefully packed every letter and note he had written to me when we were in school. He had given his ID bracelet to me to wear, and I had a couple of snapshots, everything placed in a small box on the floor of my wardrobe. I took the box to him, we said our farewells and I never saw him again.

"He said that you looked very pretty," my mother told me. I stared at her, speechless. Why would he say such a thing? And to my mother! Secretly, inwardly, I was happy that I was wearing a pretty dress, one in which I knew I looked *cute*! I certainly didn't want him to think that I was pining away, for I wasn't.

Afterwards, I began to question, to wonder why he had found it necessary to come to Güines for such a trivial thing. He knew no one else in the city, except some Havana University acquaintances. He could have written to me, asking me to mail the few things he had given to me.

I remembered how jealous he had been, when he no reason to be; and I wondered if he might have heard a rumor about Dr. Aguilar. Could it be possible that he had come to see for himself if I had a new boyfriend? Had he expected me to be glad to see him, to ask for another chance; or was I just being silly?

At any rate, the handsome young man who had been my boyfriend was completely gone from my life, never to return; and I never knew for certain what was in the small, square box he had wanted so badly for me to open. Did I continue to be curious? No, because I had not cared that much. How would it be possible for such a young girl to care deeply for someone she rarely saw? When I thought about him at all, I realized he had done all the talking when we were together. He hadn't asked about my interests, what I liked to do, whether or not I had plans after La Progresiva. He didn't know me at all.

In retrospect, I am very grateful for my mother, as overly cautious and protective as she was. I think she was one of God's angels, watching over me; for I am sure now that His plan was unfolding all around me, even though I could not see it at the time.

CHAPTER TWELVE

New Beginnings

Following the breakup in January, 1955, I had just turned eighteen. As a distraction, I became more involved in activities with my friends at La Progresiva. Among them, The Folkloric Club, one of the many organizations offered by La Progresiva, was joined by several of the girls.

Within the club was yet another, The Experimental Group. The instructor chose members for this organization. I loved to dance, and there was no shortage of partners. Every Saturday morning, we met in *La Plazoleta de los Tamarindos,* The Plaza of the Tamarinds, fruit trees of the tropics. In the center of the rotunda stood a huge tamarind tree that spread above us like an open umbrella.

One day the instructor chose me to dance with him to *The Slovenian Waltz,* a very fast, difficult piece. How excited I was to be chosen, but I had never danced to this music. I followed him, and I made no mistakes! Can you imagine how I felt? Well, I can tell you that I felt fantastic!

One of our presentations was in the International Hotel located at Varadero Beach, Matanzas, which is one of the most recognized and most beautiful of Cuba's beaches. The Rotary Club was holding a reunion in this lovely place. How exciting it was to be one of such a group, and I was thrilled to find myself dancing on the platform with them in that fabulous hotel.

Before I enrolled at La Progresiva, the school had sponsored another group of student entertainers. A talented combination of singers, dancers, actresses and actors, called The Artistic Embassy, traveled and performed in various cities and communities.

While I was still at Candler College, this group appeared in Güines, at the amphitheater behind The Kate Plumer Bryan Memorial, the American school where I had attended as a child. Fortunately, I was able to come home that weekend and see their performance. They were outstanding!

I don't remember which group held the talent show shortly after I broke up with my boyfriend. The director chose me to sing the low part of a quartet, a talent I never thought I had.

Of all the songs available, the director chose "My Foolish Heart," a popular song of the 1950's. I was not interested in having another boyfriend, but a really cute boy lived in the dorm. He was a serious student, very shy, who had never spoken to me; but I had told my friends I thought he was quite handsome.

His name was Francisco, but we called him *Pancholo*, which is one of the many nicknames for Francisco. In Spanish, "pan" means bread. I thought that "cholo" sounded a lot like "solo," so we began to call him "bread alone." But I changed it even more. I told the girls that we would call this boy *Galleta*, which means "cracker" in Spanish.

I saw him every Saturday night, when we all went to the boy's dining room for dinner, cafeteria style. I told my friends to look for *Galleta* and to let me know if they saw him, that I might be able to speak to him. This was not like me at all! But I was free, no longer tied down by someone who made me afraid to even speak to another boy.

In fact, when he had been with me, I was afraid to dance, afraid to be seen playing an instrument or marching in the band, even afraid to eat in the cafeteria, where they served hotdogs and other foods I adored. My friends used to tell me "Isa, eat something!" but I could not when he was there. Looking back, I can see how intimidated I had been with him, afraid to speak my own mind, afraid that he would laugh or make fun of me. But no more! I was liberated!

So the night of our big debut as a quartet, I was daring. We knew we looked good that night, all of us dressed in black skirts, wearing different-colored turtleneck jersey tops. Mine was dark blue-violet, one of my favorite colors. We had practiced, and we also knew that whatever we did was going to be good. Before we went onstage, I glanced at the audience; and right in the front row, center stage where I would stand, was Pancholo.

"Look!" I told the girls. "Cracker is sitting below center stage! I'm going to look right at him all the time we're singing! Just see if I don't!" So the girls watched me as we started to sing in English, *My Foolish Heart.* True to my word, I gazed right into the eyes of that poor, unsuspecting boy. He started to blush, and his cheeks turned as red as apples! My prank was so successful that the girls began to laugh at me, and then I was the one who began to blush.

I don't know how we got through the song, for the girls were laughing so hard it was nearly impossible to sing. All I could do was try to avoid looking at Cracker until the song was done, to avoid further embarrassment for both of us. After that, neither of us had nerve enough to even speak to the other! Alas, a thwarted non-romance!

When I no longer had a boyfriend, it was if someone had put a sign on my back: *Isabelita Ramos is available!* I'm not sure for what, because I could go nowhere or be seen alone with a boy without a chaperone! One would-be suitor, Israel Gonzalez, was a good student. He made straight A's, was president of the student council, president of this and president of that; but I didn't like him.

He wrote many letters to me. One of them was so romantic, filled with sweet, beautiful phrases. The problem was, as I read it, the words were very familiar, words that I could almost recite.

I found my book of poetry by poet José Angel Buesa and there it was, word for word, "Poema Del Renunciamento," one of my favorites. The boy never had a chance from the beginning; but after he tried to pass off the poem as his love letter, I wanted absolutely nothing to do with him.

Like Pancholo, I took my studies seriously, wanting to get a good job after I graduated. Most subjects came easily enough for me, except math. I liked the Algebra professor, Maestro Chirino. He was young for a teacher, very nice and he liked me. In spite of my occasional adventurous streak, I remained shy, sometimes introverted; but not with this teacher.

One day I was late for class, so instead of entering quietly and taking my seat, I rapped on the classroom's closed door. TAT-TA-TA-TAT-TAT— TAT-TAT! I opened the door to find that class had already begun. Instead of scolding me, something I probably deserved, Professor Chirino laughed, granting tacit permission for the class to laugh, too.

My problem with algebra was well known in class, for my grades were not the highest. I worked hard, wanting to do better. Following a difficult test, the teacher handed back our papers.

"Several students did very well on this test," he said, "especially Isabel, who received a 98," Professor Chirino stated. "Isabel, will you please stand?"

This was such an embarrassment to me. I think it was a bit of payback for the silly things I had done in his classroom. At any rate, it was a good payback. I had studied very hard for the test. My classmates applauded, and I think my face turned as red as the roses I loved.

The professor had a reputation as a strict, no nonsense teacher, who sometimes allowed his temper to show; but he was never anything other than pleasant, even lenient with me. In his classroom, I felt somewhat free to let my inner clown show, sometimes to the point of embarrassment.

I don't remember the source of inspiration for my most outlandish caper. Other girls had crushes on movie stars, maybe secretly hoarded chocolate or any number of crazy things. But I brought my invisible son to class. Yes, you read it right. My invisible son. I named him Lutero.

Lutero went everywhere with me, to church, to baseball games, to class; and he was accepted by my friends, who enjoyed the harmless fun. We had all heard of, maybe even had, invisible friends as children. I had an invisible son. Occasionally, a friend would offer to babysit with Lutero. Yes, I know it was ludicrous! Crazy! It was also great fun, especially when Maestro Chirino laughed at the concept of an invisible child in his classroom.

In time, like all make-believe, invisible creatures, Lutero went away. His appearance and departure occurred during my last year of school. He had served his purpose, so I sent him went away; and I was free to get on with other sources of entertainment.

The following summer, Professor Chirino came to Güines to visit his sister, who taught at the American School, where I had attended. While he was there, I think he also went to see a couple of other La Progresiva students; and he came to see me. I was so surprised when he showed up at my house. I didn't know what to do with him.

The only thing that came to mind was to take him to the home of my Aunt Omaira, Elba's mother, who lived only a couple of blocks from my house. I thought it might be nice to introduce them, for I certainly didn't know how to entertain him. On the way back to my house, I was terribly shy. I didn't know where to look or what to say.

He did most of the talking as we walked back to my house. Suddenly a car passed very close to the sidewalk, splashing the professor's clothing with mud. His spotless white trousers and white *guayabera* (a linen shirt, commonly worn in tropical climates back then), were no longer spotless. The Maestro blushed easily, and his face turned as red as mine. Again, I didn't know where to look or what to say; but I made a suggestion.

"Perhaps my mother can do something with your clothes," I told him. He agreed to let her try, so we went into my house to find Mami. Actually, my mother did a pretty good job cleaning his clothes, especially his pants; but I don't remember exactly how she did it, especially with him wearing them! But then my mother could do just about anything she undertook. We visited for a little while longer, and then he left.

Before I graduated from La Progresiva, Professor Chirino married a teacher who also taught in the School of Commerce. As events unfolded in Cuba, they were among those of us who were able to immigrate to the United States. He was a brilliant mathematician, and he received calls to teach at Harvard University and Yale in Boston, where he taught for some time.

(Eventually, Profesor Chirino became part of a team that designed a system to make military planes undetectable, but I never knew the details. Many, many years later, a friend told me that the good teacher was not doing well physically and that he often asked about me. She gave me his telephone number, so I called him. We had a very nice conversation, remembering old times and many of his previous students.

A couple years later, I attended a La Progresiva reunion in Miami. At the entrance to the hall, seated in a chair, older and weakened, was Profesor Chirino. I presented him to my husband. As the professor hugged me, he whispered in my ear.

"Is your husband a doctor?"

"Yes, he is," I replied.

My old teacher smiled and said, "I knew it!"

I don't know why that was important to him, but he seemed pleased, which made me happy. He died a few years ago, a good man, one I will always remember and respect.)

One weekend that summer I attended a Quince Años party. I was a few years older than the birthday girl, whose father was a doctor. I knew many of the guests; and among them was a tall, dark and handsome doctor, whose path I kept crossing. Dr. Armando Aguilar, one of the most eligible bachelors in Güines, was also a friend of the birthday girl's father. It has been the dream of many mothers that their daughters would marry doctors, and the mother of a party guest was one of them. She had set her sights on Dr. Aguilar for her daughter.

At the party, Dr. Aguilar sought me out; and we talked for a while. All the girls who had boyfriends at the party were accompanied by their mothers. Since I had no boyfriend, I had been able to come alone.

When the woman who wanted Dr. Aguilar for her daughter saw me talking to him, her face turned white! If her eyes had been daggers, I would have become a bloody heap on the floor!

But let me tell you! That streak of daring or mischief that sometimes burst from me, took over. I had the best time talking to Dr. Aguilar. I smiled and laughed, probably flirted a little bit more than I normally would have. Unhindered by my mother's presence, I had a marvelous time!

After the party, I found myself thinking about the handsome doctor a lot, more than I wanted to. It had been several months since my last meeting with my ex-boyfriend, and I had no desire to be anyone's "girlfriend." Boyfriends could be stifling.

Still, this man lingered in my thoughts; and I often recalled the evening I had felt him staring at me, where I had stood in the ticket line at the movie theater. I remembered the way chills had swept up and down my body when our eyes had met.

Now I was eighteen, going on nineteen, free to let my thoughts go wherever they wished. They seemed to visit this eligible doctor quite often. One day I came up with a legitimate reason to call him. When he answered the phone, I was a little breathless.

"Dr. Aguilar, this is Isabelita Ramos. I'll be going back to La Progresiva, in Cárdenas, soon; and my friends want to hold a going-away party for me. I would like to invite you, if you are free to come." There was a moment of surprised silence.

"Hello, Isabelita. Yes! Yes, of course I would like to come to your party. Just let me know where and when." I was surprised, scared, excited, all those things all at once!

"I will let you know as soon as they tell me."

"Thank you for the invitation," he added. I thanked him for accepting and we hung up.

He was coming to the party! I was so excited! There was one problem. No party had been, nor would be, planned. Now what was I going to do? I had to come up with a plausible reason to cancel the party-that-never-was! I thought and thought about it. So a week or so later, I called him back, another great opportunity to talk to him, to hear his voice.

"Hello, Dr. Aguilar? This is Isabelita Ramos."

"Oh, hello! How are you?"

"I am fine, thank you. You remember that I invited you to a party?"

"Yes, yes."

"I am sorry, but the party has been canceled. There isn't enough time to get everything organized. I'm sorry."

"Oh, I'm sorry, too," he said. "I was looking forward to it."

That made me very happy!

There were occasional unplanned meetings during the next couple of summers. One evening, as my mother and I sat on the porch of our twin house, I glanced across the park that stretched along the street. Sitting in front of a house on the other side, shining in the sunlight, was that beautiful Bel-Air Chevrolet, the chariot that belonged to the local Greek-god! In this case, CUBAN Greek-god!

"Look, Mami," I told my mother. "Over there is Dr. Aguilar's car. He is making his house calls, and I think he might come by here when he's done." My mother, engrossed in a newspaper, glanced up, said nothing, and returned to her reading.

"Mami, give me part of your paper. If he comes over here, I don't want him to think that I am waiting for him. I'll just be reading; and he won't know that we saw him." Mami gave me a sheet of the paper, and I unfolded it. I held it up, lowered just enough for me to watch for Dr. Aguilar. It wasn't long before I saw him get into his car, and I watched until he turned onto our street. He pulled to a stop in front of our house, got out of his car and walked up to the porch.

"Hello," he called. I lowered the paper, hoping that it was right side up.

"Oh, hello," I replied, studied surprise in my voice. Not for anything in the world would I have let him know that I had been watching him. I turned to my mother. "Mami, this is Dr. Aguilar."

"Oh, hi," Mami said. "How are you?" She was so nice to Dr. Aguilar! And he was very polite and courteous to her. From the first meeting, she liked him. I think she might have fallen in love with him before I did!

After that evening, he came by several times; and one day I invited him in to listen to music. I had a phonograph that played LPs (long-playing record albums), among them, *Our Love is Here to Stay,* by Nat King Cole. Both of us loved that song! So, *poco a poco,* little by little, we became a couple. Only time would tell what the future would hold for us. At the moment, it looked as if it might hold an entire bouquet of roses. I hoped they would be the pastel ones I loved so much.

CHAPTER THIRTEEN

Adulthood

La Progresiva continued to fill the biggest part of my life. Yes, I had a real boyfriend again, but his office and his other jobs were in our home town, not in Cárdenas. It was 1957, and I enjoyed taking part in school activities. I helped serve at the seniors' graduation party, which was great fun. I often attended movies with my friends, one of which reminds me of two associated tragedies that year.

Alfredito Echevarría, a young man who lived in Cárdenas, became friends with some La Progresiva students. He especially liked to ride his bicycle alongside me, while talking to the whole group of girls as we walked to church or to a movie. He was a bit of a show-off, enjoying tricky maneuvers on his bike.

One Wednesday night my friends and I went to a movie, as usual. Alfredito had told the girls where to sit, for he was planning to sit in the row in front of us, so he could turn around and talk to me. I still remember the movie, *Stranger in Paradise*. He did as he had planned, talking to me more than watching the movie. He was a nice boy, but I wasn't interested. A tall, very handsome doctor already had my heart.

The next day, Alfredito was killed in a car accident. I felt a sense of loss at his death, not so much personal, but for his parents and for the potential he had to live a good life. I was allowed to attend his funeral, accompanied by another girl, but this would not be the only tragedy that befell his family.

For several years, major unrest had filled Cuba. The rebellion against President Batista, the reigning tyrant, continued to escalate. Alfredito's older brother, José Antonio, was president of the Students Federation of Havana University, a group that was actively engaged in planning to remove Batista. In the mountains of Cuba, Fidel Castro was trying to raise his own forces to topple the president, but he was not a part of Manzanita's group.

José Antonio and his comrades targeted and blew up buildings and places where Batista was believed to be, their main goal being to assassinate the Dictator of Cuba. The Students Federation and Jose Antonio, nicknamed Manzanita, wanted a true democratic government, one not ruled by a tyrant.

This dedicated group of ten or twelve students, led by Manzanita, broke into the National Radio Station, timing the event to coincide with a well-planned attack on the Presidential Palace, another attempt to assassinate President Batista. The effort had two plans of attack. Assuming that the coup would take place as planned, Manzanita's speech would encourage all of Cuba to join them and rise up against the forces of corruption in the government.

They entered the radio station during a news broadcast, hoping to reach as many people as possible. Manzanita figured that he and his group had no more than three minutes, 180 seconds, before they would be stopped.

He had practiced reading his speech, timing it to the second, knowing that it must take no longer than his allotted time. He read all of it, and the station's security forces broke through the door at the 181st second. What this group of young men did not know was that the broadcast had failed to go over the airwaves. Nor had the planned coup in Havana taken place. Unfortunately, the whole operation would prove to be a comedy of errors.

Over forty of Manzanita's men were killed in and around the Presidential Palace. José Antonio Echevarría did not realize that his dream of democracy for Cuba had failed.

There are different accounts of his death. One is that he was shot in the head immediately after reading his speech in the radio station. Another is that he died with his friends on the second floor of the Presidential Palace. The most accredited version is that he escaped from the radio station and drove toward the Presidential Palace, thinking that coup had been successful.

He got within a couple of blocks of the palace, where he believed that Batista had been killed. He met a police car, and he thought they were coming for him, reacting to what he believed had been the death of Batista. He got out of the car, firing his machine gun at the patrolmen, who returned fire; and Alfredito's older brother died on the sidewalk, in the city of Havana.

The truth is that the police were not looking for him. Since they, nor anyone else, had heard his broadcast, there was no reason to connect him to the attempted government overthrow. Had he remained in his car, he probably would have been successful in his escape and lived to continue the fight against Batista.

So all the time I was in school at La Progressiva, political unrest and revolution were growing in the country. At the time of my graduation, the ceremony could not be held in the elegant Cárdenas theater, due to numerous explosions that had been triggered in various buildings. Instead, the Presbyterian Church became the setting for my graduation, a fitting location for such a grand event.

By that time, Fidel and Raúl Castro, along with Ché Guevera, were leaders of the "great revolution." Unfortunately, theirs would prove not to be in the best interests of Cuba, regardless of Fidel's loudly proclaimed love for the people. José Antonio Echevarría's passion and hope for the country he loved died with him on March 13, 1957. He was twenty-four years old.

Even with the unrest that continued to escalate, my life remained much as usual. Following my graduation, I applied for and got a job in the bank where my father had been employed for so many years. He retired that same year, but I think one of his last official acts was to see that I became an employee in his bank. Fully qualified to carry out any secretarial duties, I was prepared for anything I was asked to do.

By then, Dr. Aguilar and I had become a couple, dutifully escorted by a chaperone around town to the movies, to parties, wherever we could go. Our bond was growing closer, while the bearded revolutionary continued his forays, mostly in the mountains and country sides, working his way toward Havana.

On January 1ˢᵗ, 1959, Fidel Castro entered the city, welcomed by throngs of adoring crowds, people who waved white handkerchiefs and banners, much like the crowds waved palm branches the day that Jesus entered Jerusalem nearly two thousand years previously. That is where the similarity ended, although much of Cuba considered Fidel their messiah.

Many people of my generation thought of him as a hero. Both my husband and I believed so. I might even have cheered a little, but only when and where neither of my parents could see me. Castro had deposed the dictator, Batista; and he was going to usher in a new age of prosperity, one where everybody would "share the wealth." He promised equality, promised that he would rid the country of foreign interests and anyone who had taken advantage of the people, either domestic or foreign. A state of euphoria filled the streets.

Life for my generation remained much the same, for a while, at least. I wanted to obtain a driver's license, so Dr. Aguilar said that he would take me to Havana City where I could take driving instructions. His sister always accompanied us as chaperone. Just the two of us going together simply was not acceptable.

For lunch one day, we chose a restaurant across from the Malecón, in Havana Bay, which is still probably the most recognized feature along Cuba's coast. Rugged and striking, it bears the marks of age and weather and the passing of hundreds of years.

We finished our lunch and were leaving when we saw a group of people outside the restaurant, talking. They appeared to be, possibly, government men or someone of equal standing.

"Let's go see who it is," I said.

"Sure, we can go see what's going on." Armando agreed, so we approached the group of men. In the midst of them was Fidel Castro. I shook hands with him, and I told him that we were from Güines, and that I had come to Havana to take driving lessons. Now, after all these years, it's still difficult for me to imagine that I actually said that to the man I would come to hate passionately.

"Ah," he said. "Remember to buy a small car." That was one of his constant warnings to the people, to buy a small car in order to conserve gasoline. Just imagine. Fidel Castro was one of the first environmentalists! His concern was not for the environment, however. All of Cuba's oil and gasoline had to be imported, and he was on his way to alienating everyone in the world except other Communist countries.

Later, Armando asked me, "Did you notice his hands? They were like silk, just as soft as silk."

I think I expected his hands to be hard, firm, maybe even callused, because he constantly maintained that macho persona. He never gave up his cigar-smoking, bearded, mountain guerilla traits. I couldn't believe that his skin was as soft as a baby's bottom. How insulted he would be to hear himself described that way!

He was friendly, totally comfortable with his celebrity status. Why wouldn't he be? He had successfully overthrown the previous government, and he continued to thumb his nose at the United States and the rest of the world. It was 1960, and only a small tip of the massive Communist iceberg was exposed.

Many people of my father's age, however, were not so quick to embrace Fidel's new ideology. They didn't trust the man or his politics. When he began to embrace Communism, they knew what it meant.

My father was one of them. Shortly after Fidel's rise to power, my father bought a number of divisas, a means of currency exchange from one country to another. My mother planned to accompany him to Mexico, but changed her mind at the last moment. When he returned, he still had a number of these divisas; so he asked me if I would like to go to the United States with him.

I was thrilled! I had never flown anywhere, and I was excited about finally visiting Miami. Papo bought tickets; and soon I was flying above the turquoise waters toward the magical world of Miami and Miami Beach. My father exchanged the last of his divisas for dollars, and we did a lot with the money. Almost every day I went shopping, sometimes with my father, sometimes alone.

We stayed in the San Juan Hotel, an older hotel even then; but it was very clean and nice and centrally located to shops and restaurants. Papo gave me money, and I loved going to clothing stores and shops, most of them no more than half a block from the hotel.

On Lincoln Road, carts were available for those who preferred not to walk, but I enjoyed walking. The whole area was like a park, with flowers, palm trees, beautiful surroundings and restaurants everywhere, with stores and shops along both sides of the street.

Cuba's climate is the same, being only ninety miles from Florida; and it had many lovely department and clothing stores, as well as excellent restaurants at that time. Fidel had not yet destroyed most of what was good there. I understood a little English, but so many people spoke Spanish in Miami that I was comfortable wherever I went.

Several of our relatives had lived in Miami for some time. Many came to see us, even taking us to their homes for meals. I don't think I realized exactly what my father was planning, even then. He was in the process of converting pesos to dollars, at the rate of ten pesos to one dollar, American money. He opened an account in a Miami bank, preparing to get all his family out of Cuba, sooner, rather than later.

With the money I made working in the bank, I had bought a lot of clothes, among them a pair of beautiful white pique shorts. Some of the girls I knew wore shorts at the beach; and I saw no reason why I should not be able to wear them, at least in Florida. I had packed them in my suitcase with my other clothing, hoping for a chance to wear them in Miami, the perfect place to show off my new, very short, white shorts.

One morning I decided that the day had come. I dawdled over getting dressed, taking as long as possible, combing my hair, checking my makeup, anything I could think of to take up more time. Impatient, my father looked at his watch. "I'm ready to go downstairs for breakfast," he told me.

He did not approve of shorts or slacks on women, especially in public; and he hated bare midriffs. He did not object to low-necked dresses and blouses, even strapless sundresses, which seems strange to me now. I knew that he would not be happy to see me in shorts, but I thought that he would not make a scene in public when I appeared in them.

"Papo, you go ahead. I'll be ready pretty soon, so wait for me in the cafeteria." The moment he left the room, I quickly changed into the white shorts and a pretty blouse. Feeling like a movie star, Jane Russell maybe, I went downstairs, confident that my father would frown over the way I was dressed, but that he would allow it just this time. I was wrong. He took one look at me and shook his head.

"No, no, no! You go back upstairs and change your clothes! You are not wearing those shorts."

I sighed. My father was not going to change his mind about the way his wife and daughter dressed. So I went back upstairs, probably pouting as I went. I don't remember what I changed into, probably slacks. Papo didn't like them either, but they were more acceptable than shorts, especially on the beach. To him, the only appropriate wear for girls and women were dresses! I cannot imagine what he would think of the way girls dress, or undress, in today's world.

After a few days in Miami, Papo's business completed, we returned to Havana. At the time, I had no idea how far-seeing my father was. He understood exactly what Fidel Castro intended to do in Cuba; and he already had a plan in place to care for his family as well as possible.

Quietly and thoroughly he was moving assets, important papers, jewelry, photographs and money into the United States. In the meantime, my friends and family were planning a wedding. While my father made plans to provide a way of escape for those he loved, I thought of nothing but my wedding day and of the fairy tale life I would live with the handsome man I planned to marry.

Excitement over a new government escalated during those first few months, and I was living in my own little world of excitement. Dr. Aguilar went to my father's office to ask for my hand in marriage. On February 14th, only six weeks after Fidel's triumphal entry into Havana, Dr. Aguilar proposed to me. He presented the ring to me at my house, and then he took me (and my mother!) to a dance at the same elegant Brage Yacht Club where my Quince Años party had been held.

I wore a cardinal red, shining satin, strapless evening gown, fitted and perfect for such a special occasion. With a red stole draped around my shoulders, I again felt like a princess, one who had just won the handsome prince! It was a beautiful evening, one I would never forget. Even so, my new fiancé and I were never allowed to go anywhere without a chaperone!

The next few months were filled with wedding plans, fittings for my wedding gown and most importantly, getting our house ready for us. While I would live in my fantasy world for a few more short months, Cuba, under the command of Fidel Castro, became a Communist country. It wasn't long before interrogations, arrests, torture, executions and disappearances occurred daily.

One of the first things Fidel did was to change the money of Cuba. Pesos, the same monetary value as the United States dollar, would no longer be the currency of the land. Cubans were required to exchange the old for the new, at a great loss to those who had a lot of money.

Many who had worked hard all their lives, built businesses and acquired a work force, had it all confiscated by the government. Some committed suicide. My father, who was already sixty years old by then, had been able to circumvent this mandate, and he began to make even more plans to take his family to the United States.

Many of my friends and family attended a party that was held for me at the Brage Yacht Club the week before my wedding. It was a grand party, filled with laughter and happy memories, in spite of the way our world was crumbling around us. This party, called "Despedida de Soltera," was hosted by six or seven of my closest friends. A loose translation means a farewell to the single life.

These parties were all different, with menus drawn up and dishes named by the hostesses. Thanks to my father's foresight, I am able to include photos of the menu and the party. Even so, I had no idea to what extent our world would change.

I wish I had been more emotionally prepared. I would have held my friends closer, especially Sonia. Although our lives took different paths, I had reconnected with her; and I was happy that she came to my party. She married around the time I did, and she gave birth to a baby boy, who was not well. He died when he was very small.

The most priceless wedding gift we received came from my father. I think it was in his mind when he bought the adjoining twin houses, to live in one with my mother and to give the other one to me. This is what he did. They furnished it, including beautiful table and bed linens, the very best they had. The night before the wedding, I spoke to my mother.

"Mami, Armando and I are going next door to look at the house and see if everything is ready for us."

"I will go with you," she told me. Not even on the night before I was going to get married would my mother allow me to be alone with my fiancé! Now I can laugh, for it is hilarious that I could not even share an innocent kiss with the man who was going to be my husband the next day! So the three of us did a walk-through in what would be my first and only Cuban home during my married life.

The next day, November 5th, 1960, dawned bright and beautiful, like most mornings in Cuba. The magnificent, beautiful Catholic Church, so close to all the houses where I had lived, would be the setting for our wedding. I had six attendants, dressed in rainbow colors: in light blue were two of my friends, Nelita and Bertica; in light green were my sister-in-law, Marta, and my cousin, La Nena; in pink was Gulle, Armando's sister, and Elba, my cousin.

The girls resembled a rainbow, with pretty hats that matched their pastel dresses. Our flower girl, Lourdes, the little niece of my soon-to-be-husband, looked sweet in her dress of light pink; and my cousin, Guari's, little son, Rafaelito, was so proud to be our ring bearer. Cuban grooms had attendants only in elaborate, big city weddings.

The church was filled with people. My gown was as beautiful as any bride could desire. Made of white peau de soie, a heavier satin than was worn in summer weddings, it fell in lustrous folds to my feet; and a long, gossamer veil trailed down the back of the skirt.

The aisle seemed long, and I was nervous, perhaps even a bit scared as I held to my father's arm. But more than that, I was excited. I looked at Armando, so handsome in his wedding clothes, standing in front of the altar, waiting for me. I thought that he was perfect!

The wedding itself took a long time. I knew that I was getting married, but it was somewhat like a fairy tale, like a dream to me. Instead of a huge reception after the ceremony, we had a smaller party in the courtyard of my house, but only for family and very close friends. Even so, there were a good number, for we had a large extended family.

Lots of finger foods, drinks and music made it a joyful, noisy occasion. At some point, I'm sure long before the party was over, my new husband and I changed from our wedding clothes into our "going away" outfits. I had chosen the perfect dress, my *Tornaboda*, in Spanish. Off-white, the sleeveless dress fit perfectly, a slim sheath. It had a matching coat, with push-up sleeves; and the accessories were black. I loved it as much as the wedding dress.

In a letter Armando once sent to me while we were dating, he addressed me as "My elegant brunette." No one had called me elegant before; but in the *Tornaboda* dress, that's how I felt; elegant and beautiful, which is how every bride should feel.

While we were changing, the boys and men were busy tying cans onto the back of my husband's car, a fact we didn't notice until we were driving away. As was the custom, we drove all the way through town before he pulled the car over and removed the noisy cans from the bumper.

My husband had taken care of all the arrangements for our honeymoon, and he had chosen well. He had reserved the Honeymoon Suite, (*Recien Casados*) on the fifth floor, in the elegant Riviera Hotel in Havana City. ¡*Ay, ay, ay!*

It was so beautiful, like a dream. Prepared for us were silver and crystal trays filled with fruits and cheeses. A bottle of champagne rested in a silver ice bucket, and crystal champagne flutes stood beside it. When my husband took me into his arms, I was the happiest bride in all of Cuba....

We had a long honeymoon. That first week we spent in the Riviera Hotel, but we went out for a bit in the balmy evenings, to the Tropicana nightclub and other exciting places. One night we went back to Güines, before we spent another week at Varadero Beach, Matanzas Province and then back to Havana City for a few days at the Hilton Hotel.

Like all honeymooners must, we had to come back to the real world, to our new home. It did not seem strange to me that my husband and I lived only a wall away from my parents. It was a very thick wall, and we had our privacy. My husband had moved his office to the front part of our house, which was certainly large enough for it.

I went back to my job at the bank, where I continued to work; but there was a difference. Before the wedding, my name was Isabel Ramos Pichardo. When I returned, I learned to sign my new name: Isabel Ramos de Aguilar, which it would be for the rest of my life. I just didn't know that the rest of my life in Cuba would soon come to an end.

My mother and father

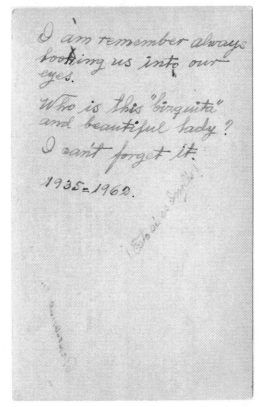

Poem from Papo to Mami

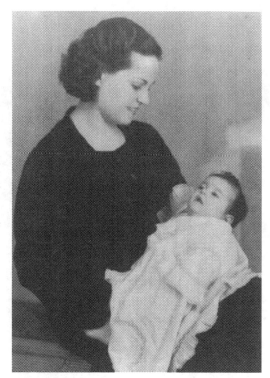

Edilia (Mami) & Isabel 1937

Isabel & Shirley Temple doll

Isabelita and cousin Kali

Juan & Isabel

Isabelita—Top row, 4th from left, Kindergarten Class-1942

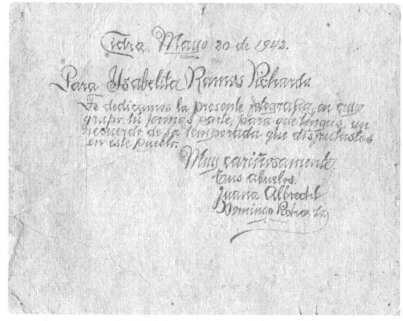

Inscription by Isa's grandfather

Isabel & Juan - 1943

Juan, Isabel, & Mother

Isabel's 5ᵗʰ birthday

1943-12-27 - Juan 5ᵗʰ birthday

Isabel's cousin, Class Valedictorian, Panchitín

1952-07- Mi Casita (my little house)

1954 - José

1954-01-15 - José

Quince Años 15th Birthday Party

Isabelita in La Progresiva

1957 -.Juan High School Graduation

Isabelita in La Progresiva

1958-05-20 - Isa (at piano) & friends

Armando Aguilar - 8th grade graduation

MERIENDA DE CONDOLENCIA

a nuestra pobre compañera

Isabel Ramos Pichardo

con motivo de su ingreso en

la gran Institución en la cual

"LAS QUE ESTAN DENTRO QUIEREN SALIR" Y
"LAS QUE ESTAN FUERA QUIEREN ENTRAR"

Domingo 30 de Octubre de 1960

Hora: 4 p. m.

Invitation to Isa'a engagement party

M E N U:

Cariños de Novios

Besos Azucarados

Delicias de Amor

Marcha Nupcial

Calor de Luna de Miel

Celos de Casados

Sorpresas de Matrimonio

Bebitos que llegan

Amor Eterno

Ponche a lo Aguilar

Engagement party menu

Ateneo Ramos Montero
Edilia Pichardo de Ramos
y
Ezequiel Aguilar Espinosa
Serafina Jiménez de Aguilar
tienen el gusto de invitar a Ud... a su
distinguida familia a la recepción
del Sacramento del matrimonio
de sus hijos
Isabel y Armando
el Sábado cinco de Noviembre de mil
novecientos sesenta, a las siete de la
noche en la Parroquia de Güines.

Wedding invitation

Isabel - Front row, 8th from left - Engagement Party

Isabelita and her father

Armado Aguilar's parents

Wedding kiss from José

Wedding kiss from Mami

Wedding kiss from Juan

Off to the honeymoon!

The Twin Houses- Aguilars' on the right.

Part of Dr. Aguilar's office wall murals

Park in front of Twin Houses

Bank where Isabelita worked (current photo)

1963-09 - Madrid, Spain,1963 - Armando, Isa and Alejandro

Armando and Alejandro, Madrid, Spain

1963 - Madrid, Spain

Madrid, the beautiful city. 1963

Isa, Armando, Alejandro & friends Madrid

1963 - Madrid, Spain - with friends

1963 - Madrid, Spain

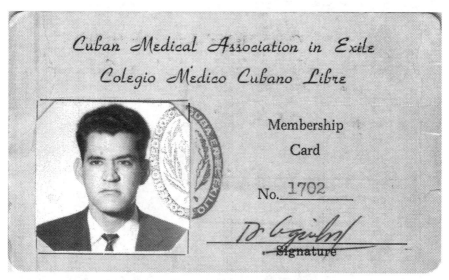

Dr Armando Aguilar Membership Card

Cuban Medical Association in Exile

Asociación de Médicos Cubanos en el Exilio

Colegio Médico Cubano Libre

Certificamos que el Doctor:

ARMANDO P. AGUILAR

cuya foto y firma aparecen al dorso pertenece al Colegio Médico Cubano Libre.

18 de mayo de 19 65

Presidente   Secretario

Dr Armando Aguilar Membership Card back

Isabelita's father in Chicago

Armando, Alex, Babe and Isabelita - Kankakee IL

Victor Aguilar - age 3

Alex and Lisa wedding day 1979

Alex Aguilar graduation photo 1979

Armando (Babe) Aguilar graduation photo 1983

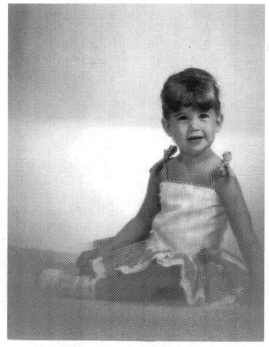

Christina Aguilar age 4 1979

Auto accident in TN 1982

Auto accident -Photo by Victor

Early 80s - Auto accident - no one hurt

Armando & Isabel - So Happy Together....

Victor Aguilar Graduation Photo 1990

Christina Aguilar Graduation Photo 1992

Alexa and Sarah 1999

Christina Aguilar and Ben DeVerger's Wedding Day 2006

L to R: Alexander, Lorenzo and Devon DeVerger,
Sons of Christina and Ben DeVerger

Original Circle of Friends, minus one

Isa and Circle of Friends II

2010 - Victor, Papa, & Alex

Sarah (greatgranddaughter) Alexa and
Olivia(granddaughters) Christina (daughter) 2011

Sisters-in-law Aidita, Marta and Isa in Florida

Isa's childhood friend from Cuba, Sonia

Sonia and Isabelita, reunited after 54 years

Isa's Grandfather's house in Cuba

Christina, Armando, Isa, Victor, Alex Thanksgiving 2014

The Aguilar Family - Thanksgiving - 2014

PART TWO

Dr. Armando Aguilar

CHAPTER ONE

The Young Man

Nueva Paz, a small town in the Province of Havana, Cuba, is the place of my birth. I scarcely remember it, for my family moved from there to the outskirts of Güines, two or three years after I was born. Güines is where I would live until I went to medical school. I later opened my medical practice in the same town, and that is where I got married, when I was twenty-eight.

My father was not wealthy; but as a soldier, he made an adequate living to support his family of five. I had an older brother, Noel, and a sister, Gudelia, five or six years younger than I. My parents sent me to a private Catholic elementary school.

A friend of my father's owned a small academy, where he tutored children who would be entering high school. When my father asked if I could enroll in these classes, the man readily agreed. Panchito admitted me into his school, which was of great benefit to me.

Little did I know that several years later, this man would become my uncle by marriage, for he was the husband of Isabel's Aunt Sara. At that time, I did not know the Ramos family.

I liked high school, probably in part due to the tutoring I received. During my last two years, I formed a friendship with Leopold Franqui, a boy from my neighborhood. We studied together, and we both enjoyed physical training. Behind my house was a great place to exercise, and we spent a lot of time there. As in most towns in Cuba, and I'm sure in the United States, we had a group of friends who played baseball; so we kept busy.

Another activity we boys enjoyed was playing marbles. On any playground or yard, boys drew circles and gathered around them, using their skills with marbles and thumbs to win as many prized marbles as possible from their friends. Could all that thumb-flexing contribute to later surgical skills? Probably not!

This was in the 1940s, before television became a household word. Movies provided our source of entertainment, and my brother and I walked to the theater as often as possible. Our trips into the center of town were uneventful. I don't recall ever hearing of children kidnapped or molested, and we were always safe.

My family and I looked forward to Sundays, when most of us went to the park. It was a large area, filled with lots of tall trees and sidewalks; and it was the perfect place to spend time with friends. It probably sounds unexciting now, but everyone dressed up, boys and girls alike, wanting to look their best.

The boys usually gathered in a group, talking and watching the girls, who walked by, all of us smiling and laughing, which was all we knew about flirting! It was a good time, an innocent time in our lives, one that can still make me smile, remembering.

On those Sundays, younger children wandered among the adults, offering shoe shines to anyone who would pay them a nickel for a good shine. A nickel! Those of us who could afford the nickel were happy to pay them, for we wanted to look as good as possible, even down to the shine on our shoes.

I did very well in high school. After graduation, it was decided that I would go to college; and the only opportunity to do that was in Havana City. Transportation to Havana was easy and inexpensive. By bus or train, both of which we used, the fare was twenty or thirty cents.

I had decided that I wanted to study medicine, to become a doctor. There were several factors that drew me in that direction. My father once took me to see a doctor when I had a very sore throat. I remember looking around his office, how clean and neat it appeared.

Many people sat in the waiting room, and it occurred to me that there would always be a great need for doctors. I liked the surroundings, and I respected the doctor's knowledge and skill. It didn't hurt that his office looked prosperous, and that he drove a very fine car!

In Cuba, not everyone owned a car; and in Güines only professional men, doctors, lawyers, people who owned lots of real estate could afford them. Since there were no automobile manufacturing plants in Cuba, all cars were imported from the United States or Europe, which made them even more expensive. I really wanted to own a car!

My friend, Franqui, and I went to Havana, to check out the university and get the information we needed. Later my father and I searched out boarding houses; and we found one. The cost, which would include food, was twenty dollars a month. That doesn't sound like much today, but then it was a quite a bit of money.

My brother, Noel, owned a grocery store; and at that time there was a shortage of rice, a staple in Cuban food. My father didn't have much extra money, but he saw an opportunity. He bought one hundred pounds of rice, and he took it to Havana. He approached the woman who owned the boarding house, and he struck a deal with her. In exchange for the rice, she agreed to let me live there for five months at no additional cost.

My friend and I both enrolled in medical school; but after one year, he discovered that he didn't like it. He decided to be a dentist, so we were no longer able to spend much time together. Our lives took different directions.

While in medical school, I discovered an acquaintance from my home town, Emilio Rubio, the younger brother of Dr. S. E. Rubio, a Güines physician. We saw each other often, and I asked him where he was living. "Here in a clinic," he told me. What is called a clinic in Cuba would be a small hospital in the United States.

"Why are you living in a clinic?" I asked. I didn't know that a medical student could do that. I thought they boarded somewhere, as I did.

"Well, the owner of the clinic was a doctor in the army. An army general is a friend of this doctor, and his son is also from Güines and a friend of Dr. Rubio. Our parents are friends, and they agreed to let us live there."

"Could I see this place?"

"Sure," he told me. So I went to see the clinic, and Emilio and I often studied together there, twice or week or so. In the meantime, the son of the general decided that he no longer wanted to be a doctor. He dropped out of medical school, so I asked Emilio if he thought I might possibly take his place.

"I'll find out," Emilio told me. As it worked out, I was able to talk to Dr. Alberto Bravo, the former military doctor who owned the clinic. He told me that I could live in the clinic for twenty dollars a month, which would include room and board. Since I was already paying that amount, I decided to move.

The clinic was about fifteen minutes from the university, which cost five or ten cents on the streetcar. That was still money I had to come up with! After a few months, my father told me that he could no longer afford to pay for my education at the university. So I decided that I would drop out for a year, get a job and save enough to come back and get my degree in medicine. By then, Emilio had joined his older brother in his practice, so I was boarding by myself.

I went to the clinic to inform them of my situation. I had begun to work regularly, helping with surgeries and anything else I could, without pay. I went to one of the doctors and told him my decision.

"I'm sorry, but I'll have to drop out of school for a few months."

"Oh, I'm sorry to hear that! Why are you leaving?"

"My father can no longer afford to pay the tuition and boarding. I'll have to find a job and save money enough to continue. I'll be back next year." I was prepared to do that, but it turned out much better than I could have dreamed. My friend, the doctor, went to the owner of the clinic and told him what I had said.

"No, Armando Aguilar does not leave here!" Dr. Bravo told him. Then he came to me. "You stay here," he said. "I will pay you the twenty dollars, and you stay here for free."

And that's how I came to be working at the clinic, in 1950, for a salary; and I was able to continue with my studies in medical school. I enjoyed my work. I took x-rays in the mornings, helped with surgeries, worked with appendectomy emergencies, all the while learning from the doctors every evening.

There were several emergency amputations, mostly from people whose fingers were caught in factory equipment. Most of the doctors on staff didn't have much experience with this type of injury, so I learned from "the boss," Dr. Bravo. He called me to come to the ER in the evenings, after regular hours, asking if I could help with amputating a finger now and then.

"Sure, I can," I told him every time. And this is how I learned. I went to classes every day, came back to the clinic to work and to study with the many doctors, even to work with patients in heart failure. I gained valuable experience.

We also went to the homes of patients who needed medical care, some who needed IVs, which I inserted and hooked up. Sometimes there were those who suffered from cirrhosis of the liver. I learned how to make a small incision, insert a huge needle and extract fluid, put in a couple of stitches and collect the five or ten dollars that was charged.

I didn't make much money, but I made enough to survive. I did have to buy books. On a street called San José, close to the university, there was a heavy-set man who taught anatomy; but he also had a printing shop, where he printed all the books.

Legally, he couldn't do that! Considering copyright laws, I'm not sure how he got away with it. There were students who never paid him, but I always did. He allowed me to pay ten or twenty dollars to take the books, and I paid him another five or ten dollars every month until I had paid for them. He had a good business!

One night, following another emergency appendectomy, Dr. Bravo asked me if I would like to go get a sandwich, to which I heartily agreed. It was very late, probably close to midnight. After we finished eating, we got back into his beautiful Buick convertible. He turned on the radio, which he always had set to Radio Reloj, where nothing but news was broadcast for twenty-four hours. But the station was not broadcasting.

"Something is not right," he told me. "Let's drive around and see what has happened. Army headquarters is close to the hotel." He knew that something was wrong, for the streets were just too quiet. He drove to the entrance of army headquarters, where we discovered that the gates were blocked by an army tank and a machine gun-toting soldier. The gunman recognized my boss and addressed him by name.

"Hello, Dr. Bravo!" He called.

"What's going on?"

"Batista is in there! There has been a coup," the soldier replied. "Do you want to go inside?"

"Sure!" My boss was enthusiastic, but I wasn't. My mind raced with the possibility that we, I, could be killed in there!

As incredible as it may sound, my ex-army boss took me with him into Army Headquarters where now-President Batista was meeting with his generals! I could not believe it! It was one or two o'clock in the morning, and I wanted nothing more than to leave the presence of the new ruler of Cuba! We were there for a short time, but I was happy when we left.

Later I relived the moments, thinking how dangerous it had been. At any given time, Batista's enemies could have attacked that building. All of us could have been killed by gunfire or rockets or whatever! I had no desire to experience anything like that again. Sometime later, I read an article in The Readers' Digest about the coup that had taken place without a shot being fired and not one combatant killed.

So there we were in Cuba, an up-coming election for the presidency scheduled to take place in a short time, with three candidates running, one of whom was Fulgencio Batista, a previous president, elected in 1940 and voted out of office in 1944. Apparently, he didn't want to take the chance that he would not win the presidency if an election were held.

In his first term, Batista had not been a good president; but the man who succeeded him, Ramón Grau San Martín, was. The four years of his presidency provided more human rights and prosperity than at any other time in modern history. Unfortunately, his successor, Carlos Prio Socarrás, was not of the same caliber. Now Batista had re-taken the government, would name himself president and the country would again know corruption and violence. We just didn't know to what extent it would change our lives.

CHAPTER TWO

Success

Batista's takeover of the government didn't affect the medical profession much, if any, at that time. I continued to go to medical school and work in the hospital every free moment. Patients started to ask for me instead of talking to a nurse, so I made a little extra money.

In my last year of school, I bought a car, a Hudson that cost me $395. With it, I learned how to drive; and I was able to go home to Güines and visit my family. Although I worked very hard at school and at the hospital, there were times I managed to have a little recreation, too.

A taxi stand did a thriving business on the other side of the hospital. Tourists who stayed in the nearby hotels hired them to go to nightclubs and other attractions in Havana, one of which was a well-known racetrack, three or four blocks from the clinic.

On a slow night, the owner of the taxis invited those of us who were off duty to go to the Tropicana night club with him. So we did! He was the chauffeur, and we got to ride for free. It was a good deal!

His cabs had parking privileges outside the club, so he parked with no concern that he would be fined or towed. We went into the luxurious nightclub, sat at the bar and watched the live show. We even ordered a beer and tried to look like those worldly tourists who came from all over the world to visit the Tropicana.

When I was working in the hospital, I reconnected with an army captain I had met before, through my father. They knew each other while my father was in the military. We were friendly enough. He had moved to Havana, where he had close connections with the Department of Children, the ONDI.

Batista had built desperately needed clinics for children in various towns. The captain told me to let him know when I graduated from medical school, for he could put me in touch with the head of this organization. There was a good possibility that I could get a job with them.

After I finished medical school, in 1953, I didn't call him. I was busy setting up my practice in Güines. However, he called me.

"Have you finished medical school?"

"Yes, I have," I told him, with a measure of pride, I'm sure.

"Listen," he said. "The ONDI is going to set up a clinic in Güines. It will be ready in about a month, so I'll give you a call then."

"Fine," I told him.

"You will have a job there as a pediatrician."

I wasn't a pediatrician, but I liked children. Again, I thought, *Fine. I'll be a pediatrician!* I already had a job, making big money, $150 a month! Let me tell you, that really was a lot of money at that time.

I enjoyed working with the children, but some of the cases were heartbreaking. The clinics were a godsend, for the need was great. There were so many of the little fellows. Without the free care provided by the clinics, none of them would have had medical care. This is one good thing President Batista did for the people.

In Cuba, as well as in other Central American countries, intestinal parasites were rampant among the children. Oh, my goodness. Among the very poor, basic cleanliness, sanitation and good drinking water were practically non-existent. Some of the children died due to dehydration and massive infections. After working there for a good while, I became Director of the ONDI Children's Clinic.

A textile factory (*La Textilera*) in the area kept a doctor on staff, for injuries in that industry were common. A friend of mine told me that the company wanted to hire a new doctor. I applied for the job, which brought the number of applicants to three. Several of my friends worked there, so they got the addresses of the employees for me. In my free time, I went to their homes, knocked on doors and asked them to vote for me.

Since I had been away from Güines in school so many years, I was afraid that the other doctors would have a better chance to be elected. It was a pleasant surprise to learn that I received the most votes, and I got the job, which paid monthly. So with that job, I then had three: my private practice, the children's clinic and now the textile factory. I was finally in a position to make some money! It felt good.

One of the first things I did was trade my Hudson for a Plymouth, which was small and not very pretty. I gave it to my brother and father, to the family. Then I bought a new 1957 Bel Air Chevrolet, a beautiful car. It was mauve and silvery, the only one like it in town; and I was so proud. I paid $2,450! My monthly payments were $85.00, and I was one of the happiest young men in Cuba!

In the meantime, Batista's forces captured Fidel Castro, tried and sentenced him to fifteen years in prison. After a year, the president relented and allowed Fidel to go free. It was the worst mistake he ever made. Eventually the bearded rebel managed to gather a rag-tag army that continued to grow as he roamed the mountains. He and his followers put together a radio system and started to broadcast every night from different locations, pleading with the people to rise up against President Batista, the dictator.

Fidel's army grew, for he had given hope to the poor, the displaced, those who had no chance of ever owning a house, land or the ability to make decent wages. Most of the factories, bottling plants, tobacco and sugar companies were owned by corporations in the United States. Workers received very poor wages, while Batista grew wealthy on their backs. Corruption in the government was rampant.

Even so, my practice grew. There are always illnesses and injuries that must be treated. The location of my private practice could not have worked out better for me. I rented a house right beside the movie theater in the center of Güines. I let my aunt and uncle move into the back part; and I set up my practice in the front. This arrangement suited both of us.

A front porch formed a buffer from the street, as well as providing a comfortable area where I could take brief breaks between patients. Around five o'clock every evening, people lined up along the sidewalk, waiting for the ticket office of the theater to open. I often managed to take a break at this time, for I enjoyed watching the people. To be honest, I was probably watching the girls! I was in my mid-twenties, single, a hot-blooded Cuban man. Of course, I was watching the girls!

One evening, my eyes focused on a particular girl. Taller than average, dark hair, strikingly beautiful face, cute figure—I found myself staring at her. She wore a brown dress, styled with wide shoulder straps that were fastened with big wood buttons. After all these years, I still remember how she looked in that dress.

I watched her for several moments before she saw me. Our eyes locked, and she returned my gaze; but then she looked away, apparently very shy, which I found appealing. I kept staring at her, mentally willing her to look at me again. She did, briefly, before she turned her back.

My eyes followed her until she disappeared into the darkness of the theater, and I knew in that moment that she was *my* girl. I had seen her before, when she was much younger. Her father had an insurance business, and I had been to his home office on insurance matters.

All my life I had worked very hard. Now I had three great jobs and a dream car. The only thing that kept my life from being perfect was the absence of a special girl, the one with whom I could build a life. I knew that I had just found her. It was only a matter of time before she would know it, too. I have to say that it did take a while.

We began to run into each other now and then. Within a year or so, we became a couple; and I asked her father for permission to propose to her. He agreed, so Isabel Ramos and I became engaged. She was young, just out of school and working in her father's bank; so we had a long engagement.

While I continued to build my medical practice, to save, to help my family, to make plans for what would be my perfect life, unrest and anticipation among the Cuban people grew every day. They hoped that a "savior," in the form of the bearded revolutionary, would deliver them from poverty and an oppressive dictator. A kind of excitement, as well as fear, filled the tropical air.

Over the years, many Cubans had moved to Florida; and a good-sized community of them flourished there. They had established businesses and encouraged relatives still in Cuba to join them. And many did, wanting better lives for their children. As it turned out, these Cubans had made good choices.

Now all of Cuba sensed that change might actually come; and they pinned their hopes for that change on Fidel Castro, a big man who smoked long cigars, wore Army-green fatigues and lived in the mountains. Word spread that he and his "army" were coming down from those mountains, all the way into Havana. Pockets of resistance bombed nightclubs and meeting places, and Batista's troops tried to quash them. However, Fidel kept coming.

In desperation, Batista's army escalated their attempts to stop the people from supporting Castro. They rounded up many, imprisoned them, tortured and even killed them. The closer the revolutionaries came to Havana, the more brutality Batista's forces used, hoping to gain information that would bring down Fidel Castro.

No one thought that the president would leave Cuba. We all thought that he would fight this "lawyer turned soldier" with his little army of 400 men and women to the end. After all, Batista had a real army and real tanks and unlimited ammunition and supplies enough to hold Castro at bay for months, maybe years, if he were determined.

The closer Fidel came to the capital, the more excitement he created. Then suddenly, we heard that El Presidente Batista had flown from Cuba in the middle of the night, taking hundreds of millions of dollars with him. I could not believe that he had actually left the country!

On New Year's Eve, 1959, Fidel Castro's "revolutionary army" rode their tanks and trunks into the city of Havana. Cuba was liberated! People thronged the streets, waving white handkerchiefs and scarves. His entry was televised, and we all bore witness to this miracle. The Cuban people would no longer be oppressed, forced to work for starvation wages, denied hope of bettering themselves.

A brutal government would no longer drag its citizens into a filthy prison, to be tortured, maimed and killed. The new government would be fair. It would become a democratic, free state, much like the United States, where people could accomplish anything they could dream. Hard work would benefit them, not a bloated, corrupt dictator who lived in a palace with gold trappings.

Life was going to be good for everyone.

The paradise that had once been Cuba would flourish again, and the balmy air that we breathed would smell sweeter, the breezes would feel fresher; and we could once more be proud of our country.

We were living in a fool's paradise.

CHAPTER THREE

The Beginning of the End

For a time, excitement and optimism filled the streets of Cuban cities. Other countries wooed the island's new leader, especially the United States, hoping to gain an even stronger lucrative foothold than they had enjoyed under Batista's corrupt reign. Cuba's production of sugar, tobacco, rum, tourism and the promise of much more held the possibility that it could once again become the "Jewel of the Caribbean."

Isabelita's parents continued with plans for our wedding. Nothing much was required of me, but to make arrangements for a long honeymoon. I was excited. Like most Cubans, I felt that this new government would be a good thing for the country. I could see my life laid out in front of me, like a well-designed highway, lined with good things: a home, a beautiful wife, children, an excellent income, friends—everything a man could envision to make him happy.

In the beginning of Castro's regime, everything was rosy. The young people were especially excited all over the country, including the youth of Güines. We experienced a new sense of freedom from oppression, and hope that better paying jobs would be available to those who had so little materially.

A representative of the former government lived across the street from the hospital where I worked. His daughter, a doctor, and I worked together occasionally, and I respected the man's opinion. So I asked him what he thought of Fidel Castro.

"He's no good. He's a Communist."

"Well, I don't like him either," I replied, "but I don't think he's a Communist." The man was right.

In the beginning, most Cubans who moved to the United States had been close to Batista and his government. Those who were smart enough, who had more experience, left Cuba with dollars. A Güines businessman, who had come to Cuba from Spain years earlier, had lived under Franco's rule. He married a Cuban girl and raised a family as he built a business, importing various woods.

Eventually, he and his two sons-in-law built a huge business in our area and surrounding towns. He became a very wealthy man. He began to make trips to the United States, with no problem. People eventually began to wonder about the trips, and one day he took his family with him and he didn't come back!

"What is this?" asked the community. "He is crazy! He built all this and he left it?" Well, the man was crazy like a fox! He took all his money, all his liquid assets, and he left the shell of a business that no one knew how to run. He had recognized the same signs in Castro that he had witnessed in Spain, under the dictatorial ruler, Franco. Eventually he relocated in Puerto Rico, where he established another business.

Aside from the exodus of other like-minded businessmen, not much changed in the first few months, except that Batista's military was disbanded. The soldiers were sent home, no longer needed. Citizens were relieved of their weapons, all guns; for with peace and harmony in the country now, there was no need for them. The word, confiscation, was not heard.

My first experience with the new government was not very promising. Someone found a photograph, taken during Batista's time, of me, having lunch at the military headquarters in Güines. I don't remember what the occasion was, but I had been invited to have lunch. I knew several military men, for my father had been a soldier for many years.

Castro's local people called me in, accusing me of being an active supporter of Batista's. "No, no," I told them. "I am a doctor who treats patients. I don't have any connections to anything else." Many people who knew me told my interrogators the same thing, that my loyalty was to medicine and my patients.

One thing I know. Havana became like a circus during the trials against Batista's generals and supporters. The trials themselves were a joke. The outcome was predictable. All of the defendants were found guilty and ordered to the wall, *"Paredón!"* Shot by firing squad. There were no appeals and executions were immediate. They were televised, shown in news footage, a graphic warning to anyone who might entertain the thought of resistance to the new regime.

I continued to work at my three jobs. As a wedding gift, Isabelita's parents presented us with the house that adjoined theirs. It was perfect for our needs, allowing ample space in the front part of the house for my medical practice. Even though Castro continued to implement additional changes in the country, I remained optimistic.

The day I watched my fiancé walk down the church aisle toward me was one of the happiest of my life. Dressed in her white gown and veil, I thought she was the most beautiful woman I had ever seen. I knew that she was mine, that we had made the right choice, that our families were compatible and that we would have a good life together. And I could not imagine living anywhere in the world except Cuba.

We returned from our honeymoon, ready to build that ideal life. Even with the changes that began to affect everyone's life, my practice grew. There would always be a need for doctors.

My father-in-law was a very perceptive man. Quietly, he set about giving away many of their possessions. He and his wife had beautiful furniture and tasteful decorations. He had no problem getting rid of them, especially since the block monitors were not fully in place as yet.

When Castro announced that pesos, which had the evaluation of an American dollar, would no longer be the currency of Cuba, Isa's father and I were better prepared than most of the people in Güines. By that time, many were beginning to realize that this new government was not going to be what they hoped.

Fidel wanted to govern even the music that was played in Cuba. For a long time, he closed the nightclubs that had attracted tourists from all over the world, and he decided what kind of music would be appropriate in his new regime. He wanted to reject anything he considered too American. Eventually he would outlaw Christmas and close the churches, most of which happened after we left Cuba.

Our medical system remained unchanged for a year or so, although I was removed from my position at the children's clinic. Even those who were in power in our home town knew me and all the other professional people. For probably a year after Isa and I were married, my practice remained about the same.

During this time, though, many of Castro's generals, those who had totally supported him, started to question his motives. Some accepted that his declaration of Communism was the right thing for Cuba, but many did not. They wanted him to implement the free elections that he had promised, but that was not to happen.

With Ché Guevera in charge of interrogations, many people were imprisoned and tortured on the merest suspicion. Raúl Castro was not much better. He actually killed more of their own people than Fidel did, although Fidel was responsible for the executions of some of his former friends and supporters.

In time, Castro jailed and even executed some of his own friends and officers. Huber Matos, one of his most trusted commanders and friend, was tried for treason and sentenced to twenty years in prison. Matos was loyal, had been a teacher; and he supplied arms to Castro's revolution, going to Costa Rica and the United States to obtain them. There was no reason for Castro to turn on this man, but he had become so paranoid that he trusted no one.

An example of his paranoia occurred after we left Cuba. Castro sent a young general to Africa, where his mission was to help the people spread Communism in their country. The Cuban people really liked this general, who was very popular with all of them. Castro could not tolerate the possibility that one of his men might become more beloved than he was. He fabricated a story about this young man, saying that he was connected with drug trafficking, which he was not. But Fidel Castro framed him and had him executed.

From the very beginning, Castro and his revolutionaries were liars. They pretended to be compatible with the Catholic Church, with priests, who married people during the revolution. The worst one, the head of the Communist movement in Cuba, was Ché Guevera, who was a violent, brutal man.

He was a true Communist in every sense. He did not hesitate to murder anyone he suspected of betrayal. It didn't matter whether or not they were guilty. If he had not been a factor in Castro's revolution, it might not have had such a disastrous outcome. We will never know.

Ché and Castro didn't like each other. Eventually they parted ways, and Guevera went to South America, where he was eventually killed. It's too bad that Fidel came to see himself in the role of Supreme Leader, a dictator who would turn a once-productive country into a virtual wasteland of poverty and despair.

With agrarian reforms, the people began to suffer even more. Castro nationalized everything, from American-owned companies to farms and cattle ranches, from bakeries to markets to banks. He removed the farmers from their homes and land. He turned them over to people who had no clue as to how to prepare the land for planting, how to plant, how to do anything!

He became furious when the crops failed, when the land was ruined. He kept telling the people that they had to work harder, to be more productive, to make sacrifices, as he continued to live in the twenty or more lavish houses he had confiscated from the once-wealthy people in Havana and other cities. He enjoyed the best Cuba had to offer, while the people he professed to love had not even bare necessities.

With embargos from the United States and other countries, food became scare. Rationing of food, supplies of all kinds, gasoline and everyday needs became necessary. Suddenly, Russians were all over Cuba, cutting down and exporting trees from our forests to Russia. They became the island's only source of support, but even with its years of brutality, corruption and murders, Russia could not make Communism work in their own country. They assisted in destroying Cuba.

During Batista's time, there were six or seven well-known young people in Güines who actively protested against him. They were not Communists, but they didn't like Batista. They had a Jeep that they traveled in together. One became the mayor, all of them professional people. They were supporters of Castro, and one day they came to our home, saying that they wanted to talk to me. I might have raised a questioning eyebrow, but they reassured me.

"No, no! We just want to talk to you. We know that you don't like the government, and that you plan to go to The United States." I knew them, so I invited them into my house.

"Yes," I said. By that time my in-laws had left Cuba, and it was my plan to leave also.

"We don't want you to go. We want you to stay in Cuba. It's going to be a great place to live. Everything is going to be fine, the government will provide all our needs, and we want to talk to you about it." They continued to talk, and then they told me what they could offer me.

"We will give you a house."

"Okay."

"We will give you a car."

"Okay."

"Your children will receive free education."

"What else?" I asked.

"All of these are good things," they said.

"Forget it!" I told them. "I already have a house, and I already have a car, and you are going to teach Communism to my children, no? Forget it! As soon as I can get visas, we are going to the United States!"

I was not afraid of these people. We knew each other as children, all our lives we knew each other. I had no fear that they would harm me or my family. We were fortunate that someone else did not approach me. Our circumstances could have been very different. The interesting thing is that all these people are now in Miami!

One of the worst things about Fidel Castro's revolution is that it separated families. Sons turned against fathers. Fathers turned against sons. Brothers turned against brothers. Girls were no longer subject to their parents' rule. They threw off all moral restraints, turning against everything they had been taught.

When Communism became the law of the land, it destroyed all family loyalties. Communism became mother, father, sister, brother to everyone; and heaven help you if you were not a loyal Communist.

PART THREE

Isabel Ramos de Aguilar

CHAPTER ONE

Surprises

I loved being married! Living in my own beautiful house, with my own handsome husband, I could not have been happier. Our home was filled with lovely things my parents had given to us, the best they could provide. Clouds of the approaching storm over Cuba had formed, but the full force of it had not yet unleashed its fury.

My husband held regular office hours in the front part of our house, separate from our living quarters and the colorful courtyard in the back. He treated many children, so he wanted to make his office and waiting room as child-appealing as possible. Our artist friend, Laura Galainena, volunteered to paint Disney cartoon characters directly onto the walls.

The smiling faces of familiar figures helped to calm nervous, ailing children when they came to see Dr. Aguilar. Anyone in Cuba who had seen Disney movie cartoons could not help but smile back at them, so bright and reassuring where they marched around the waiting room. It proved to be a stroke, actually many strokes, of brilliance!

Every morning I went to my job at the bank. It still seemed strange to me that my father was no longer part of something that had been so important in his life. Although he had retired from the daily routine of the business world, he kept abreast of political maneuvers. He understood what was about to happen to our country long before most Cubans.

There was a measure of uncertainty, but at least no bombs were being dropped. We felt safe walking down our city streets, but it would not be long before our sense of false security disappeared.

Shortly after our wedding, Consuelo, the beloved cook of my childhood, came to see me. "Do you have someone to cook for you?"

No, I don't."

"Could I come to work for you?" I was happy to see her, and thrilled that she would be cooking for us. Consuelo made such a difference in our lives. Just having her in the kitchen, busily preparing whatever delicious dish she chose for our dinner, made our house seem more like a home.

I liked to sit on the cool tile floors, something I did often. One day, as I sat there talking to her, something didn't feel right with me. "Consuelo, I don't feel good."

"Ah, ha." She chuckled knowingly and wagged her finger at me. "You are going to have a baby!" I was shocked! Me? A baby? How was it possible? After thinking about it for a moment, I realized that it was, indeed, possible! I was thrilled, excited and happy at the prospect of becoming a mother. I could not wait to tell my husband. It had not occurred to me that, being a doctor, he could already be aware!

I knew very little about babies, except that they were sweet, cuddly, sometimes cried, needed to be fed and changed. I was twelve when my youngest brother, José, was born. I had not been responsible for his care, but I had loved to play with him. I dressed him and pampered him, like a baby doll.

Having my mother next door was a comfort to me during those months. Except for my time in boarding schools, she was the constant in my life. I knew that I could always depend upon her. Consuelo did not stay with me very long; but we hired another cook, Rosalina, who was more than capable in the kitchen. We also hired a housekeeper, Xiomara.

I quit my job at the bank after I learned that a baby was on the way. Aside from the morning sickness, my pregnancy progressed without incident; and on September 11, 1961, our son, Alejandro, was born in the Ocejo Clinic in Güines.

He was a beautiful baby, with big hazel eyes and black hair. My mother fell in love with him at first sight. She stayed with me most of the time during the day, and she showed me how to care for my little son. With her help, Xiomara keeping our house clean and Rosalina cooking wonderful meals, I quickly regained my strength.

Every morning Rosalina came to me and asked, "Señora, (or Madame) what do you want me to make for you today?" Breakfast consisted of *café con leche,* which is coffee with milk, accompanied with toast or bread and butter, perhaps orange juice. Our breakfasts were very light.

Often I told her to make whatever she wished. If I wanted steak or other cuts of meat, she bought them a day ahead, for she marinated and then pounded them very thin before cooking. Once the menu was planned, Rosalina went to a little grocery store on the corner of our block and bought what was needed for that day.

By then foods were being rationed, especially meats. If none was available, Rosalina chose something else. Always, the food she prepared was delicious. She made wonderful soups, which we might have for *almuerzo,* along with black beans and rice. This meal was a bit heartier than a light lunch, but not like dinner.

While we ate, Rosalina made preparations for the evening meal. She then washed the dishes before she went home to take care of her own house. Around five o'clock she returned and cooked whatever she had planned for dinner. Sunday was her day off.

Dinners often began with soup, followed by a main course of meat, black beans over rice (a Cuban staple), a *vianda,* such as fried plantain, yucca or malanga, and always bread and butter. Dessert was mandatory, followed by small cups of Cuban coffee.

Looking back, I smile at my lack of working knowledge or familiarity with anything in my own kitchen, which was a pleasant room with white walls, bright and sunny. I knew what the yellow appliances were, but I knew nothing about how to use them.

The first four months following the baby's birth passed much too quickly. My father's plans were in place, and it was time to set them in motion. Much to my dismay, he sent my mother, my little brother, my other brother, Juan, and his wife, Marta, to Florida. He was unable to obtain visas for my husband, our son and me. Armando was a valued doctor, and we had a baby boy, both of whom Castro wanted to keep.

Not long before the day of their departure, my mother stopped by our house, on her way to or from somewhere, dressed in a beautiful black dress. She took Alejandro into her arms and pressed him against her shoulder in the universal way mothers and grandmothers caress a child. Unfortunately, she did not cover her dress with a towel to catch possible spit-ups.

As if on cue, the baby let loose a torrent of overflowing milk that spilled down my mother's shoulder. Instead of being upset at the damage to her garment, she brushed away my apologies. "I'm not going to get this dress cleaned," she told me. "I'm going to keep it just like this and take it with me to the United States. It is something of Alejandro." I don't know whether she actually did this or not.

That's how much my mother loved her first little grandchild. Her grief at leaving us and that precious baby was as intense as mine at seeing her walk away from the house that had separated us only by a wall. How could any of us bear it? After she left, I often sat in a rocking chair in the dining room, holding my baby, looking at that wall, wanting my mother.

Papo stayed for a while longer, just to look after me; but when he left, I thought my heart would break. I didn't know if I would ever see him or the rest of my family again. The furnishings and lovely accessories my mother had accumulated remained in their house. A young doctor and his family from the other end of the island were moved into it, and knowing that they would use my parents' treasured belongings just added to my heartbreak. None of this was right!

I cried a lot, but eventually I became immersed in caring for the baby and running my household. Xoimara was wonderful with Alejandro, and she loved to play with him. When he began to chatter, "Da-Da," Xoimara was thrilled.

"Look! Alejandro is crazy about me!" she said. "He is calling me 'Da-Da!'" She was crazy about him, too. Xiomara's brother, Armando Vasquez, had gone to the United States, where he became a major league baseball player. He was well-known in both countries for many years. She was so proud of him.

With my parents and brothers gone, I was unbearably lonely. So when my husband got ready to make evening house calls, I got ready, too. I packed up enough diapers and bottles to take care of the baby, and I went with Armando on his house calls, which could take a few hours. I sat in the car and played with Alejandro until my husband came back to the car, and then we went to the next house on his list.

Almost as soon as my mother arrived in Miami, she started sending things to us. She sent boxes of Kraft macaroni and cheese, which we had never tasted. We read English well, so we followed instructions on the box;

and occasionally we had mac and cheese for dinner on Sunday evenings. We loved it! She also sent cans of Campbell's soup, with which we were familiar. I remember putting the pan and dishes in the sink, for Rosalina to wash the next day; but it would not be many months before I had to learn how to do all the domestic chores, all by myself!

#

CHAPTER TWO

Black Market in Paradise

A shortage of meat led to the people of Cuba obtaining it any way they could, a form of black market that involved even some government-employed people. One of them knew my husband, which led to an improvement in our menus. It was, however, a don't-ask-don't-tell endeavor.

I went with Armando to the home of this man. I don't remember how he evaded the block captains, but perhaps his standing in the government made the difference. Together the two men loaded a quarter of beef into the trunk of our car.

When we returned home, Armando backed the car into the garage and closed the door. He had asked Luis, the husband of the woman who did our laundry, to help him unload the beef, as well as cut up and package it to store in the freezer compartment of our refrigerator. I was thrilled that some good meat was going to appear on our dinner table again.

Our house was arranged so that the garage was connected to one side. The car bay was close to the house; the back wall contained a window and a door that opened to the side yard, which was filled with flowers and plants. A winding sidewalk through the yard led from the garage's back door to one that opened into the dining room, next to the long, roomy kitchen. This arrangement proved to be convenient in more ways than one that night.

Rosalina prepared and served dinner and then went back to the kitchen to help Luis wrap the rest of the meat. We were perhaps half-way finished with our meal when the doorbell rang. Rosalina answered and came back to us, concern on her face.

"Señora, men are at the door, wanting to come inside! They say they need to inspect the indoor plants for mosquitoes! What should I tell them?" Rosalina's voice trembled with fear.

"Ask them if they will please sit down in the waiting room and wait until we finish our dinner," my husband told her. She scurried back to make the request, then returned, saying that the men had agreed to wait.

Quickly, we took our plates from the dining room to the kitchen. Luis had just finished wrapping the meat, so he gathered up as many packages as he could carry and ran to the garage, where he dropped them through the open window onto the garage floor. I don't recall how many trips it took, but we could not risk storing the meat in our refrigerator freezer. How could we ever explain where it came from if it were discovered?

Many of my husband's patients paid for their medical care with foods, sometimes eggs or garden vegetables; and we had to be careful that no one found out about even that. Everything had to be accounted for to the government, down to the amount of garden-raised produce.

While Luis made his runs to the garage, Rosalina, without the convenience of paper towels, used dishcloths and drying towels to wipe up blood from the work table, floor and counter, rinsing and wringing until every trace was gone. She dipped a mop in pine-scented cleaner and water and swabbed down the floor to erase any lingering odor of blood. After Luis made his last trip to the garage, he disappeared! I don't know where he went. He just kind of faded into the night.

My husband and I had stayed out of their way, not wanting to have even a speck of blood on our shoes or clothing when we met with the government inspectors. Scared beyond belief that the smallest thing could prevent us from leaving Cuba, we took deep breaths and headed toward my husband's office.

Two young men rose as we came into the waiting room. Sure enough, they had come to examine every house plant for mosquitoes and larvae. Malaria has always been a threat in Latin American countries, and the only way to keep it in check is to eliminate the carriers—mosquitoes. They took their jobs seriously, for they examined every pot, container and leaf, top and underneath, until they were satisfied that our plants were clean.

After the men left, we breathed a collective sigh of relief, weak-kneed at the close call. In retrospect, the daring of our "butcher shop" experience scares me, even now. One miscalculation could have meant the imprisonment or execution of all of us. Fidel Castro did not know the meaning of mercy for anyone he thought was a threat to his revolution, not even to his closest friends and confidants.

In exchange for helping us, we gave a portion of the meat to Luis. We stressed to Rosalina that she could say nothing to anyone about our purchase, not her family, neighbors or *anyone!* To ensure her silence, we also gave packages of the meat to her, as well as a bonus to her salary. I'm sure other black market deals like this were made during those early years under Communism in Cuba, but rarely and only with those who could be trusted, literally, with one's life.

Looking back on this incident, I can see an element of comedy, something like an *I Love Lucy* episode: Luis, desperately cutting and packaging the meat, trying not to cut himself in the process; Rosalina, wiping up blood, sloshing the mop, while I am wringing my hands in desperation; my husband, trying to keep everyone calm. It is humorous only in retrospect, for the mind-numbing terror of the moment cannot be adequately described.

So for a while, Rosalina was able to prepare dishes of marinated, succulent beef, in whatever manner we wished. We didn't attempt this black market thing again! Most of the time, we ate out on Sundays. Occasionally, we went to my Aunt Sara's house in Havana. We always took something with us to contribute to the meal, for food grew scarcer by the day.

More often we went to the house of a friend, Armando Fernández, a local politician. Every Sunday he opened his house to friends and family, providing a huge spread of various foods. Many people brought foods to him: chickens, eggs, vegetables, fruits, *viandas*, possibly hoping to gain favor with him. Thinking about those days, it embarrasses me that I didn't know how to cook; but it was the only way of life I knew. I was ill-prepared for what was to come.

The happiest time for us during those two years were spent in a beautiful house on Varadero Beach, the most spectacular beach on Cuba's shores. One of the Duponts had built a complex of big, lovely houses there, called appropriately, Dupont Estates. (It is possible to see photos of this area online.)

Before Castro, the houses were owned by wealthy people from all over the world, I suppose. Some were used as summer homes, but I think many were inhabited year round. Fidel allowed those who could afford it to rent them as vacation houses, as well as keeping one of the best as his own personal property. While he often bragged that he owned nothing fancier than the common people of Cuba, in truth he had confiscated well over a dozen dwellings for his private use, traveling among them to avoid assassination attempts.

We took Rosalina with us, and we also invited my husband's sister, Gudelia, who was called Gulle. The second floor was reserved for house maids, but we didn't need them. Rosalina had a wonderful room with a private bath. So did Gulle. I was enchanted with the house, which stood no more than half a short block from the ocean. The accommodations were more than amazing, like something out of a fairy tale.

We kept Alejandro with us in the huge master suite. The comfortable bed was covered with the softest pillows, pillows everywhere! The bathroom was like a spa, elegant and spacious. I could have lived just in that room!

A door from our bedroom opened into a library, lined with book-filled shelves. A comfortable sofa, placed strategically between bookshelves, rested directly across from sliding glass doors that led outside. On another wall of our room, a door opened into a long hall. Additional bedrooms were accessible from this hall, which also led to the kitchen and dining room that included a small sitting room, the only "living room" area in the main part of the house.

Sliding glass doors, like those in the library, opened from the dining room to the outdoors. Both sets of doors opened onto a path that led over an arched bridge spanning a small body of water, filled with colorful gold fish. Across the bridge stood a spectacular, glass-walled entertainment area, a living room of sorts. Octagonal in shape, I could see that it was furnished as lavishly as the main house.

Flowers and greenery surrounded the whole area, beautiful grounds that stretched all the way to the beach. I didn't cross the bridge to the glass-enclosed room. It was too far from the house for my taste, and there was something almost sinister about it to me. I was probably being fanciful, but I could not make myself enter it, beautiful as it was.

A carnival, complete with rides and entertainment, spread its promise of excitement along the beach, not far from the house. I liked the music, the noise of carnivals! Gulle didn't want to go, but the rest of us went one day, exploring the stalls and booths, sampling the food, enjoying the atmosphere. My husband held Alejandro while Rosalina and I wandered among the rides. She had never been on any of them, so I tried to persuade her to ride one with me. I loved them!

"Rosalina, don't be afraid," I told her. "You will be with me, and you will enjoy this ride!" In spite of her reluctance, she finally gave in to my pleas.

We rode one that swung us around, reversing so fast it took our breath. Poor Rosalina. Her skin was black; but when she got off the ride, her face was pale! She was so sick! I wished I had listened to her. She was miserable. I doubt that she ever again got on one of those spinning machines!

Many shops and stores had once prospered in Varadero Beach, much like Miami Beach in Florida. They were still there, but merchandise was scanty in many places. So I took Gulle with me to town, driving that beautiful Bel Air, which was still my husband's pride and joy.

I didn't know how to drive very well. Unfortunately, I didn't pay much attention to signs, either. There were two lanes leading one way, and two leading another. I took the wrong lane, making a left hand turn from the right lane, and someone in a convertible yelled at me. "Hey! What are you doing?"

I turned to Gulle and asked, "What did I do? What happened? Why was he angry at me?"

"I don't know!"

When we got back to the beach house, I told my husband what I had done. He didn't seem too excited about it. He just told me not to do it again! Well, I didn't—at least, not in Cuba!

Every day that week I put on my bathing suit and walked the few steps from the kitchen into the sparkling, multi-hued blues of the Caribbean. Pure, white sand covered the shore that led into a light blue, then darker blues, then turquoise and aqua and deep blues of the most spectacular water in any ocean, anywhere. It is indescribable, warm and luscious against the skin.

When I think of those days, it's as if I am watching a movie, with myself in the starring role. I watch a young Isabelita as she strides along the beach in slow motion, tossing her hair in the warm breeze, breathing deeply of the moist, tropical air, smiling in anticipation of the warm water. I watch her wade into the sparkling blue of the sea, and soon she is swimming, watching crystal droplets fall from her arms. It is a brief daydream of earthly paradise, one I am happy to have experienced, although for only one week, never again to be repeated.

I know that bad things happened to some of the people who lived in those houses along the beach. The natural beauty of the tropical paradise is still there; but a political snake still holds the power of life and death over the residents of the island. It will never be free, not as long as Communism reigns.

The house Fidel had chosen for his own use on Varadero Beach was to the right side of us, at an angle from ours. He was not there at the time, but the grounds caretaker told us which house belonged to the Supreme Ruler. Those people trusted no one! Fidel had many houses, and he moved from one to another, so no one knew exactly where he would be. One time he might wear a blond wig, or a different beard, or some form of disguise, for he knew that he had many enemies, many who wanted to kill him.

A narrow street, butted against white sand, wound from house to house, all of which were far apart, with wide, spacious lawns. Our week at the beach was heavenly, but it was not free. My husband paid for the use of the house. Those few days would provide my last pleasant memories of the country that had been my home all my life.

Fidel had begun to clamp down on every part of Cuban life. Inventory was taken in every house in every city, town, plantation and farm. And that is why four young, armed militia thugs came to be in my house—to take inventory. They systematically went through each cabinet, drawer, closet and box in every room of my house. My husband knew that they were coming, and he warned me.

"I cannot be there," he had told me. "It will be only you, and you'll just have to take care of it. You will have to deal with them." It was imperative that I be cooperative, which became more and more difficult as they followed me from room to room.

One held a notebook while the other called off the items, which were described and written down. Every piece of china, silverware, napkin, table cloth, skillet, saucepan--everything in the house went on that list.

"If you break something, you must replace it," one of them told me. They went through my clothes in the closet, my undergarments in drawers, shoes, stockings—and they counted everything. In our bedroom, one of the men held up a dainty, soft-white bra to his chest and made an obscene gesture. I wanted to slap his smirking face!

"Wait just one minute," I told them. "I have to ask my husband something." I was enraged, but I dared not show my anger. Carefully, I walked away from them. I don't know if they took anything or not while I was gone. I didn't care. I knocked on the door that led into my husband's office. He opened it, and I poured out my distress to him.

"They held a bra in their hands and held it up, laughing! What am I going to do?" I whispered.

"Don't do anything! Don't say anything or complain, and don't come to me again, while they are here. We don't want to do anything that will make them stop us from leaving. Don't make a fuss!" And he closed the door.

Somehow I got through it, but this was the final straw for me. From that moment, I could not leave Cuba quickly enough. Even though my parents were gone, somewhere in the back of my mind, I think I might have held a thread of hope that one day we could be reunited in Cuba. After the inventory, I didn't even think about that possibility again.

I had never lived anywhere else, and the one visit to Miami with my father was the only time I had been off the island. To think of calling another country "home" had seemed impossible, but it was equally impossible to live under the horrible fear, the dread that, at any moment, armed militia could come to take my husband away. Such occurrences were becoming common place. Now I just wanted to leave all of it.

Now, just looking into the innocent eyes of my little son, my dark-haired Alejandro, provided all the incentive I needed to leave what was no longer my safe haven. I would not stay where Fidel Castro and his Communist murderers could mold him into their likeness. Whatever the cost, I was ready to go.

CHAPTER THREE

Flight

Time seemed to pass slowly, but the problems and deprivation in Cuba escalated. I mentioned that a council was appointed in every city to appoint block watchers, captains who observed all the comings and goings of residents. These Castro loyalists recorded the times people went to work and the times they returned. The took notes of names and times that people visited houses in their blocks. If more than two or three came to one house, a follow-up visit by armed officials took place, wanting to know the reason for the "group meeting." Paranoia reigned.

If a person failed to come home at the expected time, the block captain appeared at their door to ask why. The citizen being questioned had best have a legitimate reason for being late. Those were the days when executions of suspected traitors were carried out quickly, sometimes by standing the prisoner against a wall and shooting him.

The disastrous Bay of Pigs invasion occurred in the spring of 1961, before Alejandro was born in September; and many young Cuban counter-revolutionaries lost their lives or were imprisoned. Fidel Castro no longer trusted any of the people for whom he had professed such love. He accused The United States and the CIA of corrupting people on his staff, some of whom were his best friends, one of whom he imprisoned for twenty-five years.

It was also during those months that Operation Pedro Pan was secretly organized by Catholic charities in the United States and some very brave counterparts in Cuba. Over 14,000 Cuban children were flown out of Cuba to the Unites States, using false visas, right under Fidel Castro's nose. Many desperate parents sent their children away, not knowing if they would ever be reunited. Some of them were not.

Not all of the children had positive experiences in their new country, but most of them became good, productive adults who were happy to be American citizens. Their freedom came at a tremendous cost, for some of the parents were never able to join their children. They loved those children more than they loved their own lives.

We were confronted with a major disappointment quite some time before our departure date was set. All diplomatic connections between Cuba and the United States had been broken. Flights were no longer permitted to Florida, so our destination became Spain.

My mother had bought and given to me a washing machine, telling me that it was better to wash towels in it and hung them on a line to dry. I don't know how the inventory takers missed that washing machine, but we decided to give it to my Aunt Sara. Somehow we loaded it into the car, concealed in our garage from the prying eyes of our block captain. I don't remember how my husband and my uncle wrestled it from the car and into my aunt's house in Havana without being caught, but they did.

Unfortunately, we were unable to pass along any of our possessions to other relatives, which caused a few ill feelings. It was just too dangerous. The disappointments were understandable, for there was no way to buy anything new when old things wore out, even if people could afford it.

Sanctions and embargos from all Western countries meant that nothing exported from their shores would reach Cuba. Their only source of goods came from the Soviet Union, which was in no better shape, materially, than Cuba. Corruption among the leaders in Russia, carefully hidden from the rest of the world, proved that Communism never will, cannot work.

It was almost two years before Castro's government decided to let us go; but at last we were notified that our departure date from Cuba would be July 13th, 1963. We had waited all that time, knowing there was always the chance that Fidel could change his mind and force us to stay.

A day or two before we were to leave, government officials came to take another inventory of the contents in the house that was no longer ours. It took less time than when they had invaded our privacy months earlier, with their notebooks and guns. This time they checked items against the original list, all of which was accounted for.

"You may take three changes of clothing, from underwear to street clothes," they told us. "One purse, two pair of shoes besides the ones you wear." They allowed us to take plenty of clothing and diapers for the baby, which was a blessing. We had to place everything into one suitcase for all of us. My husband was allowed to carry his brief case, which held necessary papers and our passports.

On that last day, I walked through the house my father had bought for me, trailing through each room, touching the furniture, gazing through the windows, remembering the day my husband and I brought our baby boy home. Even then, our plans to leave Cuba had been made; and we had taken a photo of him for a passport.

I thought of the care my parents had taken, selecting all these lovely things, the furniture, bedding, draperies, even down to the embroidered linen tablecloths and napkins for this beautiful house. I gazed at the rocking chair in the dining room where I had rocked Alejandro, missing Mami. I realized anew how much I loved my mother, how she loved me, how we had hugged and kissed each other from the time I was born.

Now that I was a mother, I realized that everything she had ever done, all the strict regulations she had enforced and the constant watchfulness over me had all been to protect me. I thought of Papo, his indulgent love for me, his only daughter, born when he was past the age of most men when they first become a father.

The longing of my heart was to see them, to hug them and place my precious son into their arms once more. The baby they adored was now twenty-months old, a toddler, and no longer the four-month-old infant they had left. Before they saw him again, he would be two years old!

My husband had driven his beautiful car for the last time. From the day Castro declared that Cuba would be a Communist country, the car had ceased to belong to Armando. They were simply allowing him to drive it.

My uncle, Panchito, picked us up and took us to the home he and my aunt Sara shared with their two daughters. Although it was now some fifteen years since Panchitín, their son, had been killed, the memory of him was treasured and vivid.

They would stay in Cuba, choosing to help their daughters through the deprivation and hardships that were coming. They would sacrifice their own well-being and freedom in order to support their daughters and yet-to-be-born grandchildren, who would not know the meaning of freedom.

Ironically, Panchito had been right about Castro from the beginning. While the rest of us, especially younger people, believed that Fidel would be the champion of Cuba, the one who would right all of Batistia's wrongs, my uncle predicted that the bearded "savior" would embrace Communism. He was an avid reader of history, government policies, a teacher who recognized all the signs that Fidel Castro displayed. I wish that he had made the same choices as my father.

They gave us their bedroom that last night. Our leaving was doubly hard on Sara, who had taken the place of my mother during the last two years. We had always been close, and now I was like a daughter to her. Losing me was like losing Panchitín again.

From our suitcase, I took one of my outfits, including shoes and whatever else I could part with, and gave it to Sara for one of their daughters. The next morning I dressed in a two-pieced black suit that Sara had made for me, a beautiful suit, not at all comfortable for a twenty-three-hour plane trip. My two choices of shoes were sandals and high heels. Cubans had a saying: Whatever is in fashion, wear it! So, of course, I chose the high heels! Before the day ended, I was miserable; but I wore pretty shoes!

We went out to the car, but Sara did not get inside with us. "I'll come to the airport a little later," she told me. "There are several things I want to take care of first. I'll see you in a little while." She waved to us as we drove away. I knew that she was trying hard not to cry. So was I.

The drive to the airport in Havana was a somber one. My husband seemed calm, I think; but I was afraid to believe we would actually be allowed to leave. Did I forget to mention that all contact between the United States and Cuba had been broken? That no flights were allowed to or from either country? That twenty-three-hour flight I mentioned is not a typo! We were flying to Madrid, Spain!

Aunt Sara did not come to the airport. I kept watching for her, wondering why she didn't come. Saying goodbye to us was just too much for her, and she couldn't face knowing we might never see each other again. As it turned out, we never did. She was in my earliest memories. Even now, it saddens me that our separation was permanent, just one more item in the long list of sins, crimes and heart breaks that would lie at the feet of Fidel Castro.

We waited at the airport, in the well-known "fish bowl" inside Havana's pre-boarding area, a huge, glass-enclosed room, visible from all sides. During the long hours we were detained, Panchito watched us through the glass, tears streaming down his face. The long line of desperate, hopeful Cubans was strangely quiet, everyone afraid to draw attention to themselves.

Multiple doctors were part of the security that examined women and children for contraband, anything that was not on the list of things allowed to leave the country. Any jewelry, watches or an extra item of clothing would be confiscated. Women doctors took certain children and their mothers from the line, ushering them into separate rooms, where they did body searches.

Some desperate passengers actually swallowed money, jewels, etcetera, hoping to escape with at least something of value to help fund their new lives. I blessed my father anew for having the foresight to protect his family before the need was apparent to most Cubans. Just thinking about this inhumane treatment, the greed-driven searches and final insult of Castro's regime to those he professed to love nauseates me.

Ahead of us in line stood a rather large man, another doctor scheduled to leave on our flight. His pregnant wife rested her head drowsily against the back of a chair. I think she had been given something to help her relax, for she seemed unnaturally calm, drugged.

The officials looked up at the doctor and told him that he needed an additional form, another signed paper before he would be allowed to leave. They told him where in Havana he needed to go to get the paper and have it signed, that perhaps he might have enough time to do so before his flight left. They also told him that it would leave without him if he did not make it back in time.

Desperation ravaged his already worried face. His wife, huge in her final month of pregnancy, began to cry. I was nearly in tears, myself, sympathizing with her distress. Their escape from Cuba depended upon how quickly her husband acted.

I didn't know it was possible for a man of his size to run like he did. The whole line of waiting passengers trembled with fear for him, for all of us, failing to hide our frantic hope to get aboard that plane, just waiting for us on the runway. I watched him, literally running for the lives of himself, his wife and his unborn child.

Planning ahead, we had packaged all of my jewelry, even a gold bracelet I had received at my Quince Años party, engagement and wedding rings, every important or precious item I had, along with family photo albums and treasured photographs. My husband had mailed the package to a foreign embassy in Havana where one of his doctor friends worked. The doctor then forwarded the package to my father in Miami.

Knowing that I would be searched for a wedding ring, we had bought a realistic-looking glass replacement for my engagement and wedding rings. I didn't shed a tear when the security guard took them from my finger. I hope they had them appraised!

Aside from my purse and my little boy, I carried a big thermos with enough milk to feed Alejandro on the flight. We finally made it through security all right; but before we got on the plane, a man stopped me and asked for the thermos.

"But it's for my son," I explained to him. I looked at Alejandro in my arms, trusting me to take care of his needs. "This is all I have to feed him."

"Sorry," he said. "We need the thermos."

"Please!" I begged the man. "Please let me take this for my baby! We don't have anything else!"

"No. Give the thermos to me."

There was nothing I could do but let the man take it from me. I know that tears of anger must have formed in my eyes, but I don't think I allowed them to fall down my cheeks. This one last cruelty to a child just reinforced my resolve that we had made the right choice even stronger.

Those of us who waited were filled with joy when the desperate doctor returned with the correct paper, just in time. But it was not until we all boarded the plane and felt the wings lift us into the air that we applauded and cheered for a long time, despite the lingering fear even to do that.

The doctor's wife gave birth in Madrid the next day, shortly after arriving. What a marvelous thing for them, to begin their new life without the bondage of Communism.

Finally, we would be free once more to live without looking over our shoulders, without the fear of saying the wrong word to the wrong person, afraid that we could be arrested for any infraction of a minor rule. Our almost twenty-four hour trip to Spain was truly our flight to freedom. Freedom, one of the sweetest words in any language.

PART FOUR

Madrid

CHAPTER ONE

¡Dios Mío!

Our flight to freedom turned out to be part nightmare for me. On the plane I fed Alejandro a jar of baby food, apple, I think; but he was still hungry. I asked the stewardess (That was before they became flight attendants!) if she had some canned evaporated milk I could give to my little boy. I explained to her how the airport security had taken from me all I had brought.

"I think so," she said. I held up a bottle.

"Could you please prepare this for me?" I asked.

"Of course." I was so grateful to her. She brought the filled bottle to me, and the baby drank the milk. I don't know what happened, whether the milk had been opened and spoiled, or if she didn't know to fill the bottle with half milk and half water. It's possible that with the stress of the trip, I forgot to tell her how to mix it. Within a short time, Alejandro began to cry; and I could not comfort him. I knew he was in pain, but nothing I did made him feel better.

Our seats were in the last row of the plane. They were not adjustable, so I couldn't change positions to make the little guy comfortable on my lap. Poor baby. It wasn't long before he developed diarrhea, and I spent the next twenty-three hours changing diaper after diaper, trying to keep him as clean as possible.

The aisle was the only available place for him to lie down, so I spread a blanket right beside my seat. Still, his abdominal pain would not let him sleep, and he cried for hours. I felt terrible for the other passengers, too, especially those who sat near us. The experience was not pleasant for them, either!

The drone of the propellers provided a constant background noise as the hours dragged by. It seemed that our journey would never end! An older man, whose seat was not far from ours, kept up an ongoing litany. "We aren't moving," he said. "This plane is standing still." He peered out the window, seeing nothing but darkness, no lights of a city anywhere. The fact that we had been over the Atlantic Ocean since leaving Cuba seemed not to register with him. "I know this plane is not moving!"

I couldn't sleep, but my husband managed to get a little nap or two. When he was on call in the hospitals, he learned to take quick naps when he had only a few free moments. Alejandro being so sick was hard on him, too, for he had no medicine to help his own son. In the hospitals and at his office, he often treated children with severe diarrhea. If he had tried to bring any kind of medicines on the plane with him, he would have been arrested for trying to steal from Castro's revolutionary government.

Long after dawn of the next day, the plane began a descent; but the trip was not yet over. The pilot landed at Islas Canarias to refuel. I took the baby inside the small airport and tried to clean him up, as much as I could. There was not enough time to give him a bath, and I surely wasn't going to take the chance that the plane would leave without me and my son.

The flight from there to Madrid was not long, but the total trip took twenty-three hours from Cuba. When we touched down at Barajas Airport in Madrid, I could have cried from sheer relief. It was close to mid-day, July 14th, 1963, the first full day of our new beginning, never to live again in a country ruled by a tyrant.

Our contact man waiting inside the airport was Rafael Torres, who knew Armando. He had been watching for us, and he greeted us right away. He had been sent by Nimia Llanio, a good friend of my parents. Señora Llanio, a widow, had been a lady of distinction in Güines, and she had many business dealings with my father and his bank.

She and her only son, Pancho (Francisco), had settled in Madrid shortly after Fidel formed his new government; but she and my father had stayed in touch. Papo had sent a check to her from the money my husband had managed to exchange when we first made our plans to leave Cuba. My father, as he had done from the day I was born (God bless you in heaven, Papo.) continued to make life easier for my little family in Spain, even when he was living in Miami, Florida.

"Come with me and I'll take you to the bank's counter here in the airport so you can cash your check." Señor Torres held out his hand, indicating the direction we should go.

"No," I insisted. "Not yet. Armando, smell this baby! I have to wash him and change his clothes first." We found the restroom, and I told my husband to meet me there after he cashed the check. When he walked away, I started to cry, exhausted from the long trip, overwhelmed with all of it, scarcely knowing where to start the process of cleaning up my poor little Alejandro.

"Don't cry." I looked up to see a pretty young woman dressed in a janitorial uniform. She had witnessed the exchange between my husband and me. She had probably watched many other Cubans arrive in this airport, dismayed with the daunting task of beginning new lives.

"I'll help you," she said, and she kept up a comforting flow of encouragement as she guided me into the huge restroom. She scrubbed the single big sink before she filled it with warm water. When she was satisfied that the water was the right temperature, she took Alejandro from me. She didn't ask permission. She just took him from my arms, and he didn't cry. I removed soap from my bag and placed it on the edge of the sink.

That wonderful woman undressed my beautiful little boy, and she washed and bathed him until he smelled sweet and clean again, chatting and playing with him. He loved it.

Exhausted beyond belief, I watched as she placed him on the counter and dried him with paper towels, the only thing available. From the bag I removed talc, clean diapers and clothing, socks and shoes. I placed everything on the counter beside him, and my Good Samaritan dressed him. She continued to talk as she refilled the sink with clean water. Then she washed the soiled clothes, scrubbing the stained little boots by hand, rinsed everything and put all of it in a plastic bag.

"These will need to be washed later," she said, "but they will be fine for now." I turned from her for only an instant to pick up my bag. I lifted Alejandro from the counter, looked up to thank the woman, at the very least, for I had not one cent to give her. She had disappeared.

She was nowhere to be found, not inside the restroom or in the busy corridor outside. It was in my mind to hug her, to kiss her cheek, to convey to her my lasting gratitude. I thought that I could surely see her somewhere in the crowd of travelers, pushing her cart. There was no trace of her.

At that time, I didn't have a personal relationship with God. I knew nothing of Him or of angels. I realize that not everyone believes in angels, but this woman was certainly an angel to me. Still today, I have no explanation as to how she managed to disappear so quickly, without a sound, without a word. I will never forget her. Among the beautiful roses in my life, she would represent at least a dozen.

Money in hand, my husband and Rafael Torres came for Alejandro and me. On the way to the boarding house that would be our home for the next four months, Rafael explained to us how most of the refugees from Cuba were treated. As he talked, I blessed my father all over again.

"You are very lucky," he began. "Every day a big bus picks up refugees from the airport and takes them to the bus station, where they take another bus to the Refuge Center. From there, they are directed to places where they will stay, but all of them must come back to the Center for their meals. I think they are given a little money, not much. It must be very hard for them."

I held Alejandro and listened to our driver and Armando talk. In spite of being so very tired, I was excited, wondering what our temporary dwelling would look like. Rafael dropped us off at a big boarding house in the middle of the block. Our new address was Gaztambide # 11, 5th Floor Left, Madrid, Spain. My father sent our checks to us, one every month while we were there, always on time.

Inside the building, we took the elevator to the fifth floor, the location of the boarding house. The elevator was like an open cage, with a sliding door. As it went up, people on other floors could see everyone inside. There was a limit as to how many people could ride at once, so those waiting had to be patient.

It took passengers only one way—up. Everyone in the building had to use stairs to go down. The structure was ancient, perhaps so old that the elevator had been in service when Columbus sailed from Italy to ask Queen Isabella to fund his voyage to the west! Hoping to prove that their world was round, not flat, he believed that he would find India and China. To think that he found Cuba, instead!

The landlady, Doña Mercedes, knew that we were coming and she put us in the first room, across from her suite. The room was small, but it held three beds, which reminded me of The Three Bears story: except that these beds were all smaller than a twin bed! Alejandro was already drowsy, so I placed him in the middle bed. He turned over and went to sleep immediately.

"I need to go see Nimia Llanio," said my husband. She lived close to the boarding house, about three blocks; but I was nervous, afraid for my husband to leave me. He was the only security I had, and just the thought that I could be left in a strange city, with no money, no family, scared me to death. Like I most often did when faced with a crisis in those days, I cried.

I stood there, Alejandro sound asleep in the little bed, my husband on his errand, possibly facing dangerous robbers and crazy drivers, or both! Still crying, I took the plastic bag filled with the soiled clothing and took them to the adjoining bathroom to wash them in the sink. I had washed some by hand, using soap I found there, and was hanging them over the shower curtain rod when the landlady came into the room.

"Hey, what are you doing?"

"My little boy was very sick on the plane, and I don't have many clean diapers left. I have to wash these. What else can I do?" I asked.

"No, no, no! You cannot do that here! First of all, the water is too expensive. And no one does laundry here. No one is washing clothes in the bathrooms!"

"I understand that," I said, "but what else can I do for my baby? Can you tell me that?"

"Well, you go ahead and finish with this now. In the morning I have a lady who is coming, and she will collect your laundry and do it for you. You tell her what you want, and you can pay her to do it. Her name is Mari."

What will I pay her with? I thought.

So I finished washing the diapers and went back to the bedroom, where the baby still peacefully slept. Tired, hungry, scared, I dropped onto one of the beds. Crash! The mattress fell to the floor! I wasn't hurt, but it was just one more discouraging thing in a day that was not yet over. So I left the bed like it was and I cried!

Well, like it or not, I decided I just had to make the best of it. So I opened the big armoire, which was clean, but it smelled musty and ancient. I didn't want to put what few clothes we had in it, for they would soon smell the same way.

I looked around to see what my alternatives were. I opened the cabinets in the bathroom, but they all smelled the same. I knew that the landlady would not like it if I hung things in the open.

When my husband returned and saw the broken bed, he asked, "What happened?" So I poured out my distress. His reply to me? "Calm down. We'll work it all out."

CHAPTER TWO

Waterworks!

The next morning, my husband had to go back to see Nimia, to sign some necessary papers. We couldn't call her. There was no phone in our room, only a crank-type wall phone in the hall, which we didn't know how to use. In my grandfather's house where we lived when I was a very little girl, my father had such a phone in the room which was his office. That was in the early 1940s.

(I remembered once trying to call one of my little friends. I had seen and heard my parents picking up the earpiece of the telephone and giving the operator a number. Sometimes they asked for the number of a person they needed to reach. So one day I decided to call my friend, Rosita.

I climbed onto a chair and took the earpiece from its cradle. I don't think I was big enough to turn the hand crank on the side of the big, wall-mounted wooden box.

"I want Rosita Awais' house." I spoke right into the mouthpiece, certain that it would work. That was the extent of my familiarity with wall phones, for my father had a desk phone installed as soon as they were available.)

After finally falling into bed that first night, I must have died to the world. I was exhausted, and my feet hurt badly from two days of wearing high-heeled shoes. I don't remember if any one of the three of us woke up at all during that first night.

After my husband left for Nimia's house, I had nothing to do. Alejandro was fine, and I had finally put what few clothes we had in the smelly closet. I didn't want to put the high heels on my feet again. I would have loved to go barefooted.

Two things prevented me from doing so. I didn't know if the floors of the boarding house were as clean as I wished them to be, and I didn't know what the landlady's reaction would be to my bare feet. She might tell me that she didn't want boarders who went without shoes! She had already scolded me about using too much water. What if she kicked us out?

The only thing I could think of that would be worse than this place was having nowhere else to go. After the miserable flight from Havana, I decided that I could make the best of even this room. At least we were no longer flying over the Atlantic Ocean with a sick baby. I would just try to think positive thoughts.

Within the next day or two, the landlady moved us to a room at the other end of the hall, probably because I complained about something. This floor was the only one in the building reserved for boarders. All the other floors were inhabited by individual families, just like houses. We never stopped the elevator at any other floor.

I liked the new room much better. It held three bigger beds, and the room itself was much larger. Our window lined up with a window in the building next to ours. No matter what time of day I looked out, a woman was staring at me from her window.

It was like living in the house above the bank in Güines again. The sister of the priest at the Catholic Church in the park, used to stare at me from a second-floor rectory window whenever I was on the balcony. I wondered if the women were related, or perhaps they thought they were watching television! I might have had a few *I Love Lucy* moments, but not that many.

In the following days, we bought milk for Alejandro in a bottle that did not need to be refrigerated, so I kept it on the window sill, where cool night breezes kept it very well. Every time I got milk for him, the lady was staring at me. We had to be careful about changing our clothes, getting ready for bed, even getting up in the middle of the night—because that woman was always looking into our window, which was kept open. There was no need for screens, for there were no bugs, no mosquitoes.

The boarding house had at least four bathrooms, counting the one in the landlady's suite. One was across the hall from our room, which allowed us more privacy. The other boarders were young men, all of them medical students who went to the University of Madrid, located only a few blocks away. The landlady and I were the only women.

I'm sure the young men who shared the bathroom with us were clean; but I chose a time when they were gone before I took my daily shower, which created another issue. I learned that daily showers were not the custom for most of those who lived in Madrid at that time. I suspect that the wealthy or better off financially could afford to pay for more water. When the Metro cars were very crowded, I tried not to breathe too deeply!

One day Mari, the girl who came to pick up and deliver laundry asked me about my bathing habits. "Señora, why do you take so many showers?"

"In Cuba we take showers every day. Don't you?" I asked.

"Oh, no," she replied. "I take a shower sometimes, but not every day. It uses too much water."

It is true that the scarcity of clean, plentiful water was a problem when we were in Madrid, over fifty years ago. I'm sure that the pipes were ancient. I think that cheap wine was served with all the meals because the water was not good to drink.

So the landlady had another water issue with me. When she discovered what I was doing with all the old newspapers I could find, she was unhappy with me again. One of the most important health habits I had learned living with my parents over twenty years was cleanliness—not just personal hygiene, but in every aspect of life.

It was important that we bathe every day. The floors of every room, everything in the kitchens, from top cabinets to the tile floors and everything between, were to be cleaned. The tile floors must be swept and mopped every day. Fresh clothing was necessary daily, washed and ironed, as were the bed linens and tablecloths. The way I grew up, cleanliness really was next to godliness!

Since many of these practices were not possible in our new circumstances, I did the best I could. Not satisfied with cleaning every spot of the bathroom before I allowed my little family to use the community bathroom on our floor, I covered every surface with newspaper!

Every surface, including all of the toilet, the bathtub, the floors, the sink, everything! I would do it again, under the same conditions!

And that is why Doña Mercedes was unhappy with us. She examined the bathroom and discovered that the bathroom was constantly wet, even though the students were not taking daily showers.

"I don't care," I told my husband. "I'm going to take my shower!"

"Me, too," he told me. It wasn't long before we got a visit from the landlady.

"No, no, no, no! Shower every day? No!"

"Listen, Doña Mercedes, in Cuba we take showers every day!"

"Well, if you must, you have to step into the water, turn it off when you soap up, turn it on to rinse and then turn it off!" And that is how my husband and I showered the whole time we were in Spain.

Everything in Madrid moved at a different pace. We adjusted to the new time frame and became accustomed to seeing people go to work at ten o'clock. A light breakfast would be served, the usual coffee, but Doña Mercedes also offered me hot chocolate, which I liked, with good bread and butter.

We ate in the boarding house every day. Lunch was served around two o'clock, and then everyone took a short nap, *siesta*, before they went back to their jobs, until the day's work was done. Dinner was usually eaten around ten o'clock at night. All the boarders sat at the same table, and we ate together, like a family.

Doña Mercedes was the cook, as well as the landlady. She made the most delicious dish with garbanzo beans, at least once a week. She made it with Spanish sausages and potatoes in a kind of stew. I asked her more than once when she would make the dish again. It was my favorite.

Earlier, I referred to my father's fastidious habits in cleanliness, which he passed on to me. It extended even to the furniture where we sat in public places, and I have to admit that I had a difficult time being comfortable sitting on the boarding house furniture. The dining room chairs were not so bad, for they can be washed. But the upholstered chairs and sofas were another story.

While there may have been restrictions on water in the boarding house, there seemed to be no shortage when it came to cleaning the streets. At some time during the night, possibly very, very early every morning, the streets and sidewalks were washed with huge hoses. The outside of the buildings were well-maintained and beautifully kept, regardless of in what century they were built. There was an ageless quality about them. It was only the inside that showed the deterioration and passage of time.

CHAPTER THREE

The Beautiful City

Our routine most evenings was to walk the two or three blocks to the Metro station at five o'clock. For a few pesetas, the equivalent of five cents, we could go anywhere we wanted. We tried to exit at a different plaza each day. The plazas in Madrid were beautiful, so clean. Each one contained a beautiful park filled with colorful flowers and landscaped gardens.

Small children ran and played with each other, chasing the pigeons, laughing with delight as the birds flew into the air, only to land close by again. Many of the children were accompanied by uniformed nannies, but there were several parents like Armando and me. We enjoyed watching Alejandro chase the pigeons as much as he loved chasing them.

Benches were placed for the convenience of shoppers at the various stores or for those who were just there for a stroll. Elegantly dressed people, laughing, talking and visiting with friends gathered in every plaza each evening. We watched as they stopped at small dining places called tascas, where delicious snacks were served.

We didn't have much money, scarcely any that we could afford to spend; but I loved the little sandwiches served at the tascas. One of my favorites consisted of a small omelet, wrapped around some kind of meat and placed between pieces of good bread.

This tiny bit of heaven was called *bocadillos,* and it was unbelievably delicious! Small glasses of wine were always served with these snacks. I liked very little of the food served in the boarding house, so I was always hungry. I think my husband was hungry, too. Some days we bought little packages of potato chips, just to have something to eat while we walked.

194

We made two or three turns down different streets on our daily walks to the Metro. In the middle of one of the blocks was a toy store. I was so excited about seeing all those toys in the window that I drew Alex's attention to the beautiful display. "Oh, look, look!" I pointed to the toys. "Look, Alejandro, look at the pretty toys!"

He was happy to see the toy cars and stuffed animals, balls, every toy a child could imagine. I had been allowed to take small, stuffed toys from Cuba, but nothing like those in the store window. From that moment, Alex remembered where the toy store was located on that block. He pointed and made urgent little sounds, trying to hurry us along. Then he began to cry when we left the store behind. He was two years old a month after we arrived in Madrid, and he didn't know what it was like to have a nice toy.

So I told my husband the next day that we would cross the street before we got to that block. I could not stand to watch my little boy's disappointment night after night as we had to leave the toy store. For a few days, he looked for the toy store, pointing to where he knew it was; but after that, he forgot.

When I was a little girl, we learned a Spanish song. In the first line, we sang, "Sereno," and the response was, "Yes." The second line, "Sereno, open the door, I am sleepy." I remember the melody but not all the words. During our first evenings in Madrid, the meaning of the song became clear to me.

All the buildings along the blocks had tall, iron doors or gates that were locked at ten o'clock. None of the residents had keys to those iron barricades. As they approached their homes after ten o'clock, they clapped their hands, and the gatekeeper came immediately to let them in. I thought it was one of the funniest things I had ever seen. The words of the song popped into my mind, and I understood the origin of it.

At all hours during the night, the streets echoed with the sound of clapping. Through the open windows, we could determine just how late neighboring residents came home. Lying half asleep, night breezes coming through the open window, I still chuckled at the resounding "clap-clap" of people wanting entrance into their homes.

We traveled on the Metro so often that the girl from whom we bought tickets fell in love with Alejandro. He was a beautiful, chubby little boy, with dimpled knees and elbows; and this girl thought he was gorgeous. She made a remark about his "cute little rear," and my husband and I looked at each other in shock. The word she used would never have been said in such a way in Cuba! It was our first indication that some Spanish words do not necessarily mean the same thing in a different Spanish-speaking country!

By using the Metro, we were able to see many, many beautiful, ancient buildings that dated back hundreds of years. The architecture and design of these magnificent structures were amazing. Even back in the 1960's it was difficult to imagine how such huge cathedrals and monuments had been constructed without the knowledge and equipment developed in the twentieth century.

There were statues honoring many Spanish saints and explorers. Christopher Columbus was Italian, of course, but since Queen Isabella of Spain financed his trip "sailing east to find India," he is honored with many statues in Spain. The pride of the Spanish people in their city of Madrid was evident everywhere we looked. The grounds were well kept, even pristine. Just traveling and stopping at so many different plazas and parks taught us more history of Spain than we learned in classes.

A big living room was available in the boarding house for everyone to use, and one night we had company. A man we had known in Güines, who had immigrated to Madrid, came to see us. He was the funniest man, and he kept my husband and me laughing the whole evening. We were so happy to see someone from home, and we needed the laughter, as well.

One of our favorite times away from the boarding house was in the home of Nimia Llanio, who was so kind to us. She often invited us, as well as new acquaintances we had met in Madrid, to come to her home for dinner. After serving a delicious meal, she showed us into the living room where we could visit in comfort.

A guest at one of the dinners monopolized a good deal of the conversation as we ate, and he continued to do so after we left the table. As in Cuba before Castro, people in Spain dressed for dinner, down to nice shoes and jewelry. My husband and I had only the clothing we had brought with us, so our options were few. One of my rare purchases had been a pair of comfortable sandals, for we walked many hours every day. There was no way I could walk that far in my single pair of high heels, no matter how stylish I wanted to be.

This talkative man began a discourse on the careless way some women dressed. He thought it was scandalous that any woman would appear in public, at dinner, wearing sandals! He was looking right at me! There was nowhere to hide my feet, clad in those disgusting sandals, but I kept trying. I had been unable to bring even one full skirt with me, which would have made tucking my feet beneath my chair a bit easier.

But, no! I had to sit there listening to his tirade against women who didn't care how they looked in public! He knew nothing about our circumstances, so how could he dare to judge us? Judge me? I suppose it was a good lesson to learn—never to form an opinion of someone by the clothes or shoes they wear at any given time. We cannot know what their history or circumstances are.

Flights from Havana arrived in Madrid every day. Sometimes we went to the bus station where people were brought from the airport, just to see someone from home. If we found out that people we knew were coming, we made certain that we were there to greet them. We had a million questions to ask about those who were not planning to leave Cuba. There were tears of joy and tears of sadness.

What happened to us was hard to comprehend, even months after we left Cuba. I think we took comfort from each other, since our situations were much the same. Armando and I were fortunate that we had enough money to meet our expenses without having to find temporary jobs. Every day I was thankful that my husband and my father had been able to transfer enough money from Cuba to Florida to keep us from absolute poverty.

Ignacio Hernández, a good friend of my brother, Juan, had been our wedding photographer. He and his wife, Maggie, were married the same month we were; and their little girl, Ivette, was born within a week or so of Alejandro. We were thrilled to see them in Madrid.

They both had jobs in Madrid. He worked during the day and his wife worked a night shift in a restaurant. When it was possible, we met a few times at the parks in the plazas, where we watched our children play together.

Late one night, Ignacio called the boarding house and asked to speak to my husband. Their little girl was very sick, running a high fever. His wife was still at work, and he didn't know what to do. They had no money, no medicine.

So we took Alejandro and went to their home. We had no medicine, either, and no way to get any; for my husband could not practice medicine outside Cuba. It was very late. When we arrived at their house, we clapped our hands; and the sereno immediately opened the locked gate for us.

Armando used the back of a spoon as a tongue suppressor to look inside Ivette's throat. They wrapped her in very cold, wet towels and ice to bring down her fever, and it slowly began to drop. The next day they were able to get aspirin for her. Their work situations made it doubly hard for them to care for a sick child.

In the middle of November, 1963, we were finally notified that we could fly to Miami, Florida! I was going to be reunited with my family, at last! We had managed to save a little money, enough to buy each of us a new outfit for the trip. How nice it was to wear something new!

I dressed Alejandro in dressy beige shorts, like most little boys wore at that time, and a coordinating knit, short-sleeved shirt. His dark hair was styled with thick bangs across his forehead, but cut short in the back. He looked so cute, and I was so proud of him.

The flight was not as long as the one from Cuba to Spain; still, it was across the Atlantic Ocean. On the escalator inside the Miami airport, I looked down to see a huge crowd of people waiting to greet us, friends and family, jumping up and down and shouting with joy.

"Oh, look, Armando, there's Mami! And Papo! And my brother, José!" It had been two years since we had seen each other, and there were many tears of happiness. I placed Alejandro in my mother's arms. It had been almost two years since she had held him.

"Oh," she cried. "He is the most beautiful thing I have ever seen!" She hugged him and kissed him and then started all over again. He was terrified. He cried and reached for me, not knowing who this woman was. From there, we went to the house that had become the home of my parents.

The whole group accompanied us, too many to find a place to sit in such a small house; but it was wonderful. They sat on the floor, anywhere they could; and we ate, laughed, cried, hugged each other, sharing such indescribable happiness. I wonder, now, if being reunited with loved ones in heaven might contain some of the same kind of joy. Remembering now, I smile.

PART FIVE

The
United States
Of
America

CHICAGO

Armando

Working Again

For one week, I stayed with my wife's parents in Miami before I left for Chicago, where a job was waiting for me in the Evangelical Hospital. I was eager to begin working as a doctor again. I loved treating patients, seeing them get better and knowing I had helped improve the quality of their lives. Yes, the challenge of learning to speak a new language in a new country was great, but I knew I was up to the challenge.

I hugged my wife and little boy and boarded yet another plane to the next destination toward our new life. The flight was not long, but I had time to think about the changes that had taken place in our lives during the past five years.

Until October, 1962, Cuba and the United States had continued to have diplomatic relations. With the Cuban Missile Crises, the American ambassador left Cuba, and the embassy was closed. It was the same with the Cuban embassy in the United States. From that moment, with Russia's aid to Cuba, Fidel Castro declared open hostility to the country only ninety miles from his shores.

Early on, I made my intentions clear about leaving Cuba. Once our plans to join my wife's family in Miami had been finalized, I checked for flights at the airport. None were open. The next day I asked again and was told that no flights were available to the United States, but there was one to Spain.

I bought tickets right then. Evidently the flight windows to America had been closed, but I didn't care where we went, as long as it was away from Cuba. By doing that, we were not considered as refugees, fleeing from one country to another for political asylum.

When our freedom flight lifted, most of the passengers cheered and sang songs. I was glad to be leaving, but I was worried. For the first time since I graduated from medical school, I possessed nothing but three shirts, three pair of pants, and two pairs of shoes. The responsibility of supporting my wife and little son was staggering! I had no guarantee I would be able to provide for them as I had in Cuba.

Now I was on my way to Chicago, where Dr. S. E. Rubio had lived and worked in city hospitals for the past two years. As I mentioned earlier, his brother, Emilio, and I had gone to medical school together, until he had changed his course of study. Unlike Dr. Rubio, Emilio chose to stay in Cuba with his family, hoping that circumstances would improve. They never did.

My hopes and plans were to continue to be a doctor. While we were in Spain, I had asked my father-in-law to send me a book, American Manual of Medicine. It covered everything from specialization to medicines and procedures. What's more, it was an English edition. Since I had been reading and learning English for several years, the manual was exactly what I needed to occupy my time in Madrid.

English in Cuba was prevalent. We saw American-made movies, and I subscribed to American medical magazines on pediatrics. We learned and sang songs in English. Our language instructor advised us to listen to American records, and the one we used most was *Our Love is Here to Stay,* a favorite of ours, sung by Nat King Cole.

I thought about all these things on my flight to Chicago. I remembered the day I was called in and questioned by Castro's regime. Someone had seen a photograph taken when I was having lunch at headquarters with soldiers I knew who had been in Batista's army. The new government inquisitors wanted to know if I had been a supporter of the former government.

I explained that I was not a political person, that my father had been a soldier, which had nothing to do with me. Being a medical student at the time, I was happy just to meet with someone and get a good meal, even if it had meant dining with Batista's soldiers. Eventually they let me go, but it could just as easily have gone the other way.

When I landed in Chicago, it was cold, something I had never before experienced. A number of people came to greet me. Juan, Isabel's brother, and his wife, Marta, picked me up at the airport. They had lived in Chicago for some time, and Juan knew his way through the huge city. He drove me to Dr. Rubio's home, where I was greeted warmly. The Rubio family welcomed me into their apartment, where I stayed for a few days before Isabel and Alejandro joined us.

The Rubios lived in a ground-floor apartment in an older building not far from some of the major hospitals in Chicago. Evangelical Hospital had provided an apartment for us, just across the alley from the Rubio's building. Dr. Rubio and Nora had cleaned and made it presentable, knowing from experience how exhausting and a little intimidating it could be to make the changes we were making. It worked out well, for we now had friends from our hometown and Cuban food to share, thanks to Nora's skill in her kitchen.

A few months after we moved in, an apartment on the floor above Dr. Rubio's became available; and we were able to rent it. This relocation made our lives even better, for all of us enjoyed the closer contact and the sound of familiar voices. However, it was to my advantage to speak English as much and as often as possible.

My first job in Chicago was at the Evangelical Hospital, located only a block from our apartment. I walked the short distance, not minding the cold too much, even though it took a while to become accustomed to it.

That winter was still not a problem after I got my second job at Christ Community Hospital, for I could ride in a van from one hospital to the other. But when I got a third, part time job working weekends at South Shore Hospital, I thought I would freeze to death! It was two blocks away, and I had to get up very early in the morning and walk those two blocks to catch a bus.

I put on as many layers of clothing as I could: the heaviest socks I could find, long underwear, undershirt beneath my dress shirt, tie, suit, a long, heavy coat, gloves, wool scarf around my neck and a hat. Sometimes I had to wait for the bus on a corner of the street, and that icy wind coming off Lake Michigan cut to the bone! They don't call Chicago "the windy city" for no reason!

While I worked as many hours as I could, I continued to study every free moment for the board exams. I did whatever was asked of me, from observing and assisting with surgeries to whatever else was necessary. Juggling all of it wasn't easy, but I did it.

I hadn't left my country, most of my family and my medical practice for nothing, and I was determined that I would make a new home and regain what Fidel Castro had taken from me. Actually, he didn't take it. I walked away from it, so I could raise my family free from oppression and terror.

I learned that there was a service in Florida where we could go for help to bring remaining family members from Cuba. So I flew back to Miami and stayed for a week, filling out forms, requesting that my mother, father, sister and brother be allowed to come to the United States.

A few months later, all of them came except my sister. She was single, and she had the opportunity to come; but she also had a boyfriend. She decided to remain in Cuba and marry the man, who was a Communist. It makes me sad that she chose such a hard, repressive life, when she had the chance to escape it. I never saw her again. She died in Cuba a few years ago.

My parents and my brother came to Chicago, and that is where they continued to make their home, even after I moved my family to Southern Illinois. Coming to the United States was the only possible choice for all of us, but that early time in Chicago was just the beginning of our adventure.

CHICAGO

Isabel

Snow!

My mother had aged some in the two years we had been apart. Worry about me and my little family, about family left behind, about making it in a new country—all these things had affected her. Even so, I thought she looked wonderful. Papo looked older, too, not unexpectedly, for by then he was almost seventy years old, twenty years older than Mami. The transition from a spacious, comfortable house in Güines, to a new country, new culture and entirely different living conditions took a toll on them.

In the beginning of their stay in Miami, Mami and my brother, José, lived with my brother, Juan, his wife, Marta and their baby boy. Juan moved his family to Chicago the following year, in 1962; but in the meantime, not content to be a long-term guest in the house of her son, Mami wanted to find a job. While shopping in a grocery store, she saw a woman she thought might be Cuban. The woman was speaking Spanish, and something about her made Mami comfortable enough to approach her.

"Are you Cuban?" she asked.

"Sí, I am from Cuba."

"Oh, good! I wonder if you might know of someone who needs a housekeeper. I am a very good cook, and I can care for children."

"Yes, I do," the woman replied. "My neighbors, Bob and Jackie Volpe, have a big house, and they are looking for a housekeeper. They have two children, one in kindergarten and a three-year-old. Her mother-in-law lived with them, but she passed away not long ago."

The lady put my mother and the Volpe family in touch, the results of which soon found Mami and my brother living in a new home. The neighborhood was lovely, and the house had adequate room to accommodate my mother and brother. It had a large bed/sitting room with a private bath, where Mr. Volpe's mother had stayed until she passed away, a short time before my mother met them. This room, beautifully kept, was more than adequate for her and José.

It was a Godsend. My brother enrolled in a nearby school, and soon they established a comfortable routine. Mami fell in love with the children. Joe was in kindergarten and Judy was only three, and they also fell in love with her. Every day she got Joe ready for school, and Judy stayed with her. My mother prepared lunch for the little ones and dinner for everyone each night.

At first, Mr. Volpe, who was an airplane mechanic for Eastern Airlines, was not completely comfortable having strangers living in his home. He had no way of knowing whether or not my mother and her son were trustworthy. Who could blame him? In time, however, he grew to love her, too; and he trusted her completely with his children, who loved her like a grandmother.

I wish I could remember the name of the woman my mother met in the grocery store, the neighbor of the Volpe family. She helped a lot with translation between my mother and Jackie Volpe, who worked for Sun Life Insurance Company. The neighbor and my mother became good friends. She had a lot of children, all of whom became special to Mami, too.

When my father left Cuba, several months after my mother and brother arrived in Miami, he also stayed in the Volpe house with my mother—but only for two or three days. He wasn't comfortable living in someone else's house. He wanted his own home. They found a little house with a huge yard. The owner lived next door, so he kept both yards mowed. My father didn't have to worry about that.

In Miami was a place where "Cuban Relief" was supplied for those who had fled Cuba with nothing but the barest essentials. Food stamps were provided, as well as other assistance. Once a week my father walked twenty blocks to catch a bus to this place of refuge. He liked to walk, and he was always slender and in good health. He didn't seem to mind it, but the round trip every week was long.

Among the things provided by this organization were dry milk, block cheese, crackers and peanut butter, all good sources of protein and sound nutrition. Papo didn't complain, but I wonder what he thought as he made those trips. He and Mami also qualified for food stamps. Papo had always been a good provider, had worked hard his whole life to make sure his family would never want for anything. Their new circumstances must have hurt him, but I never heard him complain.

As in most communities, especially in larger cities, Miami homeowners placed unwanted furniture near the curbs in front of their houses. Anyone who wished could drive by and take whatever appealed to them. One of my nieces, Nereyda, drove my mother slowly in front of these houses, stopping when Mami saw something she liked, then helping her load her choices into the car. I don't know how many trips they made, but Mami filled her house with beautiful pieces of furniture, bedframes, sofa, chairs, tables—everything she needed to make a home. Family and friends from our hometown also helped to transform the little house into a home.

So many wonderful things happened while my mother worked for Bob and Jackie Volpe. She began to teach little three-year-old Judy to speak Spanish. The child learned it in a snap! It was the cutest thing. Little Judy became a translator for my mother and her mother, and Mami began to learn a lot of English. My mother loved these children.

(*Even after my parents moved away, they stayed in contact with these wonderful people. They sent pictures of the children as they went to school and grew up. After Mami passed away, years later, I continued the communication. Now that her parents are gone, I am still in touch with Judy to this day.*)

It was to the little house where my mother and father lived that my husband and I went when we arrived in Miami. After Armando left for Chicago, I concentrated on my parents. Just being with them, listening to their beloved voices, relating to them our experiences on our flight to Madrid and about our months there—it was wonderful.

We spoke of happier times, of our shared worries about friends and family still in Cuba, hoping that some of them would come to Miami eventually. Mami and Papo loved getting reacquainted with little Alejandro, and he grew more comfortable with them. When Mami was working every day, I did what cleaning needed to be done in her house. It was a wonderful week, and over much too soon. Still, I was excited about going to Chicago.

On November 30th, two weeks after we arrived in Miami from Spain, I boarded another plane, carrying Alejandro in my arms. Poor little boy! He had been dragged from two countries to a third in four months, and now he was inside a third airplane.

Juan, accompanied by Armando, picked us up in his car at O'Hare. I was happy to see Juan, excited to be safely on the ground with Armando again, thrilled with so much to see on the drive through Chicago; but for the first time in years, I was not afraid. I looked out the window at huge, towering skyscrapers; and I saw, for the first time in my life, snow.

We had just turned the first page of many in the book that would chronicle our new life in The United States of America. I could not wait to see where it would lead. Although I hated to leave my parents so soon, after being separated from them for two year, I knew that the distance between us this time was not great and travel would be easier. Thankfully, this last flight was short and uneventful.

When Alex and I landed in Chicago, the late afternoon sky was gray, overcast with dark clouds. I was excited about everything! Thrilled to be with my husband and see my brother when they picked us up, excited to see the five o'clock traffic in such a huge city. The hundreds of brightly lit store windows, some of them with Christmas decorations, seemed to flash by with endless possibilities, although it would be a long time, even years, before we could afford to do any serious shopping.

I peered through the car window, looking up and up at the tall, magnificent buildings and big churches. Snow flurries filled the air, whirling and floating like tiny pieces of clouds. It was not just the joy of beginning a new life in a new land that made my heart beat fast. It was the realization that my family would never have to fear Fidel Castro again. Not ever!

The contrast between winter weather in Chicago, Illinois, and Güines, Province of Havana, Cuba, seemed symbolic to me. The balmy breezes that always blew warm, temperate weather and the scent of flowers across the island were now tainted with the evils of Communism. The cold wind coming from Lake Michigan, swirling white flakes of snow down every street and alley had the brisk, sweet smell of liberty.

From the airport, my brother took us to his apartment, where his wife, Marta, and their son, Juan Carlos, were waiting for us. That day,

November 30th, was Juanqui's second birthday. What a wonderful way to celebrate my first night in Chicago, at my little nephew's birthday party!

Alejandro and I spent that first night with them. There was not room for my husband in their tiny apartment, so my brother took him to Dr. Rubio's house. The next day, which had to be a Saturday or Sunday, my brother drove all of us to Dr. Rubio's. We crossed the alley behind their building, to the small apartment that would be our home for the next few months.

When my husband opened the door and ushered us inside, I didn't care that it was small and old, filled with used furniture. Everything was clean and smelled so nice. I knew that Dr. Rubio and Nora had cleaned the apartment, put sweet, clean sheets on the bed and crib and made it as comfortable as possible for us.

They had put new slipcovers on the couch, hung bright, new curtains at the windows and put out new towels in the kitchen and bathroom. They placed new pillows on the couch and made everything as comfortable as they possibly could. There was even a television!

Suddenly the little place was filled to overflowing with people! Dr. Rubio, Nora and their four children, my brother and his wife and son, and our little family of three, made a total of twelve. A wonderful surprise occurred with the arrival of our friends, Ignacio and Maggie, with their little girl, Ivette.

They had left Madrid a short while before we did, and their parents had already settled in Chicago. So there were fifteen people, counting the babies, crowded into our new home. By then, it was lunch time. Dr. Rubio, generous soul that he always was, went to a Burger King restaurant and brought back lunch for everyone: bags and bags of food, which he placed on the little table in the small kitchen.

I was starving, and my first Whopper was delicious! I can promise that it was not my last! Lunch included other sandwiches, French fries and milkshakes, too many things for me to recall. It was a feast! I had never before eaten anything like what I tasted that day…and to share it with so many friends from Cuba! Still, overriding every other emotion was the sense of total freedom. We didn't have to be afraid that armed government thugs might kick in the door and take us prisoners, or worse!

The days that followed included much-appreciated invitations from Nora Rubio to eat dinner with them. Their house was often filled with people, including her brother and his wife, who had also managed to flee Cuba. Sometimes Nora invited my brother and his family, as well; so the activity and laughter of children added to the happiness that emanated from the house.

I cannot say enough about the generosity and kindness that Dr. Rubio and Nora showered upon us during those days. Having experienced the transition themselves, they knew how to make the adjustment to a new country and a different culture easier for us.

One day Dr. Rubio decided that he wanted to go shopping in a Montgomery Ward store in the middle of downtown Chicago. He wanted to buy rugs, towels, linens and things for their house. He loaded his family and the three of us into his car and away he drove. In those days, bucket seats were not part of a family car. Both back and front had bench seats and no seat belts. I don't remember exactly how we were seated, but I know that the car held all nine of us!

What an experience! The store had multi-levels, connected by elevators and escalators. Poor Nora! The children ran throughout that store like they had never seen one before. "¡*Muchachitas*! What are you doing!" She called to the girls, who paid no attention to her whatsoever. "Sergio!"

Sergio disappeared into the elevator, then pretty soon we could see him coming back up an escalator, before he vanished again. "Isabelita, where are these children now? I don't see them!" The poor woman was frantic, looking first one way then the other. I kept a pretty close watch on Alejandro, who would have fled, too, given the opportunity. We had not traveled thousands of miles to guarantee safety and freedom, just to lose him in a crowded Chicago mall!

CHICAGO

Isabel

Never a Dull Moment

In the days that followed, Marta and I had a good time going through my new home, looking at the furniture and appliances, if they could be called that. "Look at this, Marta!" I pointed to the refrigerator. "What is that?" All we could do was laugh! It was horrible, a little square box with a round motor attached. It must have been one of the first ever made!

Shortly after we arrived in Chicago, Bertica, one of my Cuban friends, got in touch with me. She had left Cuba and come to Chicago quite a while before we did. She found out that we were there, so she got in touch with me. I invited her to come to my apartment for lunch.

Not only did I prepare lunch, I made a banquet! I don't remember how I managed to buy enough groceries to do it, but I made Cuban dishes that we loved. "How did you learn to cook like this?" Bertica asked. I was happy that she appreciated my cooking. So we ate lunch and then I washed the dishes and put my kitchen in order.

I took the broom and swept the kitchen floor, and then I took the mop and mopped it, wanting my friend to be impressed with my newly-found housekeeping skills. Bertica didn't care about all that.

"Stop!" Bertica told me. "I came here to talk to you, to show you my car and to take you for a drive! Not to see you clean the floors!" So that's what she did. I was so impressed with her nice car and her driving skills. She drove me all around our area of Chicago, showing me buildings and incredible things that I had not yet seen. Bertica was an amazing woman.

Spending a few hours with her in Chicago that day so many years ago was a bright spot for me.

Although we had very little materially during the two years we lived in Chicago, my husband and I were incredibly happy. He worked overtime when he could, and we had everything we needed. That first winter was unmercifully cold! It might have just seemed colder to us, as we were used to the warm winters of Cuba.

Some of the incidents I will describe are not intended as complaints. They merely relate how drastically our way of life had changed in just a few short months. Even with the bitter cold, the changes were glorious!

I recall one particularly cold day when my husband and I dressed as warmly as we could, bundled up two-year-old Alex, and set off to walk the block-and-a-half or so to the closest grocery store. He was a big boy, so heavy and awkward to carry, which we had to do. He was much too young to walk that far in the cold.

We took our time inside the warm store, buying only what we needed. Still, the few bags were quite heavy. On the way home, the frigid wind blew so fiercely that we finally had to stop, for we could not carry both the bags and our son. My husband placed the bags against the corner of a building, and we hurried home as quickly as possible.

"Let me warm up a bit, and I'll go back for the groceries," my husband said. He stood beside the little heater and let his hands thaw, absorbing as much warmth as possible before he went back into the cold, Chicago wind. Neither of us believed that our groceries would be where he had placed them, but they were! To me, finding the food that we would depend upon for days still remains a perfect example of God's miracles, one of the many I have witnessed in our lives.

Most mornings, after I fed Alex his cereal and ate mine, he was ready to take a nap. So I covered him well, went back to bed and slept until he woke up. I dressed him warmly and put on the warmest clothing I could find and carried him to my brother's house, which was about a block away, down the same alley.

Juan and Marta were expecting their second baby soon, and Marta and I enjoyed each other's company. The whole time they lived there, they slept on a sofa bed, for Juan Carlos' crib was in the bedroom, where the new baby's crib would also be. I stayed with Marta and Juan Carlos every day, until Juan came home from work. I was so grateful when he took me back home in his car, which was cozily warm.

Their apartment was in a newer building, and it was nicer than ours, just much smaller. She had the blessing of a washing machine in the little kitchen, and that's where I washed our clothing, too. Neither of us had a dryer.

I took our wet items home, spread them across the kitchen chairs and table and put some things on hangers near the big heater. When the clothes were finally dry the next day, they were as stiff as if they had been dipped in starch! Some of them could have stood alone!

Never in my old life could I have imagined that I would one day be trying to dry my laundry in my house. In just a few months I had learned how to do so many things, even cook, and I was proud of myself. I kept our apartment clean. In truth, there was not much for me to do, so I had to stay busy doing something!

In February, my brother's second little boy was born, and I took care of Juan Carlos while Marta was in the hospital. We placed his crib end-to-end with Alex's, which worked out well. They still did not get along. Sometimes I had to separate the cribs, for they would fight with each other across the ends!

It was a challenge to feed them at the same time. On the table I placed two bowls of cereal with a spoon in each one. I held the boys in my lap, an arm around each one. I fed first one, and then the other, from their own little bowl. I suppose they were too hungry to fight! It's too bad video cameras were not available at the time, but then we could not have afforded one! Juan brought Marta home in a few days, and we all celebrated the homecoming of little Jorge Luis.

Dr. Rubio knew a physician who was the same size and stature as my husband. Having gone through the same experiences, Dr. Rubio also knew how difficult it was to come from a year-round warm climate to one of frigid temperatures, especially when forced to leave with few clothing changes.

When he told his friend about us, the man gave him two suits, complete with shirts and ties, for my husband, which made a huge difference in his wardrobe. The doctor also had a little boy who was outgrowing the toddler stage, so he gave some nice clothing to Dr. Rubio for Alejandro.

Unfortunately, there was nothing for me; but I didn't care. I was so happy my husband had some nice suits to wear to work, and I could dress my little boy in something besides the things he was outgrowing. Not only that! The doctor had included a few toys for Alejandro, the first new things he had to play with since we left Cuba. I think I was more excited about them than he was.

In spite of the cold, those first few weeks were quite an adventure for me. On Saturday mornings I cleaned the apartment. Juan and Marta, accompanied by their two little boys, picked up Alejandro and me in his old car; and the six of us went shopping for groceries on Saturday afternoons.

I sat in the back seat, holding the baby, trying to keep the two-year-olds from fighting. That was an adventure in itself, let me tell you! For some reason we could never understand, Alejandro loved to scuffle with Juan Carlos, who did not enjoy it much. But they were both so cute, with bright eyes and dark hair, two little bundles of energy.

I had my hands full with them and the baby. One afternoon Alejandro grabbed the door handle and pushed, trying to open the door! We were driving along the expressway, with traffic streaming beside us, in front of us and behind us! Thank God the door didn't open, one more of His blessings that just kept coming into our lives, even though I was not serving Him at that time.

Gradually, it became less cold, and the first warming days of spring arrived. Alex was able to walk along beside me to Marta's, and she and I could enjoy time outdoors with them on the patio outside her back door. We could listen for the baby, now three or four months old, if he woke up from his nap. One day after lunch, we stepped outside with the boys to enjoy the sun.

"Oh, no!" Marta's eyes widened, and she covered her mouth with her hands. "I closed the door, and it locked behind us!" she said. "And I left the key inside, and I don't have my purse! We can't get in! Oh, what if the baby begins to cry, I can't get in!" Oh, my goodness! We tried everything we could think of to get the door open, without results.

Desperate, she went to the front of the building while I waited with the boys outside her apartment. Marta explained to the person who answered her call that her baby was locked inside her apartment, and she had no way to get in. Well, none of the tenants had keys to any of the other apartments; but someone had a telephone number for the owner of the building. The call was made.

She came back to the alley and we waited outside Marta's door, praying that little Jorge Luis would not wake up. It seemed like hours before the owner arrived with a key to open the door. In truth, it really was a long time. When we were finally inside the apartment, we hurried to the boys' room to discover that the precious little baby was still sleeping soundly. I think it must have been the longest nap he ever took, for usually he cried all the time! Makes me wonder if angels were watching over him. Or us!

Spring continued to advance, and I could not believe the changes I saw taking place all around me. Trees began to show the most beautiful shade of light green on their branches, and birds appeared. The gray of winter gave way to a bright blue sky, and warm, sunny days made me think of Cuba, where trees never lost their leaves, except during a hurricane, and then the whole tree could disappear! Chicago residents took these miraculous spring days for granted, but I gloried in them.

When we learned that the second floor apartment above the Rubio's was available, we were thrilled. It had a large living room and kitchen, as well as three bedrooms and a bathroom. I was as happy with that apartment as I had been with any of the nicer homes we had shared in Cuba.

How could I not be happy? On most of those warm, sunny afternoons, women in our immediate neighborhood gathered on Nora Rubio's porch, talking and enjoying each other's company while the children played. Marta often joined us, as well as Nora's sister-in-law and her children.

Gracielita Viziola and her mother, Tina, lived two buildings to our right. The wife of another physician, Gracielita was very young, younger than the rest of us, and the only one without children. Our husbands were all doctors, and there were many more in the community because of such close proximity to major hospitals.

Dr. Pianilli's father-in-law, also a doctor, had lived in our apartment before us, so there was almost a sense of family among all of us. Shared experiences and common interests can be as binding as family ties.

Another thing about Nora Rubio: Not only did she have us over many times to eat, she often had other dinner guests. I don't know how she did it, but the meals she prepared and served to a houseful of people were extraordinary! And the food!

All the dishes we had loved in Cuba, meats, vegetables, plantain, rice and black beans--incredible! I have mentioned the generosity of Dr. Rubio and Nora before, but the way they welcomed us and other Cuban compatriots made our lives so much easier that first year.

CHICAGO

Isabel

Working Girl

As the days passed, Armando and I talked about getting a car, and we started looking for one we could afford. At a local Ford dealer, we found a blue one we liked, but we were not totally sure about it. As we discussed the pros and cons, Armando explained to the agent that I didn't know how to drive.

"She passed the test in Cuba, and she drove a little bit there; but she hasn't had much actual driving experience," Armando said.

"Well, she can take the exam here." That agent really wanted to sell us the car! So I took the exam right there, and I passed. I walked out with a brand new driver's license; and Armando drove us home in our new used car. But just because I had a license didn't mean I knew how to drive!

The Chicago freeways, with multiple driving and turning lanes, were not easy driving for this inexperienced Cuban woman! There were some scary moments, not only for me, but for all those drivers who honked at me when I was in the wrong turn lane. I was grateful that none of them hit my car!

My husband usually drove to work, but I could now do my own grocery shopping on Saturdays, often taking Marta and the boys with me. I loved being able to have a measure of independence, and it was fun for me to be able to show off my driving skills to Marta.

Some of those skills were not apparent in my early driving experiences, such as the day I made a left turn onto a one-way street. "Isa, what are you doing!" Marta screamed at me. She didn't know how to drive then, but she knew something was not right!

"I don't know!" Cars honked and honked! I turned at the next intersection, and then we were OK, but it was a little scary for a few moments. I cannot adequately describe how happy we were and how much Marta and I laughed during those months. We were not only sisters-in-law, we were friends. We still are.

Another driving lesson occurred the day I parallel parked, uphill, outside a pharmacy. I pulled the emergency parking lever, and Marta, our three little boys and I went inside the store. We completed our shopping, came back to the car and got inside, ready to progress to our next destination. I started the car, put it in gear, but it would not move. I tried and tried, but I could not make that crazy car move one inch! In desperation, I called to a man we saw walking up the street.

"Sir! Sir, can you please help us? My car will not move! I don't know what's wrong with it!' I got out of the driver's seat and let the man get inside to see if he could make the car move. He reached down and pulled a lever, grinned, pulled the lever again and got out of the car.

"Ma'am, you had the emergency brake on. You have to release the brake before it will go uphill." He smiled again, and walked away, while I felt like an utter idiot! I had simply forgotten to release the brake! We never knew what form our Saturday shopping adventures would take, but we had several of them.

My husband and I moved into the second floor of Dr. Rubio's building, right above them. The third floor was rented by another physician, Dr. Pianelli, an Italian who had a beautiful voice. He sang for his own enjoyment, but we loved to hear him sing his favorite Italian melodies. The sound floated down the staircase, and listening to the rich tones of his voice was like having our own private concert.

An outside street entrance on the first floor provided private access to the second and third floors. Visitors rang the doorbell, and someone upstairs had to unlock the door for the caller. It provided a measure of safety for all the residents in the building.

Alex and I were alone in the building one evening, which was unusual. My husband, Dr. Rubio and Dr. Pianelli, along with a number of other doctors, were at a meeting held in the Evangelical Hospital, just around the corner. I was suddenly aware of the sound of footsteps on the stairs, but no one had rung the bell. Someone had broken the street door and was coming toward our apartment door! Then he was there, demanding to be let inside!

"Let me in!" He screamed and yelled and pounded on the door, asking for someone whose name I did not know. Scared to death, not wanting this crazy man to think I was alone, I told him that the man he wanted was in the shower and could not come to the door. I asked him to please wait for a little while, and then I called the police. Not knowing what else to do, I called my husband.

"Armando, someone is trying to get inside the apartment! He's banging on the door, and I don't know what to do! I called the police, but they are not here! Come quickly!"

I hung up the phone and called to the man outside to please wait for a little bit more. I grabbed the key to our bedroom door, took Alex into the bedroom and locked the door, thinking that at least it would be one more locked door between the man and us. I hoped it would give the police more time to reach us.

Meanwhile, the man kept yelling and pushing at the locked living room door, trying to break it down. I had not been so afraid since the night Rosalina and Luis had cut up the meat in our kitchen, months earlier! Suddenly I heard my husband's angry voice, yelling at the man. (A good deal will be lost in translation, here!)

"Get out of here, you filthy man! This is my house! What are you doing here! Get out of here right now!" I had never heard my husband so angry, and I had never heard his voice filled with such rage. At that moment, it was the most beautiful sound I had ever heard.

The police arrived at about the same time and escorted the intruder downstairs. I looked out the apartment window, amazed at the scene below. Gathered in front of the building were all the doctors who had been in the meeting with my husband! With Armando, they had run from The Evangelical Hospital to our apartment building, just around the corner— and arrived before the police!

What was unbelievable to us was that the officers, after they finally arrived, let the man go. They told us that he was just drunk and had simply come to the wrong address. We watched as the man wove his way down the street, eventually disappearing from sight.

During the previous five years, I had lived in fear, terrified that Castro's thugs would come for my husband, not knowing when they might show up at our house with machine guns. I had not realized that danger could threaten my family in our new home. However, the difference was that the threat did not come from the government, which protected personal freedom for all, even lost, intoxicated idiots! I don't remember how long it took for the street entrance to be repaired, but I'm sure it was done quickly.

My husband and I had discussed the possibility of my getting a job, but there was no one to care for our son. That's when we came up with the possibility of inviting my parents to come live with us. Our apartment had three bedrooms and a bath, offering plenty of room for three more people. I was beyond ecstatic when Mami and Papo agreed to come!

So about six months after I left my mother, father and little brother in Miami, they came to live with us in Chicago. I now had the best of all possible worlds. My parents' presence in the apartment gave me freedom to get a job, which I did. One of the hospitals where my husband worked hired me as a secretary.

I honestly don't know why they hired me! I was learning English, but I was not yet fluent in the language. There were many women of all ages working in the office, which was quite large. They seemed to like me, and they continually laughed at my attempts to speak English. I didn't mind at all. They were so sweet and kind, and they made it as easy as possible for me.

In the dining room one day, I told them how hungry I was every morning, that I sometimes ate a ham and cheese sandwich. When I said "sangwich," they broke into laughter; but it was not mean-spirited.

The first woman I worked for wanted me to translate doctors' transcriptions from a dicta-phone. Problem was, some of the doctors were of different nationalities or came from other parts of the country; and every one of them had a different accent! I was still learning English, and I could not understand any of them! From there the office manager sent me to another office to type out biopsy reports.

One day a doctor told me that he had just taken a biopsy of a liver. "Do you like to eat liver?" he asked. I never ate liver!

"Doctor, please," I said to him, "I don't know how you can do that!" I think I might have shuddered! The man started to laugh.

"Do what?" he asked, still laughing.

"Take out a piece of someone's liver!" I learned that a liver biopsy was done with a long needle, but the whole process sounded dreadful to me.

The older man who picked up outgoing mail was, well, not handsome. I hate to say ugly; but he was certainly not attractive, although very nice and friendly to everyone in the offices. His name was Alex, and he liked to stop and talk with the girls. One day I mentioned that it was my birthday. I think it was the next day that a birthday card from this man arrived at my house.

My husband was a little jealous, and my mother was not happy about it either. "Who is this Alex?" they demanded. I had to laugh.

"You would have to see him," I told my husband. "Then you would know there is nothing to worry about."

So, unbelievable as it sounded to me, I was living in Chicago, working in one of the hospitals where my husband was employed. We were in the process of becoming Americans. My life just kept getting better and better.

From the moment my parents moved in with us, my mother took over the day to day care of the apartment five days a week. She cooked every day, did the laundry, made the beds and took loving care of Alex. My father helped in any way he could, and my brother, José enrolled in a nearby school. When I arrived home every evening, the table was already set for dinner and the house smelled so good with the delicious food that was ready to eat.

My mother had bathed Alex, who had turned three in September, and dressed him in clean, freshly ironed clothes. She ironed everything! In Cuba, my family had always made a practice of using lightly-scented cologne on babies and small children, called *Agua de Violetas*, from Augustín Reyes. It is a violet scent, sweet and clean. It could be sprinkled sparingly on garments as they were being ironed, and the scent lingered. I liked to lightly spray bed linens, and I still do. When I picked Alex up every evening and hugged him, he smelled so delicious I just wanted to gobble him up!

I was so happy to have my parents in our house. After our long separation, I could not get enough of their company. I never took them for granted again. My mother was a skilled homemaker, and with her loving presence in our house, I began to feel like a princess again.

It would have been nice if there had been a garage for our car, but there was only on-street parking in front of every house. My husband was so proud of our almost-new car. One night someone ran into it, doing a lot of damage; but they did not stop.

When my husband discovered what had been done to his beautiful blue Ford, he was very calm. He did not get angry. He did not yell or any of the things many, probably most, men would have done. He surveyed the damage, called the police and dealt with the problem of getting repairs done.

Quietly, my mother observed her son-in-law. "What a man," she told me. "What a man." She held Armando in such high regard, and her respect for him grew even greater as she watched him deal with whatever came his way. There was a quiet grace about him, surprising when I realize all he had come through.

In looking back, something I have done a lot, I can understand his quiet demeanor under stress. By that time, he had basically put himself through medical school, built a practice in Cuba, managed to stay alive during the Cuban "revolution," take care of me and our son, then get us out of Cuba. In comparison, how important was a banged-up car?

Thousands of Cubans had endured more difficult times than we were going through. We had escaped just in the nick of time, while others had been jailed and killed. Even many who managed to come to the United States were never able to regain the quality of pre-Castro life they had enjoyed in Cuba. I am proud of all my husband did in those days and in the years that followed.

We developed a routine that was good for all of us. We worked hard and managed to be extremely happy. Occasionally little causes for celebration surprised us. We received an unexpected invitation from one of my husband's colleagues, another Cuban doctor, who had been in the United States for several years. Dr. Poveda had already established a successful private practice by the time we arrived in Chicago. I was ecstatic when Armando told me that Dr. Proveda and his wife, Juanita, had asked us to accompany them to a nice hotel for dinner and dancing.

For such a special occasion, I wanted to wear something pretty and new. I had not shopped for evening clothes since before we left Cuba; and I was excited about looking through beautiful dresses and touching lovely fabrics again. I didn't regret leaving Cuba at all, but I thought wistfully of the gowns that had been hanging in my closets when we left, especially the scarlet red that I had worn the night Armando placed an engagement ring on my finger.

I put those thoughts out of my mind. Armando and I went shopping, which we always did together. We found a little place called "The Three Sisters," which was not my first choice to look for something nice. However, I kept an open mind; and I found a short black dress that fit me perfectly. It was marked down more than half price, twenty dollars! I loved the way I looked in the dress, and Armando loved the price! He liked the dress, too; so we were both happy.

On the night of the dinner, I put on that sweet little dress and stepped into the same black high-heels I had worn on the flight from Cuba to Spain. Among the jewelry my father had sent to Miami before he left Cuba, I found the perfect pieces to accessorize the dress. When I left our apartment, carrying my black envelope purse, I felt like a million dollars. The feeling was worth the wait!

We had a good time that night. The dinner and music were wonderful, and getting to know this couple led to some interesting discoveries. Dr. Poveda met his wife here in the USA, and they were married here; but she grew up in Cidra, Matanzas, Cuba, where my mother was born and lived. Juanita was younger than my mother, but they had known each other's families.

Although I had not known Juanita personally, I learned that she had been a good friend of my cousin, Orlando, the one who had been an outstanding dancer his whole life. Juanita knew Güines well, for she had visited our home town often.

On another occasion, the Povedas invited us for dinner at their home, a beautiful large house in a lovely suburb of Chicago. We met their children, two boys, between the ages of nine and twelve, and a very little girl. I don't remember their names.

About ten years later, Armando and I met Dr. Poveda at a medical convention in Miami, where we learned that his wife had become ill. At that time, his two sons were attending Southern Illinois University in Carbondale. Looking back, it truly is amazing how our lives continued to cross paths with so many people from places we had known in Cuba.

In October, 1964, Dr. Rubio moved his family to the small town of Kinmundy, in South Central Illinois. He would set up his first private practice there, but it would not be his final stop in this new country. We wished him well, but I was going to miss their companionship.

October 31ˢᵗ, Marta and I and our boys dove headfirst into a totally new experience—Hallowe'en. In Cuba, Hallowe'en was not a major holiday. Earlier in my story, I described the two times I had taken part in it, neither of them very memorable.

Neither Marta nor I had the money to spend on fancy costumes, so we created our own. Marta dressed Juan Carlos in an old, wrinkled sport coat, a brimmed hat, added a mustache and a white pen that resembled a cigarette; and the little boy looked like a miniature hobo/beggar/street person. Take your pick.

I did the same with Alejandro. I pulled a multi-colored crocheted hat (mine) over his head and dressed him in my big corduroy shirt. I stuffed newspapers all around his body and kept them in place with a wide belt, also mine. We added a mustache below his little nose, and the two little guys were ready to go trick-or-treating! They laughed and giggled so much that Marta and I could do nothing but laugh with them

Like all the other goblins, we walked along several blocks, stopping at lots of houses, having a marvelous time. I'm sure that Marta carried little Jorge Luis, who was nine months old by then; but I don't remember if she dressed him for the occasion. I do know that, as usual, our husbands were working.

In years to come, there would be yearly trick-or-treating with Alex and the three additional children who would be born to us; but that October was our first. I can never forget how excited those two toddlers were with all the candies they collected that evening. To tell the truth, it was a very sweet treat for Marta and me, as well. We were becoming truly Americanized, and we loved every moment.

KANKAKEE

Armando

Decisions

Dr. Gonzalo Pera and I worked together during my first year of internship in the Chicago hospitals. We decided that we needed to find a place where we could work, make more money and still have time to study for our state board exams. We looked at different hospitals, which were not too interesting.

During our search, we went to two state hospitals. The first one was for mentally handicapped children. Both of us decided that we needed to find a hospital with a broader range, so we looked at a state hospital in Kankakee. We discovered that among the physicians were two from Cuba and two from South America.

We met with the director and asked what the hospital could offer us in the way of employment. It was also a mental hospital, but he told us that they would hire us to care for the medical needs of the patients. The hours were from eight to three in the afternoon, and the salary was $1,000 per month, which was double what we had been making in Chicago!

So we took the jobs. Dr. Pera moved his family to Kankakee shortly before we did, only a few months before our second son was born. Dr. Pera and I worked there for a year. In the mornings we made rounds for a couple of hours, and then we were free to study. They provided a room upstairs for us, where we studied until it was time for lunch. Following our free meal, we went to a medical staff meeting for half an hour and then went back to studying.

Dr. Pera chose to stay in Illinois, but I wanted options to practice in other states. I flew to Maryland, where I took and passed the state board. A short while later, I flew to Vermont and passed their exam, too. I was more interested in Florida and California because Spanish was a prevalent language, and many Cubans lived there; but I wasn't allowed to take their exams. At that time, only American citizens were able to practice medicine in those two states. Since then, the law has been changed, and now any physician can apply and take the board exams.

So I went back to the state hospital in Kankakee, where I continued to work and study for the Illinois medical board exams, which I passed. While I was away, Isabel cared for our home and our sons, and she did it well, as she did during the three years we lived there.

We enjoyed our time in Kankakee, but it would not be our permanent home in Illinois. We had not yet found that perfect place, the spot where I could establish a private practice, the area where we wanted to raise our family. It would take us a little more time, but I knew that we would find it. We never looked back, only forward.

KANKAKEE

Isabel

Baby Makes Four

Major changes took place for us after our two years in Chicago. My parents moved to another apartment. José was growing up, now a teenager, and they needed more space. That worked out well, since we would be moving anyway. I would have loved for them to come to Kankakee with us, but they decided to stay in Chicago, where my brother and his family were established.

Armando bought another car, an ugly green Chevrolet, which made life easier for both of us; but I hated that car. In July, 1965, we packed what few belongings we owned and drove to Kankakee; but that's not all we were taking. I was pregnant! Our second baby was due in October.

We moved into a small house, one of four in a double duplex. It sat on the corner of an intersection in a nice neighborhood. A carport extended from one side, so we could park off the street. Beside and behind the four-house square was a continuous common ground, an area where Alex could play.

The house had two bedrooms, with a convenient bathroom, a nice-sized kitchen and living room, plenty of space for our growing family. We bought a few pieces of decent second-hand furniture. I loved looking for and finding bargains, and I became an expert at it. We discovered a re-sale shop where I found six items: among them two dresses and a skirt, nice things. I was so happy to find something new. But the next time we entered the shop I saw nothing that appealed to me, and we never went back.

Mina Pera and I had become good friends when we lived in Chicago, and we visited each other often after Armando and I moved to Kankakee. She was fascinated with my unborn baby. She loved to gently rub my abdomen, crooning Spanish phrases, such as *"Mi pequeño bebé."* My little baby.

Mina liked her kitchen, and she loved to cook. Our husbands were always studying together, so Mina often invited us over for dinner. How I loved that! She fed me well. They had three sons, good boys who would grow into wonderful men. Even the younger one was quite a bit older than Alex.

Before long, we found a piano that would fit in our living room. When my brother and his family brought my parents to visit us, other transplanted friends from Güines came, too; and it was always a party! Our little house rang with Cuban music, and we ate Cuban food and danced as we had in Cuba, all of us so happy to be living in America. With Juan's bongo drums, José's guitar, my piano, and maracas played by anyone who knew how, we had our own band.

By then, I had become a good cook. I learned a lot from my mother during the short time I spent with her in Miami. In a notebook, I wrote down as many recipes as she could give me. I enjoyed making and serving good food to my family and friends during these gatherings. They helped to set tables and drinks while I completed finishing touches to the food, and then we all sat anywhere we could find a place. Those were happy days, especially since every one of us had lived through some scary, horrible events.

When it was time for our baby to be born, my husband drove us back to Chicago, where I had begun prenatal care. He drove a little faster than he normally would have, for this second baby was well on the way by the time we arrived at the hospital. On October 1, 1965, Armando Ezequiel was born, weighing six pounds two ounces. With his dark eyes and dark hair, he was a handsome little fellow from the beginning.

My mother accompanied us back to Kankakee, where she stayed with us for a few weeks. Like she did when Alex was born in Güines, she helped me care for our new baby, immediately christened Bebe by Mina Pera. The name stuck, and that is what he was called the rest of his life. Mami cooked and cared for us, and she made my life so much easier, just as she had done when Alex was born. By the time she went back to Chicago, I was able to resume my role as fulltime wife and mother.

In the duplex next to us lived two sisters, Eleanor, who was a widow, and Buffy, who was single, but had a boyfriend. Every day he picked up Buffy and took her somewhere. They looked so happy together, and I enjoyed watching them, probably weaving happily-ever-after stories about them.

The two sisters were crazy about my boys and they took a lot of photographs of them. One day Alex, dressed in good clothes, grabbed a connected garden hose in their yard and ran all over the grass with it, happy and laughing, while the sisters took numerous photos of him. I was unhappy with Alex for getting his good clothing soaking wet, but there was nothing I could do, except laugh with the sisters, who thought everything Alex did was funny and sweet.

Diagonally across the street from our apartment stood a huge house, probably built close to the turn of the century. I don't remember the last name of the couple who lived there, but Daisy was the woman's name. Her elderly parents lived with them. Daisy and her husband had no children, which might have been a reason she fell in love with mine.

Alex went to pre-school for a couple of months and the next fall he entered kindergarten. Daisy and I took turns taking him to school, which was a tremendous help to me while Babe was a baby. I was fortunate to have such pleasant, helpful women nearby when the boys were so little. In 1967-68, Alex went to first grade in a Lutheran school.

A pastor from a Christian church came to visit us several times to invite us to attend his church. We visited it sometimes, but were not regular attendees. His wife was a piano teacher. They lived pretty close to us, so we enrolled Alex with her for lessons.

Babe was a handful, even when he was a baby. I once took the boys shopping with me to a J.C. Penny department store. I carried him, strapped into his "pumpkin seat," which is what the handled carriers were called at that time. I placed the seat on the floor beside me while I tried on a pair of shoes.

I stood in front of the small floor mirror, looking at my feet in the shoes, turning this way and that. I glanced to see that the baby was all right, and he was gone! I absolutely panicked! I looked in every direction, and I caught a glimpse of him as he crawled under a seat, heading away from me. Everyone around me was laughing at the sight of that tiny little fellow, having his first adventure.

He was no more than six months old at the time, which was only a precursor of what was to come. He did everything early, from crawling to walking to running. I wonder if he might have had an internal clock, something that urged him to get an early start on the excitement of living, an awareness that he had to experience everything as quickly as possible. I don't know, but I have wondered.

We were so happy in Kankakee. If we were not going to Chicago to see family and friends on a weekend, they were coming down to be with us. (For a while, going to see my parents reminded me of the many times they moved while in was at La Progresiva. Every time we went to see them, they lived in a different place, from apartments to houses!) For Alex's fifth birthday we had a tremendous picnic in the park. All of our family and friends from Güines who lived in Chicago, as well as Gonzalo and Mina Pera with their three sons, Gonzalito, Carlitos, and Tonito, came to the party.

We had made other friends in Kankakee, among them Raúl, Beatriz and their three sons; so we had a wonderful gathering of friends and family at the birthday picnic. There were many picnics in that park. We had a playpen for Babe. I can still see him, his dark eyes looking through the mesh of the playpen, watching the other children run and play games, laughing and shouting. We did not dare turn him loose without one of us at his side constantly. It was the best of both worlds to us, for there were no Castro brothers to crash our party, to threaten us with a filthy prison or death. Life was good!

One day we and the Peras took a trip to Springfield, to see the tomb and former home of President Abraham Lincoln. It was memorable to me, for I was constantly learning more and more about our new country. (Dr. Rubio insisted that we study and apply for citizenship as quickly as possible.)

While my husband continued to study for his medical board exams, he and I studied the course on becoming citizens of the United States. I remember how scared I was as I studied, wanting to learn and remember everything that was required, how afraid I was when we finally went back to Springfield to take the tests.

I will never forget how excited and proud we were when we finally stood with the other applicants, raised our hands and swore allegiance to the United States and to the Constitution. We were finally citizens, and neither my husband nor I have ever looked back with regret.

SALEM

Armando

Caravan South

After Dr. Rubio and his family moved to Salem, we lived another year in Chicago and three in Kankakee; but we had stayed in contact with each other. I called to ask his opinion of areas in Southern Illinois that might be receptive to receiving another doctor. He suggested several possibilities, and he invited us to come and stay with them for a few days while we considered our options.

Two Lavernia brothers, both physicians we had known in Cuba and mentioned in the first part of our story, had established a successful practice in the small town of St. Elmo, not far from the Vandalia area. Their clinic was impressive. We visited with them, and then went to Lawrenceville, where we looked at a big clinic, one of the nicest we saw.

My wife and I drove around several towns. Dr. Rubio suggested that we look at Odin, the small town west of Salem. They had no resident physician. So one night he drove his family to Odin, and we followed in our car, where we all drove around the little town. We stopped at the local diner and filed inside. With six Rubios and four Aguilars, we must have looked like an invasion!

We ordered dinner and began to discuss the possibilities. I liked the area all right, so I asked my wife what she thought.

"No!" Her reply was adamant.

"What about Salem?" I asked Dr. Rubio.

"You can certainly try," he told me. We looked the community over pretty thoroughly, from the busy downtown area to schools and housing.

Salem was a pretty little town, nowhere near as large as Güines, in Cuba, Madrid, Spain, Chicago or even Kankakee; but I liked it. I felt that it would be a good place to make a home for our family.

So the decision was made. I had no guarantee that I could develop a successful practice here, but I was well-acquainted with hard work and determination. Several physicians were already established in Salem, some of them for many years. Dr. Rubio, whose first office was in Kinmundy, had opened another office in Salem; and the community seemed to have embraced him and his family.

I rented an office in a small business complex, located in the 600 block of East Main. Dr. Ed Perry, who had grown up in Salem, became an optometrist and returned to his home town, where he opened an office in this same location. We became friends, and I worked from there for quite a while.

At first, a couple of the local, older physicians in town were not as welcoming as the majority. I could understand why they might have been a little territorial. After all, we were the second Cuban family to arrive in Marion County. Perhaps they thought they were about to be inundated with hundreds of Spanish-speaking, Cuban exiles!

At any rate, it did not take long for the whole medical community to welcome me into their brotherhood of physicians. Within a relatively short time, my office hours were filled with patients. Like Dr. Rubio, I worked all the time. Sundays were our only days off.

It occurred to me that working together might be a good idea, so I approached him about it. "If we formed a partnership," I told him, "we could take turns having weekends and alternate evenings off." At that time, doctors still made house calls and were on call all night long.

Dr. Rubio liked the idea, and we began to work together. When we decided to build the Medical Clinic, I realized that Dr. Rubio and I were perfect examples of what could be accomplished in a country that offered opportunity. Both of us had left everything we owned behind us, including good, lucrative practices, as well as loved family members, for the chance to live and work in freedom. We had become the epitome of the American dream.

Even as I became more and more acclimated to our new country and home, events and images from our recent past sometimes popped into my mind. Patients with similar conditions, sometimes mothers bringing their children into my office could trigger a sudden, vivid memory.

One that remains with me after all these years is that of a distraught mother with two small children who came into my office in Güines. As I examined the child who needed my attention I asked the woman why she was so upset.

"My husband has disappeared, and I don't know how to find him," she told me. "Soldiers came to search my house, and they found my husband's old hunting rifle that he had not turned in. Someone must have reported that he had not turned it in. They arrested him and took him away."

"They didn't tell you where they were taking him?"

"No," she said. "That was yesterday."

"Did you go to the police?"

"Yes, I did, but they told me that they don't know where he is!"

I comforted her as much as I could, gave her medicine for her child and told her to come back the following week, which she did.

"Have you located your husband?" I asked. Tears filled her eyes.

"Yes. I went to the police again and they told me where my husband was being held. They let me see him, and he told me that they are going to kill him!"

"No!" I exclaimed. "Do you really believe they will kill him for such a small thing?" Even after witnessing executions on television, I could not believe that this woman's husband might be killed, for nothing more than having an old gun he had used for hunting.

"Yes, I'm afraid so."

I reassured her, not wanting to accept that Fidel and Raúl Castro, who claimed to love the people, would be so heartless to this woman and her children. I was wrong. After the decree that every citizen had to surrender arms and weapons, anyone who had a gun of any kind in their possession would be considered traitors. The punishment was death.

I saw her a few days later, wearing a black dress. I was heartsick, for I knew that her garment of mourning meant that the revolution had claimed another innocent man. He was only one of hundreds, even thousands, who were murdered in cities and towns throughout Cuba for small infractions of their rules, sometimes over a rumor. Castro's "revolution" had become a raging, murderous bloody beast.

I made a conscious effort to put all of that out of my mind, to concentrate on the good things and new, supportive friends who had come into our lives. For the most part, with the passing of time, I was able to do that. I tried not to think about family members and friends who had chosen to stay in Cuba or had not been able to escape. Of course, that was not always easy to do.

One cannot live successfully in the present while dwelling on the past. I committed myself to working hard, to taking good care of the people who came to me for medical treatment and to provide a good home for my growing family. The best thing I could do for all of us was to look forward. And that is what I continue to do, to this day, to the best of my ability.

SALEM

Isabel

Another New Beginning

So. We would be moving once again. I was perfectly content in our little house in Kankakee. My husband was making what I thought was a good salary. We had many friends. Our families lived a short distance from us. I loved the city and living near the metropolis of Chicago.

What I had seen of Southern Illinois did not impress me. The brightest spot during the few days we spent looking around was our time with the Lavernias, who owned a medical clinic in St. Elmo. Just being with them renewed treasured memories of sun-filled days on Rosario Beach during my teen years.

Nidia, my friend who had caught chickens with me on Rosario Beach that day, married Enrique Lavernia, one of the two doctors now in St. Elmo. A third Lavernia brother was not a doctor, but he worked with his brothers in the clinic. Nidia's mother was the one who had prepared *arroz con pollo* for us, the chicken dinner to which my mother did not allow me to go! Both Nidia's parents, Hilda and Quintín Quiñones, lived with them.

Quintín is the man who owned the big yacht, the one that got my brother and me in such trouble the day we went for a sail without first asking my mother! It goes without saying that everything they once owned had been left behind in Cuba, no doubt still being enjoyed by Castro or his friends.

We found a house on Allmon Street in Salem. It was nice enough, but it needed a thorough cleaning and new paint. When the day came to move our furniture to Salem, my husband, with Alejandro beside him, drove the blue Ford, pulling a U-Haul trailer. I, driving the green car I didn't like, followed closely behind him. Before we left, I gave emphatic instructions to Babe, the little dynamo who was inactive only when he slept!

"You sit perfectly still, and don't you move!" Something in my voice must have convinced him. Interstates were not yet built, so it was a two-lane drive down Routes 45 and 37 all the way to Salem. Babe scarcely moved during the whole trip. I think we stopped once for gas. I pulled carefully behind my husband, not letting him out of my sight.

We had scarcely entered the city limits of Salem before a police car pulled up behind us, lights flashing. We both stopped, and the officer told my husband that he had been driving over the speed limit! Welcome to our new home! At that moment, I was probably the most discouraged woman in Salem, Illinois.

My husband explained to the officer that he was the new doctor in town, that he was unfamiliar with the streets. I never learned the officer's name, but I know that he had a big heart. He didn't give my husband a ticket! We drove to the Continental Motel on the east side of Salem, where we stayed for the two weeks, while cleaning and painting were being done in the house. The motel was relatively new, and Robbins Restaurant, owned by a local business man, was next door. It served good food, and we took most of our meals there during those two weeks.

Although I rather liked living in our new house, cooking, cleaning and doing laundry and putting the boys to bed in their own room, I thought Salem was much too small. I had loved the city of Havana, in the beautiful country of Cuba. Kankakee was not nearly as large, but it was close to Chicago, a city I had found exciting from my first night there.

The bigger the city, the better I liked it; and Chicago was to be my unfulfilled choice. It was just one more incidence over which I had no control, not since the days when Fidel Castro had established his revolution. At first, this relocation seemed like a gigantic thorn in my life; but in the following days and years, I discovered that rosebuds were just waiting to burst into bloom.

The hospital's "pink ladies" had contacted us before we moved to Salem. They had been instrumental in bringing us here. They helped find a house for us, and it was they who found people to clean it. After living in the motel for two weeks, I was more than ready to move.

The school year had already begun in that autumn of 1968. Alex was just entering second grade, and he had missed a few weeks of school; but he had no trouble with the transition. He had learned good conversational English. The house on Allmon Street intersected with North College Street, near the house of Mrs. Hancock, who operated a pre-school for children in her home.

Although Babe was not yet pre-school age, Mrs. Hancock allowed me to register him. She was so nice to me, and we became friends during those years. I walked him to and from her house every day. Later, a friend told me that she had seen me walking along the street, not looking around, staring at the sidewalk in front of me. She was right when she said that I had looked depressed, for I certainly was.

The day after we arrived in Salem, my husband began to work in the little office where Dr. Rubio saw patients two days a week. In this way, Armando was able to help patients here when Dr. Rubio was in Kinmundy. There were not many at first, but in time a good practice was established.

Within a few weeks, my outlook improved and I began to enjoy living in our new surroundings. The office front was located behind what was then called the Woolford-Marsh building, on Main Street, right in the center of Salem.

Every day my husband was in his office, I went there, too. In a short time, I became acquainted with people who worked in the stores that made up the small business district. At that time it was a bustling little city, with stores and shops where just about anything one could need was available.

Three drugstores, all within a stone's throw of each other, offered services from filling prescriptions to making milkshakes and hamburgers, buying bus tickets or makeup, stationery or Whitman's Candy Samplers. Three or four nice dress shops, a fabric shop, a couple of furniture and hardware stores, two hotels, grocery stores, two banks, barber shops—all were within steps of the county courthouse.

After their initial phone contact with us in the beginning, the hospital pink ladies became our friends. Many of them invited us into their homes for dinner, and we grew to love them very much. It was not long before I recognized the merits of living in a small town, and it seemed that I saw roses everywhere I looked.

A few months after our arrival in Salem, my husband's practice had grown enough that we decided to buy a house. We found a lovely place in Country Club Estates that we liked a lot. All on one floor, it was spacious, with a large kitchen and dining room, a formal living room and several bedrooms and bathrooms. We had not lived in such a big house since we left Cuba. By then, Dr. Rubio and his family had moved to what was called the Cluster house, directly behind us. It fronted on Highway 37, so once again we and the Rubios were neighbors.

We enjoyed choosing new furniture. We made trips to St Louis, where we chose several pieces; and we ordered some through Bachman's Furniture Store on Main Street in Salem. For the first time, we hired a home decorator. I was so proud of our new house and how beautiful it looked with new rugs and furnishings, many of which we still have.

There were not a lot of fun activities for us, outside of the boys' school programs and church. Our favorite summer evening pastime was visiting Carl's Ice Cream Parlor, located in the curve of West Main Street. Cell phones had not yet been invented, and my husband was always on call at the hospital; so it was not unusual for him to receive calls at Carl's. Many evenings we gathered up Alex, Babe and our ice cream treats and made fast runs to the hospital.

Less than a year after our arrival in Salem, the hospital Auxiliary, comprised of some doctor's wives and others who organized and sponsored events to benefit the hospital, undertook quite an ambitious program. I had no idea to what extent I would be involved with this project or how much it would impact my life.

Loving to dance as I did, I could not imagine living where places to dance were not available. So when I learned what the Auxiliary was planning, I was so excited I could hardly breathe. I don't know who originally thought of it, but the Broadway-type show they brought to the community was unlike anything that had previously been undertaken.

It might have been that someone knew someone who had a connection to the right people. The program, called *Oh, Doctor...!*, written and directed by John Dean, of New York City, would be performed at the Salem Community High School gymnasium in November, 1969.

Dozens and dozens of musicians, vocalists and dancers, as well as stage hands, carpenters and costumers were needed to pull off such an ambitious production. A seventeen-piece community orchestra provided accompaniment for the musical, and a Rock and Roll band played a segment of 1960s music.

This band organized and practiced in the garages of their parents, beginning in the early 1960s. They called themselves *The Invaders*. Original members were John Gaston, Don Nesmith, Steve Mulvaney, Rick Chapman and Bobby Vogt, with Bob Turnage as vocalist and band leader. The band continues playing for different venues today, with original members still active, except Bobby Vogt.

I wish I could remember how I happened to be chosen and who asked me to be a part of it. After forty-five years, some of the details have slipped my mind; but I will never forget the excitement of those two nights, when I was one of the performers in a real Broadway show.

I was a showgirl! A kick-line dancer, wearing black net stockings, a skimpy black costume complete with sequins and feathers! Rehearsals were brutal, but exhilarating; and I got so skinny! During that time, I was probably in the best physical condition of my life.

During rehearsals, Verna Van Horn and I sat together on the stairs backstage; and we became the best of friends. We laughed and giggled like school girls, and she was instrumental in helping me to develop friendships with many, many women who were in our kick line, as well as other performers in the show.

Our dress rehearsal was almost as exciting as the two night performances. I will never forget the faces of my little boys as they watched their mama kick and preen and dance in perfect timing with a long line of identically dressed women. They were mesmerized! I can only imagine how stunned they must have been to see their mother on stage, dancing with many other women! I can still see their faces, with their big eyes focused on their *Mami*, their mouths open in shocked amazement.

The boys and my husband all attended the first night's performance, which took place on November 21, 1969. To my disappointment and his, my husband was called to the hospital just before my stage debut with the kick line, dancing to *Ain't She Sweet,* in the sixth segment of the show. We danced without making one mistake, not one out-of-sync step or kick!

Luckily, he returned to the high school in time to see the last part of the eleventh segment, which included our kick line dancing to *I'm a*

Yankee-Doodle-Dandy. The Finale, which followed, included the whole cast performing *One of Those Songs,* which had also been the opening number. The applause at both performances was tremendous. Breathless and exhilarated, we took our bows, knowing that we had danced our hearts out, and that we would never forget our two evenings of Broadway.

SALEM

Isabel

The First Good Years

Although I had gone to Christian schools all my life, neither I nor my husband had made a real connection with the Lord. We decided that we wanted to go to church, so we started visiting churches. We went to several. Then one day Wayne and Gwen Stanford came to see us. During the conversation, they invited us to come to First Baptist, on Main Street. We visited the church some, but not regularly.

One night in April, 1971, I sat alone in our house, feeling a little depressed, maybe a little sorry for myself. The boys were in bed, asleep; and as he usually did, my husband had gone to the hospital to make late night rounds with his patients.

Someone had sent a Spanish edition of *Decision Magazine,* to me, a publication from Billy Graham's organization. To this day, I don't know who sent it; and now I receive an English edition. That night I picked up the magazine, and as I was reading, conviction came upon my heart.

The article I read was based on the Gospel of Matthew, chapter 7, verses 13-14: *"Go in through the narrow gate, because the gate to hell is wide and the road that leads to it is easy, and there are many who travel it. But the gate to life is narrow and the road to it is hard, and there are few people who find it."* (NIV)

As I continued to read, something happened to me, something special and wonderful; and I knew it was from God. I don't know how I knew that, for no one had ever told me about salvation or how to pray. All I knew was that the experience was incredible. I was so sure that God was within me, it was as if I had gone to Heaven for a few minutes.

I said nothing about any of this when my husband came home, not even as we were talking after we went to bed. We knew nothing of spiritual things, so how could we talk about it?

I didn't sleep all night. I lay beside my husband, thinking about this incredible experience. I knew that God was with me, and I was filled with joy. The next morning I called a friend and told her what had happened to me. She explained to me God's plan of salvation, and I understood immediately that I had become a Christian. The following Sunday morning I made my profession of faith in the Baptist Church, but that was just the beginning.

The day after my conversion, I called my parents in Chicago. First I talked to my father. "Papo, I asked Jesus to come into my heart, the same Jesus you told me about when I was a little girl. And Papo, I received Him!" I could hear in his voice how happy he was for me. My mother came to the phone, and I told her the same thing.

"Isa, I am glad for you! You know, I've heard that Billy Graham is holding a crusade here in Chicago. I wish we could go. I've heard so much about him. But I don't know how we can do it. We don't have a ride." I could hear the longing in her voice.

"Mami," I said, "I'm going to pray that someone will take you to see Billy Graham, and that you and Papo and the person who takes you will all be saved." That's what I did. I prayed with my whole heart for all of them. Doesn't God promise that if we pray, believing, our prayers will be answered?

The next day my parents called to tell me that my brother, José, and his wife, Aidita, took them to the crusade. I will never forget how my father's voice sounded when he told me what wonderful things had happened to them.

"Isa, your mother, your brother and I answered the call when it was given, and we went to the front to receive Jesus as our personal Savior. Isa, I was so close to Billy Graham that I saw what looked like fire in his eyes, like nothing I have ever seen before. We heard the whole service in Spanish. It was wonderful, wonderful."

Papo went on to tell me that Aidita did not go forward, but later I learned that she became a Christian in the Baptist Church where they started to attend. I respected her even more for not going forward with the family at the Billy Graham crusade, just because they did.

My mother's faith grew daily, and it changed her life. Following, are just two examples of her extraordinary faith, which took place a few years later, after she and my father returned to Miami. One windy Sunday morning she and my father visited a Baptist church close to their residence. When the offering plate was passed, she dropped two dollars into it, all she had with her. As they turned a corner on their way home, a gust of wind blew a flurry of leaves along the sidewalk. My mother looked down and could not believe her eyes. A twenty-dollar-bill danced among the leaves. Amazed, she reached down and caught it.

She gave thanks to God for multiplying her small offering by ten times. Her faith continued to surprise me over the years. Jumping ahead a bit, after she and Papo returned to Miami, my husband and I took our annual summer trip to see them. Like always, she asked what I would like to eat. She told me what she planned to cook, all of my favorite foods.

Many of my relatives and friends had heard that we were coming, and several showed up at my parents' apartment at dinner time. I was setting the table when they knocked at the door. My mother welcomed them and told me to invite them to eat with us. Now, my faith in God's promises was and is strong, and I believe His word; but on this day I was concerned. The unexpected guests found places to sit all over the small apartment.

"Don't worry, Isa," she said to me. "Give everyone a plate." She served the food and I did what she told me to do, seeing that everyone received a plate of food. I probably shouldn't compare this day to when Jesus fed thousands with a few loaves of bread and a few fish, but it seemed similar to me! Everyone ate, and there was food left over. We even had dessert!

I had always known that my mother knew some Bible scripture. I remembered hearing her quote things from Psalms at times; and I also remembered something else my father had once told me. He told only me that when he came to The United States to have his eyes treated, he knew that Jesus had healed them. At the time, I didn't understand exactly what he meant, but he was very serious. I knew that he was telling me the truth, even though I didn't grasp the importance of it.

God kept blessing. Eight months after my conversion, as five-year-old Babe was watching a Christmas program on TV, he listened to a pastor and his family as they were giving their testimonies. This touched Babe. When the program was over, he came to me, crying, telling me that he wanted Jesus to come into his heart. I prayed with him, and he lifted his eyes to my face. "Jesus is in my heart, Mama," he said.

I was preparing supper, but I called Dr. Baldwin, the pastor of First Baptist at that time, and he came immediately to our house. I left him to talk with Babe in the living room. After a short time, the pastor came to me and said he had no doubt that Babe understood what he had done and what had happened to him. The next Sunday morning Babe gave his profession of faith. He was so little that Dr. Baldwin stood him on a front pew so the congregation could see him. It was one of the happiest days of my life.

A few months later, following a children's class at church on a Wednesday evening, I opened the door to a very excited Alex. "Hi, Mama," he said, "I am a new Alex!" He explained to me that his teacher, who was the football coach at Salem high school, had led him to the Lord. That left only my husband who had not given his heart to Jesus. I continued to pray for him, for I knew that God was faithful. I had confidence that he would answer my heartfelt prayer.

Needless to say, but I'm glad to say it: While I was not happy about moving to Salem, Illinois, God blessed us so much in those first few years. How could I help but grow to love the community and the people who accepted us, befriended us, took us into a church and loved us?

The following weeks and years were filled with the beginnings of new friendships and more new experiences as a result of The Follies. Verna Van Horn drew me into her circle of friends and acquaintances. Eventually, a large number of us, including husbands, belonged to a group that played volleyball at Oak Park school once a month.

Among them were Jan Williams, Marla Perry, Barbara Ferris, Dixie Haney, Patty Nieman, Irene Davidson, Ruth Ann Wilkerson and Verna Van Horn. There were others, but I simply can't remember everyone's names. My husband and I often had dinner with some of the couples over the years, and we formed some lasting friendships.

Marla invited me to join a Bible study. At first our group numbered seven. Marla Perry, Jean Flannigan, Marty Wilzback, Sue Beeson, Paulette Gregg, Judy Sherman and myself. Eventually Marla remarried and moved to Tennessee; and Verna joined the group, which kept our number at seven.

Originally, we met in each other's homes once a week for Bible study, and we celebrated our birthdays and Christmas the same way; we still do.

Verna and I had a special friendship, right from the beginning of the program's rehearsals. We formed a bond that was never broken. We made shopping trips to the Galleria Mall in St. Louis, where we shopped and ate and laughed and had the best times together.

One day we went into the Merle Norman shop in Salem and tried on wigs and makeup. We laughed at each other like school girls, and we both bought wigs! I still have mine, somewhere.

A year or so after the hospital's Broadway presentation, Verna became pregnant with her son, Danny. I fell in love with two of her maternity dresses, one pink, one black, both stylish, even elegant for maternity wear. Then in the spring of 1971, I discovered that we were going to have our third child, and Verna loaned me those two beautiful dresses. I believe that women feel better about themselves when they wear pretty clothes, especially so when they are pregnant.

On February 13th, 1972, our third son was born. Victor Javier's eyes were dark from the beginning, as was his hair. Like his older brothers, he was a beautiful baby. He loved both his brothers, but he was especially close to Babe.

A few weeks after Victor's birth, my husband accepted Jesus Christ as his savior. He knew I had been praying that he would find the joy my experience with the Lord had given me, but he was a very private person.

"Don't think you are going to see me in front of the church, crying and shaking hands with people," he told me. He was adamant about it.

During final prayer one Sunday morning at church, I stood with my eyes closed, praying that there would be a good response to this revival message. When I raised my head, I saw exactly what Armando had assured me I never would see.

My handsome husband stood facing the congregation, tears running down his face, shaking hands with his church family. I could hardly believe my eyes! God is so good, and I know that He answers prayer, as

He answered mine that morning. Since then, I have continued to pray for family members and friends; and I give my testimony every time I have an opportunity.

In the following months, Verna's husband and Armando became friends; and the four of us enjoyed going out for dinner together, laughing and visiting, building a strong relationship. Dr. Van Horn, a local dentist, was one of the nicest, friendliest men we ever knew. He wore a constant smile, and he had a genuine love of children, who numbered many among his patients. Well regarded throughout the community, his dental practice was a definite asset to Salem.

Their daughter, Linda, and our Babe were friends from their early days in Mrs. Hancock's pre-school. Their friendship endured through high school, and they even attended homecoming together.

Verna and I were not afraid to attempt new experiences, well, new for me. We took golf lessons at the course in Sandoval. We bought everything we could possibly need: golf clubs, bags, shoes, balls, tees. Verna played fairly well, but I was a disaster at playing golf! We had such fun, laughing like crazy at our escapades.

My husband and I joined the Salem Country Club. He really didn't have time to play, and I played only a couple of times with another friend, Mary Duncan. I was, truly, very bad at golf. No golfer worth the name would have wanted me for a partner or to play in a tournament.

It is true that no one is immune to tragedy. Dr. Van Horn passed away suddenly, still in his forties. The loss of such a good man, at such a young age, was heartfelt by all who knew him. As friends do, we rallied around Verna and supported her in every way we could.

As trite as it sounds, time passes, and life goes on. Several years later, when Verna became engaged to Larry Linder, we were happy for her. It was my pleasure to host a celebration for her in our house, where our circle of friends wished her every happiness and joy.

Nothing reaffirms life as much as weddings and new babies. On October 7th, 1975, our family became complete. From the day she was born, Christina Isabel was our little princess, feminine to her core. Practically from birth, she loved beautiful clothes, music and dancing, everything that had brought me such joy when I was a child.

Like Alex and Babe, my two younger children became Christians at very young ages. Victor was saved at church when he was seven, under the pastorate of Dr. Hampton. I always prayed with my children, and Christina was saved when she was at home with me. She was five years old.

All four of my children were brought up going to Sunday school and church every Sunday, where they learned scripture and heard Old Testament stories. I believe Sunday school is still important, but many churches no longer offer it as an option. I wonder if the loss of this old tradition might have something to do with the paths taken by so many young people today, paths that lead to heart ache and destruction. I wonder….

In our sons we see our husbands, our fathers, our brothers. They may have some of our traits, talents and characteristics; but, as men, they relate to their fathers. In our daughters, we look for bits of ourselves, I think. Maybe a flash of the eyes, a similar dimple or smile, maybe even a hot temper. When our daughters become adults, we are still their mothers; but we also relate to them as women. Not until I had children did I realize how much my Mami and Papo loved me.

We want to protect our children, to shield them from every bad thing, from every hurt and pain, from illness. My husband and I were about to learn that we have limited abilities in these areas. We would learn just how little control we have over some areas of our lives, and that, in those times, only the love and grace of God can carry us through them.

SALEM

Isabel

The Valley of the Shadow

Not long after we moved to Salem, my parents and my brothers' families left Chicago. I think Mami and Papo, with José and his wife left first, closely followed by Juan and Marta. They all returned to Miami, where there were other relatives and where they no longer had to face Northern Illinois winters.

José and his family stayed with Aidita's parents for a while before they found a place they liked. Juan and Marta fell in love with a nice house that met their needs, complete with a swimming pool. They lived there for many years, were there when hurricane Andrew devastated nearby Homestead, Florida.

After their children grew up and got married, Juan and Marta no longer cared about the pool. Juan was diagnosed with Parkinson's disease around that time, so they sold their house and moved to a smaller place with less upkeep.

It took my parents time to find a suitable place. They first rented a little apartment next to the home of Papo's nephew. From there they found a house close to the home of the Volpes', the family in whose house Mami had worked for several years. The third move proved to be the last one, to a first-floor apartment in a building close to Juan. This is where they lived for the remainder of my father's life.

We went to see our family in Florida every summer, something we looked forward to each year. The time I spent with my mother and father were more precious than I realized, for Papo died on Friday, February 18,

1977, at the age of eighty-two, only a few years after they went back to Miami. Saturday and Sunday visitations were held for him in *Funeraria Caballero*, a huge funeral home in Miami.

The number of friends and family at the visitations amazed me. Relatives from New York and other parts of the country, all the friends who had once lived in Güines, people from *La Progresiva,* extended family members and friends of theirs—it was incredible.

Papo had lived in this country less than twenty years, but he was loved and respected by hundreds. The progression of vehicles that accompanied his body to the cemetery was a fitting tribute to my beloved father, one he deserved. No one could ever have asked for a better father. Before the year was over, I would wish for the comfort of his presence one more time.

That same year, Alex was a junior in high school, Babe and Victor both in grade school and Christina a toddler; so we were kept on our toes and busy every moment of every day. Our house in Country Club Estates was quiet only at night, and it was not unusual for my husband to receive calls to the hospital at all hours, even then.

Alex liked sports, and he played varsity basketball in high school; but golf was what he loved to play most. He set a record, making two "holes in one" when he was pretty young. One of those he accomplished on the 1st hole. He seemed to have a natural ability for golf.

Babe played on the Selmaville grade school basketball team. There were practices after school every week day. Like most families, my husband and I thought it would continue this way until all four of the children grew up, got married and moved into homes of their own. How wonderful that dream, simple as it is, would have been. The dream died the morning I received a call from the principal at Babe's school.

"Mrs. Aguilar, your son is ill. He has his head down on the desk and says that he doesn't feel good."

I called my husband and we drove to the school as quickly as we could. We brought Babe home and watched him closely, hoping he would feel better soon. He sat down to watch TV, and he told us he saw two of everything, double-vision. Armando picked up the phone and called Dr. Kenneth Smith, a neurosurgeon at Cardinal Glennon Hospital, who came to see patients in Salem. Armando was acquainted with him through the clinic and Salem Hospital.

Dr. Smith saw Babe right away, and he arranged for him to have a brain scan at Cardinal Glennon as soon as possible. From the very first, my husband knew that something was dreadfully wrong. The diagnosis was every parent's nightmare. A tumor had formed in the right portion of Babe's brain. Neurosurgeons agreed that surgery was the best course of immediate treatment, and the operation was scheduled as soon as possible.

I didn't know what to do. I could not believe there might be something terribly wrong with one of our children. *Those things happen to other people, not to us.* It was the first prick of a thorn that drew blood from my heart, from my soul, a prick that I often thought would surely take my life.

On the day of the surgery, the younger children were not with us. Dr. Baldwin, our pastor, Armando, Alex, my mother and I waited together while the surgeons worked on our little Babe. After a long while, Alex went outside the hospital and took a walk. When he returned, he told us what he had seen.

"While I was walking, I noticed shadows cast on the sidewalk by the sun," he said. "I don't know what it means, but I know it was telling me something." He paused. "Mami, it was the shadow of a big cross, a huge cross."

I never forgot what Alex described, and there have been times when I wondered if the shadow of the cross was a sign meant to warn us of tremendous suffering to come. Or was it a promise to us that the Christ who lived beyond the suffering would be with us during whatever circumstances we would face? I have found the promise to be true.

It seemed like a long time, but time is relative to a given situation. When Dr. Smith came out to talk to us, his news was not good. Looking back, I realize what terror my husband must have been holding inside. As a doctor most of his adult life, he had seen every possible physical condition that can attack our frail human bodies. Times too numerous to count, he had been faced with delivering bad news to people in waiting rooms.

Dr. Smith told us what kind of tumor was growing in Babe's brain, and I will never forget the devastation and grief that swept over Armando's face. Helpless to make his son better, he wept. "He will not live a year." The words seemed torn from his throat.

It is difficult to describe all I was feeling, even after all this time. Unbearable grief, stunned disbelief, shock, denial. "Yes! He will live a year!

He will live more than that!" From that moment, I refused to believe that my precious Babe would not live to be a man.

The first few months of recovery were difficult for him. He went through a course of radiation. The left side of his face was drawn, much like the victims of stroke. Dr. Rubio and Nora sometimes took Babe to St Louis for his treatments, even taking him to a unique restaurant as a special treat. They were always so good to us.

Babe resumed his life, much as he had known it. He went back to school, did well and enjoyed being a part of things again. Christina, only two years old when the first surgery was performed, adored her brother. He loved to kiss her, sometimes drooling a little, perhaps a bit on purpose, I think; and she would push away from him. With time, the symptoms went away.

"Oh, Babe! Babe!" She protested, wiping away his kiss, and Babe always laughed. Christina had no memory of her brother before he became ill. His attitude toward his illness was astounding for one so young. He talked about it with anyone who asked, even pulling away his wig to show off his baldness after he lost his hair. Somehow, we adjusted. Babe's radiation treatments became the new normal.

During Alex's senior year in high school, he fell in love with a sweet girl named Lisa Hofelich. They were so young, so much in love and they wanted to get married. I think we, along with her parents, discussed all the reasons why they should wait to marry; but in the end we all agreed to allow it.

They were married on May 26th, 1979, only days before the graduation ceremony. The graduates were seated alphabetically, so Alex and Lisa sat side-by-side. When diplomas were presented, Lisa followed Alex across the stage. It was a happy moment, one we treasured, a symbol that good things continue to happen, even when circumstances are not the best.

In the summer of 1979, we took our annual vacation to see relatives and friends in Miami. Armando had bought a new white Cadillac that same year, and we sailed along the interstate like a schooner on a smooth sea, Babe, Victor and Christina in the back seat. I think cars had seat belts then, but they were not yet mandatory. None of us was buckled in.

Those tiny televisions had just come out, the ones that plugged into the car cigarette lighters. We had bought one, and I was trying to find reception on the little screen. As we drew near Nashville, TN, the screen suddenly flashed a picture.

"Oh, look, Armando! I got reception!" At my exclamation, my husband turned his head toward the device in my hands. Before there was even time to register what was happening, the car ran off the interstate highway, down a steep embankment, flipping end-over-end three times. I looked toward the back seat in time to see Christina's legs flying overhead.

The car came to a rest on its top. The next thing I remember is crawling out of the passenger side door. I stood up and saw a stocky-looking man, standing only a few steps from me. I reached out and touched his chest, felt the warm sun on the red shirt he wore, beseeching him to help me. He pointed toward my car.

"Look," he said to me. "Your children are alright. Everything is fine." I looked back at the car and saw that my husband and three children were out of the car. I turned to speak to the man again. He was gone. Shaken, I rushed to check on my family. Except for a tiny scratch on my foot, there was not one injury to any of us.

"Where did the man go?" I asked them.

"What man?"

"The man that was standing right there when I got out of the car!" I pointed to the spot where the man in jeans and red shirt had been standing, only a few feet from the car. "Didn't you see him?" Neither my husband nor any of the children had seen the man I saw, the man I touched.

"But he was right *there!*" I insisted. They looked at me as if I had lost my mind. To this day, I know I saw that man, and I know what he said to me. (There was a sense of *déjà vu* when I thought about him again, later. I was reminded of the woman who had come to my assistance when I was in such despair in a Madrid, Spain, airport, holding a soiled, sick baby. Not everyone believes in angels, but I do. How else can I explain a sudden appearance and impossible disappearance?)

Several cars had pulled onto the interstate's shoulder, and a few people had come down the steep incline to see if we were hurt. A call had gone out for assistance. While we waited, Victor roamed around the car, snapping pictures with an old camera. My husband had put a new battery in it; and before we left home, we had given it to Victor, just so he would have something to do on the trip.

The car was totally demolished, doors ajar, unbelievably smashed. After the wrecker pulled it upright and took it to the police station, we checked our luggage in the trunk, which had to be pried open. Everything was intact. I checked the contents of my makeup kit, thinking that everything inside must surely be ruined; but not one article was out of place or broken.

Within a couple of hours, we had been taken to the airport, where we picked up a rental car; and were soon on our way to Miami, as if having a horrendous car crash was nothing unusual! The fact that our wrecked car had air conditioning accounted for the windows being rolled up, but what kept the children and us from being ejected through them like bullets, as happens so often in violent crashes? What kept us from being bruised and battered, from suffering broken bones or bloody cuts?

After all Babe had been through, our agonizing over him, all the prayers that been offered in our behalf for the past couple of years—is it possible that God, in His infinite love for us, had granted us mercy, that He might have sent at least one angel to soften that car's landing? I don't know, but I thanked Him then; and I have continued to thank Him, even during the hardest moments.

All that being said, we had a good time with our family in Miami. Not one family member or friend could believe us when we told them about our "most wonderful adventure." It was one I never wanted to repeat!

On December 22nd, 1980, Armando and I received an early Christmas gift. Alex and Lisa became parents of a beautiful baby girl. They named her Alexa, and she was perfect, a gift from God that we needed at just the right time. Like all grandparents do, we doted on that sweet baby, ecstatic at each new tooth, her first step, all those things we always remember.

The next few years held four more surgeries for Babe, but he lived as normal a life as possible. He enjoyed high school, taking part in everything he could. His graduation picture is of a handsome boy, showing very little, if any, residual effects of the first surgery. The semester after he graduated, he enrolled in Kaskaskia College.

A long-held dream of my husband's was to build a new house, one situated closer to the clinic and the hospital. We found a perfect lot on the north side of Salem, one that was located, nearly centered, between the two places; and the building process began, which took close to a year, I think.

Victor and Christina were both musically talented, and Christina, especially, loved to dance. We enrolled her in dance classes; and from the time she was five years old, she took ballet and tap and loved every kind of dance. When we moved into the new house on Hawthorn Road, Victor was in eighth grade and Christina in fifth at Franklin Park school, across from the Medical Center and Doctor's Nursing Home.

The new house was completed, and we moved into it in 1984. That same year, my mother became unable to care for herself adequately. The family decided that we were better able to look after her, so my brother, José, accompanied her to Salem. My husband and Dr. Rubio owned Doctor's Nursing Home, adjacent to their clinic, no more than one or two minutes from our house.

Mami stayed in our house the first night, and the next day she moved into her room in the nursing home, where my husband had already made arrangements for her care. I was concerned that she might not like it, and she didn't. She preferred being with me. However, her condition was such that I could not take adequate care of her, my desperately ill son and two children, both active in school, sports and private lessons. In time, my mother grew to accept her new home. I brought her to us for meals when I could, and I tried to spend time with her every day possible.

All these events transpired close together. Even though Babe's condition deteriorated, he was excited about moving into the new house. The boys hauled several boxes of clothing in the back of a pickup truck, at least one of which they lost. When I discovered that the box contained my favorite purple sweater, I sent them back the way they had come to look for the box, which had already been retrieved by someone.

It sounds almost ludicrous that I would remember that sweater, with all that was going on around me. Dozens of boxes filled with papers, photographs, books and things that I wanted to keep had lost their importance. They were stacked and stored away in the finished basement, where most of them still are, to this day.

In the new house, Babe, Victor and Christina had rooms upstairs. It was so nice to be living in it, finally; but the shadow and dread that hovered over us dimmed the joy. During the two weeks following our move into the new house, Babe slept poorly, often coming downstairs to our bedroom, holding his head in agony. Armando always got up and gave him pain medication; and I knew that my husband wished he could take his son's suffering into his own body, just as I did.

One Sunday morning at church, something happened to Babe. He listened intently as the choir director related how the words of an old hymn came to be written. *It is Well With My Soul* was penned by a man whose wife and children were lost at sea, leaving him desolate. At some point he sailed to the spot where the ship had gone down, and, while gazing at the sea waves, he said, "It is well with my soul."

Then the choir began to sing, and the Holy Spirit seemed to fill the building: "*When peace like a river attendeth my way, When sorrows like sea billows roll, Whatever my lot, Thou hast taught me to say, 'It is well, it is well with my soul.'*"

Slowly, Babe raised both his arms, a silent testimony to his faith in God. This was not a common practice in the congregation, not then and not now. But the outpouring of love and encouraging words, as well as the hugs Babe received from most of the church that morning, were heart-warming.

Our boy grew worse, and we took him back to Cardinal Glennon Hospital, where a final surgery was performed. This one took over six hours, and the waiting was torture. Several people from our church were with us, along with our pastor. When the doctor came out to talk with us, I consciously didn't listen to the details he was explaining. My husband and I tried so hard to be brave, not to cry in front of anyone. I'm not sure that was the best way.

When they finally allowed us to see Babe, he was in a bed. Alex saw him first. "How're ya doin', Babe!" Babe responded to him, circling his thumb and index finger indicating that everthing was "OK."

Of course, it was not. While he was still at Cardinal Glennon, he went into a coma. There was nothing more they could do for him. We brought him to Salem Hospital for a while, but there was no change. He needed full-time care; so my husband admitted him into the Doctor's Nursing Home, right beside the Medical Clinic. Armando was able to look in on him during the day, and Mami kept her own vigil.

For seven months our lives revolved him. We were so concerned about each other: me, for my husband and children, the children, for their parents, my husband, for all of us…and every one of us, for Babe. When school was dismissed every weekday afternoon, Victor and Christina walked across the street to the nursing home, where I was sitting with Babe. Most afternoons they did their homework in Babe's room, which held a sofa and small table.

I took them home and made dinner, saw that they were well-fed, spent time with them before they bathed and got ready for bed. Armando took care of them while I went back to sit with Babe, usually until midnight or later. This was our life for seven months.

At first, the nursing staff found my mother in Babe's room a few times, always gently removing her, assuring her that they were taking good care of her grandson. Eventually, they set up some kind of barrier that allowed her to sit outside his door where she could see him, and then she was content. Although she suffered from confusion, she knew that the boy lying in that bed was her grandson. She loved all of her grandchildren so very much.

One night, actually around three o'clock in the morning, the nursing home called us to come to Babe immediately. Something had happened with the aspirator, and our son was critical. Armando dressed and left as quickly as possible. In desperation, I called Helen Leckrone to come stay with Victor and Christina, and then called my dear friend, Janet Barker, to please come. When I arrived at the nursing home, Janet was already there. We stayed outside Babe's room while my husband and the nurses worked with him; and she went in with me when they called for me.

Graphic details of what was happening with our unconscious Babe are not necessary; but he was so pale, so white when we went into his room. Janet watched him with me, and then we went outside. Janet prayed with me for a long time, asking God for grace and strength. Dr. Rubio, my husband, so many were there to try to help in every way possible.

Janet was faithful to pray for all of us, and I have never forgotten her love and patience with me during that time. I don't know how I would have survived without the love and prayers of so many of our friends.

One night, as I sat beside Babe's bed, I rested my head close to his and gently touched his cheek. The thought came to me that he might be worried about me, about his family, so I talked to him.

"You're all right, Babe," I said, "and Mama is all right, too. Papa and I are going to be just fine." I stroked his beautiful face, and I saw tears run from one eye, down his cheek. He heard me! I am certain that he heard me and understood what I was saying. As I watched him, I thought about the day he was born, the toddler he had been, the little boy before the brain tumor.

I think in that moment, in my own mind, I let my son go. I didn't have to say the words, but I knew that he could not continue in the state he was, that he would never wake up and be our Babe again. He was approaching the gates of Heaven.

Then, quietly, on April 22nd, 1985, our second son, Armando, lovingly called Babe all his life, slipped away from us. He would have been nineteen in October. I know that he went into the loving arms of Jesus. I am as sure of that as I am that I gave birth to him. Without that assurance, how could I live?

Family and friends supported us in every way. Many relatives came from Florida, even from New York, to attend the visitation and funeral services for Babe. Among the hymns I requested was *It Is Well With My Soul,* one that continues to give me comfort. Also at my request, Karen Watson and Myron Lloyd sang the beautiful song, *More Than Wonderful,* recorded by Patty Sandy and Larnell Harris and beloved by many that year.

Helen Leckrone had written encouraging notes and letters to me during the long months while Babe was in the nursing home. Later she told me that Babe had talked to her about his concern for me, that he knew how much I loved him and how I would miss him. I remembered the moments when I had reassured him, and I knew that I had done the right thing.

During those days right after Babe's passing, I did not experience the dreadful agony and grief one might expect on losing a child. Instead, it felt as if God were lifting me up, keeping my feet above the fire, as if His mighty arms were completely wrapped around me, enveloping me with His compassion, grace and tender mercies. I was comforted in ways impossible to explain.

And so it was that our lives continued without our second son, named for his father, Armando, our Babe. He has been gone from us for thirty years, but there are times when I feel his presence. I gaze at the large portrait of him on the wall, and my mother's heart talks to him. I think he hears it.

Life Abundantly

In the days and months that followed, I realized how traumatized my two younger children had been by Babe's illness and death. Christina was only ten years old by then, and Victor was in seventh grade. He had been closest to Babe, and the loss of his older brother shattered him.

Victor graduated from Franklin Park in 1986, and he would enter high school in the fall. But Babe had been such a presence during his four years at SCHS, remembered by students and teachers, alike. It was more than young Victor could overcome. So we enrolled him at a Lutheran boarding school in Missouri for his freshman year. That year softened the edges for Victor, and he began his sophomore year in Salem High School, where he excelled in sports. He played varsity basketball and he ran track; but he was exceptional in high jump.

In 1990 Victor graduated from SCHS. He enrolled in Hannibal-Lagrange University, graduating in 1996, with a B.A. in Business Administration and a Minor in Marketing. These degrees have served him well in his career as Account Manager with major corporations.

Alex and Lisa had their own little family to comfort them. My husband and I did all we knew to help Victor; and eventually he was able to accept his loss, I think, but never fully resigned all during his school years.

Christina has a natural affinity for music. At the age of five, she started taking piano lessons. She loved those ebony and ivory keys! She learned quickly, and her teachers enjoyed working with her. In elementary school band she played the flute, which she continued to play in the concert band in high school. She also played saxophone in the jazz band, but her love for the piano never waned.

Dancing comes to most Cubans as naturally as breathing, and I was thrilled when moving to music made Christina as happy as it did me. We enrolled her in classes: tap, ballet, jazz and modern dance. She became proficient in Flamenco, a Spanish dance, her first year at Butler University. Dancing took her to a different sphere, and it was almost as if she became another person when she danced. I never tired of watching her practice for recitals and performances.

As I adjusted to living with the void left by the loss of our second son, my group of friends continued to rally around me, supporting and nurturing me in ways I cannot number. We continued to meet once a week, celebrating birthdays and holidays, as before. I am still blessed to have them in my life. The current members of the group, which used to number seven, are now only six: Janet Barker, Sue Beeson, Paulette Gregg, Katie Helm, Judy Sherman and me. (Original member Marla Perry, remarried and now resides in Tennessee. Verna Van Horn Linder, who became the seventh one after Marla moved away, is deceased. We and Marla consider that she is still our seventh member.)

Gradually, our family returned to a measure of normal. My husband continued his practice, making daily rounds at the hospital and seeing patients in the office and adjoining nursing home. Victor, in high school, and Christina, in grade school kept me busy. One of the highlights for Armando and me took place during that time. We became two of the chaperones who accompanied the Spanish class to Europe. Even though Christina was still in grade school, we were allowed to take her with us.

From New York, we flew to London, England, where we visited some of the famous touristy sites for two or three days. We even saw a play, *54th Street,* in a live theater.

While boarding the ferry along with another high school group from Indiana, one of the luggage carts fell into the water of the English Channel. All of the suitcases, except one, were recovered; but Victor and Christina were among those whose luggage fell into the water, soaking every item inside. The luggage was sent to our hotel in France, where efforts were made to dry the clothing; but some things, including shoes, were not completely dry. We placed them inside the window sills to air dry as much as possible, for we were going to another city the next day.

From France we traveled by train to Spain. I did not like it! The noise and speed of the train made me uneasy. To tell the truth, I was afraid. I spent the night with Christina in a sleeper-car full of girls, while Armando, Victor and the other boys were in a separate car. I don't remember sleeping much. The swaying of the car at such a high speed on the rails was not comforting to me.

We toured many beautiful cities in Spain, places we had not visited when my husband, Alex and I had fled from Cuba in 1963. Madrid was part of our itinerary, but we weren't able to visit any of the areas we had seen back then. When we returned to France, we toured through beautiful country sides and saw several towns and cities, but Paris was the highlight, for more than the Eiffel tower!

Somehow, Victor and a couple of his friends managed to slip away from the group. They got lost and had no idea how to get back to the hotel. They flagged a cab that stopped for them, but they couldn't speak French and the driver could not speak English. He finally agreed to take them, and with hand signs and signals he managed to deliver them to the right hotel. I don't know why at least one of the boys didn't remember the name of the hotel. I do know it took a long time and a lot of money before they arrived.

The good thing about all that drama was that I slept through it! We were exhausted with the constant travel and activity and the responsibility of the children. I have always enjoyed traveling, but this trip was the least pleasant for me. My career as travel chaperone for a bunch of teenagers was short-lived. The boys and girls were delightful, but every day was exhausting. Due to the number of cities and areas we were required to cover in a short time, we didn't have a chance to rest adequately before the next day's agenda. That one experience as group chaperone was enough for me.

A few years later, Armando and I traveled to Europe on our own. We flew from New York to Barcelona, Spain, where we boarded a ship and sailed the Mediterranean, with Italy as our main destination. The ship docked at several beautiful Italian cities all along the coast. The whole experience was wonderful, but we especially enjoyed Rome.

Armando and I became separated in the Vatican. It is vast, and I believe he actually became lost among all those magnificent corridors, statuary and antiquities. I was uneasy, even scared, until he reappeared. It's easy for me to imagine all kinds of dramatic situations in unfamiliar places.

The ship returned us to Spain, to Madrid for our departure. If there had been time, I would have loved to find Gaztambide, #115, where we had lived in 1963 for four months. I will never forget those precious first days of freedom from Fidel Castro's revolution. Incredibly, our flight back to the states began at Barajas Airport, where I had met the angel who helped me with my sick baby so many years before. The circle was complete.

On May 11th, 1990, ten years after the birth of Alexa, another baby girl was born to Alex and Lisa. They named her Olivia. It was wonderful to have a baby in our lives again. Armando and I loved being grandparents. We looked forward to having more, which would happen in the course of time.

In 1993, Christina graduated from Salem High School. She enrolled in Butler University, and she graduated with a Bachelor's Degree in 1997. She continued with her education at the University of Illinois and received her Master's Degree in Spanish Literature in 2003.

It was gratifying to us and to her when she was employed by SCHS as a Spanish teacher. She also formed and coached a dance team made up of students, which entertained at basketball half-times. Christina sometimes performed with them, and it was with joy and pride that we watched her do what she loved most—dancing.

On August 5th, 2006, Christina married Ben DeVerger. They live in St Louis, Missouri, where their home now includes three sons: Ben's fourteen-year-old son, Devon, who is an incredible big brother; Alexander Armando, born April 1st, 2008; and Lorenzo Javier, born January 21, 2014.

Their second son, sweet Angelo, was stillborn on September 17th, 2011. Watching our daughter and her husband go through the loss of a son was a thorn that tore our hearts. Of all the possible hurts that threaten our children, this is the one we most dread, the one that leaves the deepest scars. Only God's love, comfort and the promise of being reunited gets us through it.

Christina's passion for music continues. She plays keyboard at her church regularly, something that gives her joy, a means of worship for her that can inspire others, as well.

Becoming great-grandparents holds special joys and blessings. On February 19th, 1997, our granddaughter, Alexa, gave birth to a baby girl, Sarah. I loved that she chose this name for her daughter, the name of my special aunt, *Tia Sara,* who had been such a presence in my life in Cuba.

We were not yet finished with cancer. Specifically, cancer was not yet finished with us. In 2008, I was diagnosed with breast cancer. Fortunately for me, it was in an early stage. I had surgery to remove the tumor, followed by courses of radiation and chemo, which caused me to lose handfuls of my hair within a short time.

Rather than wait for all my hair to fall out, Sue Beeson, my beautician friend, came to my house and gently shaved my head. She was the kindest, sweetest woman to me that day, assuring me that my hair would return, which it did. Going through the treatments was not pleasant, but in comparison to Babe's, it was nothing. There has been no recurrence, but I continue with follow-up treatment.

That same year, we became great-grandparents again, which was a wonderful reaffirmation of life. Christina's son, Alexander, (often called Xander) was born on April 1st, the first boy to join our ranks of grandchildren. Less than a month later, on May 11th, Alexa's son, Gabriel, (Gabe) was born. The next year, on December 31st, 2009, Audrey was born to Alexa. So we had three babies join the family in less than two years. They are all delightful children.

In 2011 I went to the emergency room with an episode of atrial fibrillation, a chronic condition I've had for a long time. Several periods of fibrillation had taken place recently, and I knew what to expect; but this time there was chest pain. I was in the hospital for one and a half hours, getting a chest x-ray and blood tests done.

The next day, the radiologist wanted me to repeat the chest x-ray and get a CT-scan. After looking at everything, he called my husband and me into his office. He told us that I had a nodule in the right lung. We were concerned because of the breast cancer I had battled three years earlier.

He and my husband agreed that I should see a pulmonologist for a second opinion. The pulmonologist made a January 5th appointment for me with the radiology department at Barnes Hospital in St. Louis. Following this second CT-scan, the doctor called us into his office. Both scans were on his desk, for us to compare. The first scan, taken a few weeks earlier, clearly showed the nodule; but the new scan was different. The nodule was not there!

"It's gone! It's gone!" The doctor's voice was so excited, I got excited, too!

"Are you sure?" I asked. "Please explain this to me again. What do I need to do now?" I thought there might be more tests to be done.

"Now you go home and enjoy the rest of your life."

I know that I have mentioned miracles. I also know that many physicians hesitate to say the word. But I praise God, give Him all the glory and thank Him with all my heart, because the nodule that was in my lung disappeared. Praise the Lord!

CATCHING UP

Sonia

In the early pages of my story, I mentioned my first best friend, Sonia Romero, who lived near our house. I related how she loved my piano, how much she wanted to take lessons, which was not possible. Six years later, she surprised me and my mother when she came to see us only days after my fifteenth birthday, surprising us even more when she sat down to play perfectly, a classical music recital on my piano.

Since I went to boarding school, I didn't see Sonia again until she came to the pre-wedding party, thrown for me by my friends. She married and had a sweet baby boy. I went to see them soon after the baby was born and discovered that the child was not well. While working on this book, I learned from my husband that he had treated the baby, and it was he who had to tell Sonia that her little son would not survive.

What I have since discovered about Sonia shows what an amazing woman she was and still is. She has lived her adult life under the rule of Communism, but she has done so with dignity and skill.

Sonia's burning desire to learn how to play the piano fueled her courage to work toward that goal. She once stood outside a piano teacher's house, listening to students play. She noticed that newer students practiced in a room in back of the house, many with a poor sense of rhythm. One day she approached the teacher and told her what she had observed. Already aware of the problem, the teacher suggested that Sonia come help with these students, which she did. The teacher was so impressed with Sonia's skill that she offered to give her piano lessons at no charge. That was the beginning of Sonia's incredible career.

I learned only recently that Sonia had been giving piano lessons as she progressed in her music studies. One of my Cuban friends, Maria Victoria, who resides in California, told me that her sister received piano lessons from Sonia. These lessons would have taken place before the mass exodus from Cuba, probably while Armando and I were still there. Sonia let nothing interfere with her determination to learn all she could.

Eventually she attended the Music Conservatory and became a concert pianist, in Cuba called a *concertist*. She took a year of Repertoire of Classical Music. In time, Sonia also received Master's degrees in two subjects, Cuban Literature and Spanish.

Cuban Alicia Alonso was an internationally renowned ballet dancer, performing all over the world. When she retired from public performing, she opened a dance studio at the Liceo in Güines.

Two days a week she gave lessons there. Through large studio windows, Sonia often watched students practice; and it wasn't long before the idea of a formerly successful exchange popped into her head.

As with her first piano teacher, Sonia bartered with ballerina Alicia Alonso: classical piano to accompany her students as they practiced in exchange for ballet lessons. Her heart and strength of will and spirit continue to be an inspiration to me. Sonia didn't let anything or anyone defeat her. Eventually she became an Inspector in Classic Dance and Music. She is truly an amazing woman.

How the lives of so many former friends and neighbors from Güines continue to intertwine is entertaining, as well as amazing. Maria Laura, another good friend of mine from Cuba, lives in Boyton Beach, Florida, not far from Miami, where many, many Cubans live.

Years after we left Cuba, Sonia's daughter, Carilyn, moved to Florida. She is a physical therapist in a hospital, where a major part of her responsibility it to treat patients in their homes. Sonia knew Maria Laura from the years they both attended La Escuela de Maestros (School of Teachers) where Maria Laura, whom we call Chucha, studied Elementary Education and art. She became a kindergarten teacher. Carilyn had heard that her mother's friend lived in the area, so she located the address and took her mother to reunite with Chucha.

Just last year I was privileged to visit with Sonia and her daughter in Maria Laura's home. It was as if fifty years disappeared, as if we had never been separated, As all of us do when revisiting old friends and old times, we three women spent time looking at old photographs. Among them were pictures of cartoon characters that Chucha had painted directly onto the plaster walls of my husband's office, in the house my father had given to me as a wedding present.

The photos were black and white, but the detail and expressions of the Disney characters were remarkable. Maria Laura's artistic skill was unsurpassed. The little characters had seemed to leap from the walls, their brilliant colors and smiles ready to help any timid child to relax. When Carilyn saw the photographs, she spoke.

"Mami, I've seen these before! I've been in this room! One day I went to the doctor with Grandma, and these paintings were on his office walls."

As it turned out, the physician was Dr. Barroso, the same doctor who had moved into our house immediately after we left Cuba—the one who slept with his wife in our bed, ate on the dishes my parents had given to me, sat in our chairs and saw patients in my husband's medical office! After all those years, what were the odds that I would meet someone who had seen and remembered those paintings? And that the "someone" would be the daughter of my childhood friend?

There were tears when Sonia and I were reunited, of course, and lots of remembering, catching up. Fortunately, I was able to hear her play the piano one more time, a treat I had not experienced since I was fifteen years old. She played classical pieces from memory, and she could play any song she heard.

I don't know if Sonia and I will be able to see each other again, but we now have lots of photos taken during our visit. I have her cell phone number, so we can keep in touch. We will never forget our childhood friendship and how much we still mean to each other. I have heard a rumor that she may be planning to join her daughter in Florida. I can think of nothing that would make our trips to Miami more pleasant.

A school for gifted children, not surprisingly titled "The Lenin School," enrolls those who possess superior intelligence, who consistently make high grades. Sonia's children had been admitted to this school, a credit to her passion for learning and her dedication to being the best she could be. I suppose I cannot fault this school, for many now professional people have graduated from it; and many of them have left Cuba.

Freddy Morris

After I lost contact with my very first boyfriend, Freddy Morris, at Candler College, I never saw him again. As I mentioned earlier, Freddy was the son and heir of a Philip Morris Tobacco Company magnate. Not long after Fidel Castro became the Supreme Ruler of Cuba, he nationalized all the businesses, companies and factories, regardless of who had owned them. This included the Philip Morris Tobacco Company.

I never learned what course Freddy's life took after we became adults, but I had heard that he was to inherit millions of dollars from his father, upon his twenty-fifth birthday. The amount was staggering to me.

I don't know if Freddy had been able to leave Cuba before Fidel Castro banned travel out of the country; but either way, he would have lost his vast inheritance. Castro's government would have taken the majority of it, had Freddy remained in Cuba. Regardless of when he went to the United States, the money stayed in Cuba.

I learned that Freddy had once come to see Juan, my brother, at his office. I think this occurred after Juan, unfortunately, had developed Parkinson's disease, a progressive neurological condition that eventually took his life. That was the last trace I had of Freddy Morris.

In spite of attempts to discover what eventually happened to him, whether he had/has a family, children, grandchildren, I have not been successful. A friend told me that Freddy had passed away, but I have no details. He remains only the long-ago memory of a nice boy, a friend who tried to give me little gifts that sent me to the office of the dreaded principal at Buenavista.

Candler College and La Progressiva

Every year we attend school banquets in Miami, celebrating the anniversary of La Progresiva. Two or three times a year I receive bulletins that feature photos from other alumni and reunions, some held during the summer in people's homes, sometimes on cruises.

A few years ago, I reconnected with some friends in Miami who had attended Candler College and Buenavista. That was a special meeting for me, and we try to meet at least once a year. We are a very small group now. Time often lends a golden aura to the ordinary events of our youth, the things we took for granted; we enjoy talking about and reliving these events from those far-away days.

There are two organizations established by people from Güines, one in California and one in Miami, both of which publish magazines. The one from California is *Las Villas*. Miami's magazine is titled *Ecos Del Mayabeque*. Armando and I look forward to issues from both cities. We read them from cover to cover. We enjoy these meetings with former friends and neighbors very much, where everyone reverts to speaking Spanish, remembering with fondness the years we spent together when we were young and mostly care free.

My Grandfather's House

Knowing that the house which belonged to my mother's father and mother still stands is a source of pleasure and gratification to me. A few years ago, two of my many cousins in Cuba restored the house and now live in it. This was not an easy process for them. None of the working class of Cuba's people can afford much of anything. There are still food lines, product lines, etc. under the Communist regime. If the commodity runs out before everyone in line is served, they must return the next day or another day, whenever the products become available. So obtaining paint and other materials to improve the condition of the house was difficult and expensive.

My grandfather's desk, the heart of the house, remains on the spot where it stood when I was five years old. I don't know if other original pieces of furniture have survived all these years or not, but the desk stands where my grandfather once sat behind it, writing his newspaper articles.

The family Bible is also there, as well as copies of old newspapers and other materials. I can picture is so clearly, my grandfather sitting there in his white suit. Just thinking about them recreates the picture in my mind: he and my grandmother in the living room, where I could see them from my clean bed, the Bible in his lap as he read to her.

The older cousin living in our grandfather's house is Ondina, my mother's niece and good friend. She is quite old now, but she loves to walk down the steps to the street that runs in front of the house, just as my grandmother did so many decades ago. She enjoys visiting with the shop keepers and having ice cream, regardless of how much her younger sister worries about her.

Ondina is the cousin who often came to visit with my mother, the one who first discovered my chocolate-covered face the evening I was supposed to be in bed. I had eaten every bit of the chocolate bar my mother had saved to make hot chocolate. I can still hear the peal of laughter that had burst from Ondina when she saw me.

My grandfather would be so proud to know that some of his descendants still live in that little house. Castro destroyed so much of what was good in Cuba, but he was not able to destroy all family ties and loyalty to a way of life that came before him

Home

Our life in Salem has been satisfying. Armando's medical career here has fulfilled his driving desire to improve the health and quality of life for thousands of his patients. That desire began when he was just a boy, and it has never left him. I never aspired to be anything other than a good wife and mother, and I like to think that I have accomplished a measure of success in that area. I know that my husband shares my love and pride in our children, grandchildren and great-grandchildren.

Many of our good friends have passed away, and we can no longer physically do some of the activities we once enjoyed. Armando retired a few years ago, but he missed his work so much he went back to it! One of his co-workers jokingly asked if he intended to return his retirement gifts, but they were happy to have him back, making rounds at the hospital again. Last year, 2014, he retired for good.

Several years ago, Armando and I looked at condos located in Pelican Bay of Naples, Florida, which were much more expensive than those available in Miami at the time. We were able to sign a contract for one that was not yet under construction. Since then, condos and high-end apartment buildings have sprung up like mushrooms; but their prices are more like exotic orchids!

For the past several years, we have enjoyed two or three week stays there every winter. We keep a car in Naples, so we can drive across the narrow state to see our friends and family on Florida's east coast. We also go once or twice in the summer and fall. The convenience of the condo helps both of us to relax, and the pool is wonderful. The beach is excellent, where the tropical air is the closest thing we can find to our once-beloved Cuba.

Our children enjoy the condo, too. It makes us happy that they are able to spend time on the beach there. It is likely as close as they will ever come to Cuba. Alex was too young to remember anything about the country of his birth. All he, Victor and Christina will know of it is what we tell them. Perhaps they will be able to grasp more, as they read this book.

Throughout the telling of our history, we have stated how grateful we are to live here, in The United States of America. I wish all of my family members and my husband's family members had been able to leave Cuba when we did. Even so, it was a miracle that Castro allowed us to depart, especially coveting doctors as he did.

I hope there is something in my story that might give readers a new appreciation of having been born here. Everyone has thorns in their lives, but they can always discover roses along their journeys, as I have. I must say that there have been many more roses than thorns.

In June, 2015, I underwent open-heart surgery in Barnes Hospital, St Louis, MO. This procedure set back the completion and release of my book, but my recovery is right on schedule. I am doing very well, and I want to thank the many who unfailingly prayed for me during this time. All is well.

I praise God for His constant, abiding love in our lives, for never letting go of our hands, for drawing us close to His side when the paths grow rough. I wish for my readers the same Joy and Peace that I have found in Him, and I thank you for reading this chronicle of our lives in Cuba, Spain, Chicago, Kankakee and, finally, Salem, Illinois.

God Bless and keep you.

Writer's note.

Isabel Aguilar has led a full, rich life, and she has touched numerous people, as well as family and friends with her kindness, prayerful caring and devotion. I asked several to contribute something about their relationship or contact with Isabel, who would rather be called Isa and referred to as *Isabelita.*

The Spanish language contains male and female verb tenses, as well as formal and personal forms of address. To *Isa,* Isabel is a very formal, impersonal use of her name, which I, personally, think is quite beautiful.

From Her Circle of Friends

Janet Barker~ "Isabel Aguilar and I became friends when we met at a Bible study. We both had a hunger and thirst for God's Word. That was the glue that made us very close friends. One special memory stands out in my mind. It was one of those times when the rug of life had been jerked out from under me, Isabel sensed that I desperately needed her. She came to my house and brought me so much comfort. I will never forget how much that meant to me."

Sue Beeson~ "Isabel means so much to me, as she has throughout the years. The faith that she has shown in her life, no matter what came by her way, has been like a beacon of light to me! Through tragedy and disappointment, I have heard her quote Romans 8:28: 'And we know that God causes all things to work together for good to those who love God, to those who are called to His purpose.' The most amazing time was when she lost her dear Babe.

Because of that unbelievable statement, at such a time, any time there was tragedy in my life, I always thought of how strong Isabel was. If she could be that strong, after the loss of her child, what was I complaining about? I could be strong, too!

I remember when we lost a restaurant and had very little money. Isabel knew how I loved pretty things, which we have in common. We like to look nice. She gave me some of her beautiful clothing and loaned me jewelry; but most of all, she gave me hope!

We met when we were very young, and now we are old. We have laughed together and cried together. We have supported, prayed and held each other's hands. Why, we even discovered scripture together! Our friendship has always been centered around the Lord Jesus. How blessed we are!

I love Isabel so much. I hope she always knows that, and that I always pray for her. She is now facing surgery, this next scary thing in her life. We both KNOW that He will be with her through it all! She knows that

I will be praying for the Lord to give her peace, the peace that passes understanding that only He can give.

You are my sister in Christ, Isabel. May we always be of one heart and one song in our minds for our Lord, our God." Your Susita

Paulette Gregg– "When I was asked to share about my Friendship with Isabel, I didn't know where to start. Izy has always been so very special to me in so many wonderful ways. Even though we came from far different backgrounds, we never let that be an obstacle for our friendship. We realized in God we were HIS kids and backgrounds didn't make a difference.

I love Isabel because of everything she is and stands for. For instance:
    *When I needed support she was there,
    *When I needed compassion, she was there,
    *When I needed understanding, she was there,
    *When I needed Love, she was there, and
    *When I needed a FRIEND, she was always there.

As a group we have gone together thru the lose of Dr. and Isabel's precious son, "Babe", Judy's husband, Roger, and our dear friend, Verna Linder; and God has used each of these mountains that we climbed over to grow us strong in HIM, our Faith, and of course our friendships. We have so many special memories it's so hard to find just one to share so I just wanted to say:

Thank You, Isabel for being my Friend. I love you from the bottom of my heart, always praying for you and your precious family."

Katie Helm– "For the past thirty-five years I have heard bits and pieces of fascinating stories about Isabel's life and her family's escape from Cuba. I am so excited to have the rest of her story written in the pages of this book.

I met this beautiful Cuban woman at a women's Tuesday morning Bible study and prayer group in the early 1980's. Isabel was one of the young mothers who gathered to learn more about God and His word. From the first time I met Isabel until now, her passion for life, her family and her relationship with Christ remain evident in her life. Her simple, childlike faith in God and His word have grown strong through the years. Her sense of humor and infectious laugher is contagious.

Through the years, seven women from the original prayer group have remained good friends, now mostly celebrating each other's birthdays, our children's weddings and the births of grandchildren. Over the years, we have laughed together, cried together, celebrated together and prayed together for the needs of each. A rare bond exists between the seven women whose faith in Jesus Christ brought them together and sustained that friendship through many years of trials, joys and sorrows. I consider it an honor and privilege to call Isabel my wonderful friend and prayer partner."

Marla Perry Lackovic~ "Isabel Aguilar has waited a long time to reveal the many memories she has stored in her heart and mind, stories that tell of the great strength, faith and courage that it took for her family to leave their homeland and all their possessions, knowing they would never return. Life was changed forever. Since then, her life continues to be an example of God's great guidance and love.

Part of her journey includes "7" wonderful Christian women who started a Bible study group and became lifelong friends. I and the others have cherished these friendships for almost forty-eight years. In caring and prayer, all have experienced God working in their lives. Through the difficult times and the good times, Isabel has been a true and loyal friend.

Isabel, your book is now a testimony of how God works in the lives of those who love Him."

Judy Sherman~ "Isabel has been more than a friend to me over the years. She has been more like a sister. We are part of a special group of girls that God put together to help us with our ups and downs through life. I call her my prayer warrior, and I have called upon her many times.

I still remember how frightened I was to be alone in my house after my husband died. Isabel suggested that we have a girls' pajama party. Of course, the "J" is silent in Spanish, so Isabel pronounced it "payama party." I had not laughed, like we did that night, for a long time. I had a good night's sleep, and I felt safe with Isabel and my friends in my house. She, indeed, has a special place in my heart. I cannot wait to read her book, for I know she has much to tell. I love you, Isabel! In Christian love."

Friends and Relatives – Former Residents of Cuba

Enrique Ramos Suárez~ "Isabelita has been for me a perfect example of a faithful person. In addition to her pleasant character and graceful personality, she is so strong in her spiritual convictions that she always radiates a kind of peace, a peace that comes only from real believers. Her hands are always attached to the hand of her Lord."

Nery Ramos Melero~ "I always remember Isa as a very attractive young lady, a little shy, but at the same time, very friendly. Her love for music was and still is remarkable. She is still as she always has been. We love her very much."

Guarina Ayala~ "The fondest memories of our beloved childhood and early adulthood are those that always include Isa, my first and favorite cousin, always the 'Belle' of the ball. Yet, much beyond her natural gifts of beauty, elegance and grace, I caught a glimpse into the soul of a beautiful and humble being, who dutifully fulfills her role as a loving daughter, sister, wife, mother and humanitarian, as seems to be the creed of our clan.

Although the later years find us separated by geography, she must surely know that she is always at the seat of my heart, where the love of first cousins such as we are, often rivals that of siblings. She will always be as my third and youngest sister. May God always bless you and yours, Isabelita."

Sister-in-Law, Aidita~ "I have biologically two sisters, but in reality I have three wonderful sisters. Isa has been a real sister, a friend. We can share our precious moments, our laughs, our thoughts, our worries, our pains... and the beauty of it is that it stays there between us!It is a privilege to have you as a Sister!

Love you very much Today and Always!" Aidita

Brother, José Julián~ "Thank you, dear God, for having blessed me with a loving sister like no other. Isa has always been like a mother to me, caring and providing Christian guidance during my trials and tribulations.

I admire her, because she is a true woman of God; and as such, she has positively inspired me, as well as many others around her. Even during the darkest hours of her life, she never renounced her faith and love for our Lord, at a time when others would have felt forsaken by Him.

I love you deeply, Isa. You will always be in my heart. May our dear God continue to bless you and your family." ~Your dear brother, José (Chico) Team 11:11

Marta Ramos~ "When the revolution came to Cuba, I lost my sister; but God prepared for me another sister when I married Juan, Isabel's brother. Since then, Isa has been not only my friend, but my second sister, who I love very much."

Carmita Rubio~

"Finding an old friend is like finding a lost treasure." Anthony Douglas Williams"

"Our journey through like is certainly defined by the stops we make along the way and the friends that we acquire on the journey. My life has been an incredible journey, filled with joy, great friends, disappointments, trials, and unexpected events. Unfortunately, along the way, I lost touch with one of the dearest friends of my life, Isabel Ramos Aguilar. We were unaware of each other's whereabouts from 1951-2014.

Having been born to a very loving and stable family who owned a sugar mill in Cuba, my life was idealistic, to say the least. My parents wanted the very best education for me; therefore, in my early teen years, they sent me away to Candler-Buenavista Boarding School in Havana, Cuba.

This part of my journey became a pivotal point in my life because it was there that I met a very dear friend. Isabel and I were the tallest two girls in our dorm, so as logic often goes in the educational arena, the head mistress chose to have us become roommates. Little did she know that she was teaming "partners in crime!"

To be quite honest about the situation, Isabel and I were privileged, spoiled girls who had led sheltered lives until we got to boarding school. This part of life's journey afforded us the opportunity to be adventurous and daring—something that had never been allowed in our homes. Remember. This was back when kids were seen, not heard!

It did not take Isabel and me very long to adapt to our new setting and to develop our daring reputation. All of those senseless boarding school rules had to be challenged, and Isabel and I were the chosen rebel leaders. In fact, the other girls assisted us when there was something that needed to be done.

One of our most favorite feats was to obtain midnight snacks for all the girls in our dorm. The plan was well laid out and all stops were in place to insure that our mission would be successful. After midnight, when our dorm mates were strategically placed at various lookout points, Isabel and I, carrying pillow cases, would sneak down three flights of stairs into the basement kitchen to raid the refrigerator and food storage pantry.

After pillow cases were filled with fruits, cookies, and any other goodies we could find, we would sneak back up the stairs and divide our loot with our friends. After feasting, Isabel, other friends and I would listen to romantic Spanish music (Los Chavales de España) on someone's radio and dream about our future boyfriends until the wee hours of the morning. (Did I forget to mention that radios were not allowed?)

As life would have it, Isabel and I were separated after just one year together, yet the friendship bond that was formed during those few months was strong enough to last a lifetime. Unfortunately, Isabel and I were separated longer than we ever dreamed. As political problems emerged in Cuba, both of our families had to flee the county. For sixty-three years, the only remnant of our friendship was the memories of those days and nights we had spent together at the boarding school. So often, I would think of her and wonder if I would ever see her again.

By a strange stroke of luck, we had a friend in common who lives in Miami Beach. In talking with Emma, I mentioned Isabel and she told me she knew how to contact her. When the contact was made, plans were put into place to see each other as soon as possible. When Isabel arrived in Miami for us to reconnect, it was as if we had never been apart.

That's the wonderful thing about real friends. You can be separated for decades, yet reconnect and continue on with the journey. When Isabel and I saw each other, we talked and talked for hours, just as we had back in our room in the boarding school. I feel so blessed that we are able to pick up where we left off and have this friendship give us the opportunity to build more golden memories together.

Isabel, it is my prayer that God will see fit to give us time to build more sweet memories."

From her immediate family—

Great-granddaughter, Sarah— "My great-grandma is a Champion Pamperer. She never fails to make everyone feel comfortable and welcome at her home. My most distinct memories of her during my childhood are sensory ones: The smell of Violeta, the soft mountain of pillows on her bed, the touch of her manicured fingernails playing with my hair and the delicious *arroz con pollo* she prepared.

I always loved hearing about my grandma growing up in Cuba and the stories of her big, beautiful house in such a foreign, tropical setting. After hearing about how much she adored the piano, it made me want to play, too.

I loved going to my grandma's house because of the big Jacuzzi tub, the comfy beds and the yummy meals, but more importantly, it was a place where I always felt loved and cared about.

My Grandma Isabel is beautiful, stylish, a good mother, wife, and grandmother, an amazing piano-player, a consistently good cook, a great storyteller and a devout Christian. But what I love most about her is the unfaltering care and love she has for people in our family."

Granddaughter, Olivia~ "I am proud to be the granddaughter of Isabel Aguilar. At a young age, I spent a lot of time with her, and she taught me so much. She not only taught me the importance of love and kindness, but she was also always there for me when I needed her. I remember staying over at her house and how she would always play games with me and style my hair and paint my nails. I am excited to read about her childhood and how she became the woman she is today. She is by far one of the most important people in my life and I love her very much."

Granddaughter, Alexa~ "When I reflect on my relationship with my grandmother, Isabel Aguilar, I feel so blessed to have had a woman like her in my life. My "grandma" has provided an example to our family of what it means to be an indomitable woman of spirit. Here are a few qualities I will always remember:

- Her strength. My grandmother has suffered much in her life. When there is a true crisis in our family, she rises to the occasion, turns to the Bible and her faith, and carries on. She has shown me how it is possible to live through great sadness with grace and faith.
- Her ability to show love through a wonderful meal and a beautiful, comfortable home. I spent many nights at my grandparents' home as a child; and when I think back on those visits, I remember crisp sheets, hot chocolate prepared just right, warm baths and perfectly ironed clothes. My grandma has taught me that love can be demonstrated, not just by hugs or kisses, but by tireless efforts to make the people around you comfortable and content. Now that I am an adult, wife and mother, I can only imagine the long hours she spent making her house the haven it was for everyone. She has taught me how to take pride and care in a beautiful home, a delicious meal, and in making a guest feel comfortable.
- Her beauty. How many times have friends commented on my grandmother's style, her perfect appearance, her carefully coordinated clothes? It doesn't matter if she was fleeing Communist Cuba, living on a meager salary in Chicago, or cleaning her Salem house; my grandma has always done it style. I love to look at pictures taken of her through the years and see that same fashionable woman shine through the decades. She is a perfect

example that aging does not have to mean losing beauty, and that maintaining a beautiful appearance is something to take pride in.

- Her history. One of my favorite things to do with my grandma is to sit down at her kitchen island and listen to her tell stories of her life in Cuba as a girl, a young woman and as a young immigrant mother in Chicago and Kankakee. English is not her first language, but yet she is able to transport me, with words to a tropical island so that I can just imagine her and my grandfather on the wide boulevards and beaches of Cuba or dancing to piano music in a tiny Chicago apartment. Her stories of her beloved family and homes have provided a priceless gift: a link to my history and a land I will likely never know.

- Her marriage. The decades she has spent with my grandfather provide a wonderful example of two very different people—my grandfather is reserved and disciplined, my grandmother vivacious and expressive—can depend and lean on each other to build a life and a family.

My grandmother is an amazing woman. I love her dearly."

Daughter, Christina "My mother is a woman who captivates others not only by her striking outward appearance, but also by her faith-filled spirit. She certainly has influenced me spiritually as she pursues her life living for the Lord, which is a lifestyle that I want to maintain in my own family. She is a prayer warrior and it's been incredible to see how God has revealed Himself through her consistent prayers for others.

I have loved hearing about Mama's experiences growing up in Cuba, especially about fashion! I frequently hear about the brown dress with the wooden buttons, the one that captured my dad's attention! She is one classy lady and has had impeccable taste in fashion, which is something that I love thanks to her. She always has taught me to look my best and present myself in a classy manner.

I also attribute my love for the arts, especially music and dance, to her. I remember our yearly trips to Miami to visit our relatives. My uncles and my mom would have a Cuban jam session at my uncle's house. It was so cool to see my uncle, José, playing the guitar, my uncle, Juan, playing the bongos and Mama playing the piano. I'll never forget those memories as a little girl.

Thank you, Mama, for being an incredible mother and grandmother. You are one unique and special woman who we all admire and love so much."

Son, Victor~ "Having this special woman as my mother is a continual blessing. She truly is a woman of faith and commitment to the Lord and to her family. I look back at the countless conversations we have had, and I realize how much she has taught me, how much I have learned from her.

I learned about her inner strength from listening to her speak of her struggles with leaving her home in Cuba, to settling in a new country, all while learning English. With two active little boys added to the mix, her need for strength increased!

My memories of watching my mother and our extended Cuban family in Miami gather in my Uncle Juan's house for "jam sessions" remind me how much she loves music and laughter. She is a gifted piano player, carrying the beat that encouraged everyone to dance, to smile, to laugh.

Mama has truly been an inspiration to me from my early years to the present, one of the strongest and most loving individuals I have ever known. One thing I have come to realize after all these years is how much she and I are alike. We have a very special connection, a bond that reflects how compatible we are. We have similar personalities and actions. Listening to countless hours of her speaking about her youth and experiences in Cuba when she was a teenager, I realized that, like me, she was a bit rebellious, might even be described as quite a character by some.

I think that the greatest gift I have received from my mother is strength. I attempt to take this gift and instill it as much as possible into my everyday life. Knowing of her hard struggles, the pain and suffering of some experiences in the past and present, helps me be a stronger, better man. For this, I give her my gratitude and love.

My mother is a woman of faith, a dedicated wife, mother and grandmother who prays for family and friends each day. She is committed to the Lord and has always shared her faith and the Bible with each of us. She has taught me that we can get through trials and tribulations through faith in the Lord.

My father is one special, lucky guy to have found my mother. Their commitment to each other is one to take in, to take to heart. Knowing their incredible journey together, from their lives in Cuba to building a strong foundation in Salem, is quite amazing.

There are countless stories I could share about my mother, too many to describe in this short message. She is an amazing, beautiful woman. I love you, Mama."

Daughter-in-law, Lisa- "My mother-in-law is very important to me as she has been and continues to be a big influence in my life. She was there from the very beginning of my adult life and gave me an additional mother to model myself after. Many of the things I do today in my daily life are from her example and influence. She not only has taught me many things about being a homemaker, but also about being a woman.

Isabel is the perfect homemaker and has given our family many standards and traditions. She is the center of the Aguilar family. She is a loving mother with the deepest love for her family. She knows how to make her home elegant, how to make children look almost model worthy, has always had wonderful fashion sense and is a great cook. I have many memories of coming to pick up my children from her home and they would be so spotlessly clean—just perfect! I mean "Perfect": adorable clothes and hairstyles and smelling of Violetta.

When I think of her house, I remember many meals and holidays where the house was looking like it came from a magazine and everything was immaculate. There were all the little touches that made it beautiful. The beds were made so that not even a wrinkle was obvious, flowers were everywhere, the table set just so, and now I find myself doing the same. I learned from her that if you are going to do it-you might as well do it just right. Many delicious meals were made at Isabel's and most of them were Cuban. I now prefer Cuban cuisine to any other, and have learned to make some dishes myself. The day I made a perfect flan was one of my proudest moments!

Teaching me about being a mother and wife is only one aspect of my relationship with Isabel. She also has influenced me as a woman. She always listens to me when I ask her advice or just want to chitchat. I appreciate her real interest and encouragement that I get from her every time we see each other. She is always telling me how proud she is of me and that I do things so well and she loves me. She does the same for our children. I appreciate that so much! Isabel may look very feminine and gorgeous but don't let that fool you. She is also very tough. I have seen Isabel go through some very hard times and come out of it stronger than ever. That is a wonderful example to give to me. Life is tough, but we can be tougher!

I also am incredibly grateful that she (and Armando) raised Alex to be such a wonderful son, husband, and father. I love Isabel for being all these things: a great role model, a great mother, and a great mother-in-law!"

Son, Alejandro~ "My mother Isabel Edilia Aguilar, known to all family as Mama, is a special person to many including me. Mama has been and continues to this day being a wonderful role model of a caring, dedicated, devoted and loving mother. She is also an example of someone who shines and flourishes when life's challenges are upon us.

My earliest memories include Mama providing and meeting her children's needs without fail. I was always well fed with loving delicious meals, well dressed, and comforted when needed. Cooking for and feeding her children has been a borderline obsession with Mama. As my baby pictures show I may have been fed a bit much as a toddler which is a standing family laugh. Her family's needs were and are her primary focus. We always had delicious and nutritious meals. I was blessed in my childhood having a mother who cared for all children's needs.

Mama's ability to address head on life's sudden challenges continues to surprise me to this day. Her steadfastness and faith was evident during my brother Armando's long illness. Her fortitude and continued commitment to maintain family order during those difficult years is simply amazing. At this same time period she was daily addressing her ailing mother without fault.

Mama is a mother any child would be lucky to have. I'm a better person in large part because of her. Her love for family, fellow man, and faith is an example for all to admire and emulate."

Husband, Dr. Armando Aguilar "One evening at five o'clock, I was standing on the porch of my office building, watching the line of people waiting to buy tickets at the movie theater. It was located next to the theater, and on most nights the line was long, filled with those waiting to see the next new movie.

As I looked at the people, my glance settled on a beautiful girl, the first time I had seen her. She was alone, and I knew that she saw me looking at her. I was very impressed with her; I felt like a dart went straight to my heart. At that moment, in my heart, I knew that she was the girl I wanted to marry.

At that time, she was still in school, so the only times I saw her were when she came back home to visit her parents. We became friends, and I started writing to her at her school. I remember vividly that when I wrote to her, I started my letters with 'My elegant brunette.'

After fifty-five years of marriage, I feel the same way about her as I did the first day I saw her. She has been an amazing, lovely wife and a committed mother. She has a huge influence on my spiritual life. Each day we gather in the sunroom and have our devotionals together. This is part of our everyday life, where we have that special bond with each other.

I thank God every day for this lady in my life.

I love you, my elegant brunette.... Armando